D0948384

Advance Praise for *Rise of the Fourth Reich*

"History shows evil left unconfronted and unpunished always returns, and usually even worse than it was before. It took seventy-five years after the judgment at Nuremberg for bio-medical fascism to make a comeback. Without a new Nuremberg like what Daniel and Steve are calling for, it'll come back a lot sooner than that."

—Jesse Kelly, nationally syndicated radio host and host of *I'm Right* on The First

"Steve and Daniel are remarkably courageous and wise. Read this book and find out why you are living through something we promised would 'never happen again.'"

—Charlie Kirk, Turning Point USA

"Steve and Daniel have written a definitive and frankly terrifying indictment of perhaps the most unique and systemic evil I have witnessed in my lifetime. Like many of you, I also balked at the provocative title at first—for we should not invoke such history or imagery lightly. Then I started reading the book, and sadly came to the conclusion it was a worthwhile comparison. If you read this book, you will, too."

—Glenn Beck, Radio Hall of Famer and multiple *New York Times* bestselling author

"Deace and Horowitz have teamed up after years in the trenches of the war on truth to fire away at those who have been working to strip people of their civil liberties as they install a new way of life under totalitarian control. Both authors knew they were being presented with a series of implausibilities from the start of the crisis and have not let down their pursuit of those driving the false agenda and what is really the state of affairs with the pandemic illness. The book is well-conceived and easy-to-read. It will serve as an excellent gift to others to help them understand the mind-blowing reality we are all living through—be sure your copy is read many times."

—**Peter A. McCullough, MD, MPH,**
coauthor of *Courage to Face COVID-19:*
Preventing Hospitalization and Death while
Battling the Biopharmaceutical Complex

RISE OF THE FOURTH REICH

CONFRONTING COVID FASCISM WITH A NEW NUREMBERG TRIAL, SO THIS NEVER HAPPENS AGAIN

STEVE DEACE
DANIEL HOROWITZ

Post Hill
PRESS

A POST HILL PRESS BOOK

ISBN: 978-1-63758-752-2
ISBN (eBook): 978-1-63758-753-9

Rise of the Fourth Reich:
Confronting COVID Fascism with a New Nuremberg Trial,
So This Never Happens Again
© 2023 by Steve Deace and Daniel Horowitz
All Rights Reserved

Cover design by Conroy Accord

Post Hill Press
New York • Nashville
posthillpress.com

Published in the United States of America
3 4 5 6 7 8 9 10

Also by Steve Deace

Rules for Patriots
A Nefarious Plot
Truth Bombs: Confronting the Lies Conservatives
Believe (To Our Own Demise)
A Nefarious Carol
Faucian Bargain: The Most Powerful and
Dangerous Bureaucrat in American History
Do What You Believe: Or You Won't Be
Free to Believe It Much Longer
Why Thanksgiving?: The Pilgrims Started Thanksgiving for the
Same Reason They Came to America—Because They Loved God

Also by Daniel Horowitz

Stolen Sovereignty: How to Stop Unelected
Judges from Transforming America

This book is dedicated to the truth.

TABLE OF CONTENTS

ACKNOWLEDGMENTS

*Even when I walk in the valley of darkness, I will
fear no evil for You are with me; Your rod and
Your staff—they comfort me.* [Psalms 23:4].

The authors of this book would like to begin by giving thanks.

First, of course, to God for bestowing upon us the wisdom, time, energy, and resolve to complete this work and withstand the blowback it will righteously cause. For in a time of lies and deception, nothing is more dangerous than telling the truth.

Fighting the Spirit of the Age does not always win friends, wealth, or fame—and it can even wear down a man's resolve to stand by the right causes and finish the race. Faith in God is what has sustained us through the endless emotional investment in the future of our country.

The simple fact is neither of us could've embarked on this endeavor, or fulfilled our callings, without the full support of our soulmates.

For Daniel, that is Kelila Beth Horowitz. As God declared, "It is not good that man is alone; I shall make him a helpmate opposite him." For Steve, that is Amy Ramsey Deace: "I am my beloved's and his desire is for me."

To begin with, working in the field of politics and media is a twenty-four-hour job and is extremely emotionally draining, especially when (in Daniel's case) caring for three rambunctious boys and a toddler girl—or (in Steve's case) raising two teenagers. Adding the publication and promotion of a book on top of the day job was something that succeeded only thanks to the immense patience of our beloved wives.

Daniel wishes to thank his bride for keeping the house intact while he spent extra time fighting for their beloved republic and cherished values. He owes her a vacation honeymoon—big time.

Steve also wishes to thank his wife for sparing him the extra time, providing her valuable feedback as the content was being assembled, and not rolling her eyes when he said, "I've got an idea for another book."

We also must thank Todd Erzen, who coauthored the number-one bestseller *Faucian Bargain: The Most Powerful and Dangerous Bureaucrat in American History*, for his painstaking work transcribing hours upon hours of the witness interviews that are about to burn a hole in your conscience. This contribution cut down on our production time considerably.

Speaking of colleagues, we both definitely need to thank our media partner, TheBlaze, for allowing us to do what very few other platforms of significance would've dared permitted—providing us the megaphone to challenge the prevailing narrative pushing this scamdemic from its wretched beginning.

Next are the doctors and lawyers who have separated themselves from the herd mentality and actually risked their careers to treat people with care and represent those facing human rights violations. It is impossible to mention the dozens of doctors who ran toward the fire to treat those injured by both the COVID virus and the vaccine without omitting some names.

But we thank all of you who came on our shows the past few years and taught us everything we know about the science surrounding the issues in this book. Everyone likes to say they would have opposed the Third Reich's immoral medical directives, but these few dozen doctors are the few we can say with certitude would have been on the right side of history.

However, on a personal level, Daniel would like to single out one doctor who has helped him in his personal life beyond any degree he can ever repay. Dr. Eric Hensen, an otolaryngologist of Lonestar ENT, treated hundreds of people in his show audience for free with more devotion, time, care, and expertise than 99 percent of the other doctors treated their own long-standing patients. He treated Daniel's family members and friends throughout the pandemic, helping every one of them get through the virus knowing they had the caring and expert hands of Dr. Hensen on the steering wheel.

Although we need a Nuremberg trial for those doctors who participated in the atrocities, people like Dr. Hensen who bucked the system and saved countless lives will receive their reward in heaven. Well done, good and faithful servants.

Finally, we'd like to thank all of you patriots out there who read our daily articles, listen to our podcasts, watch our shows, and send us feedback on social media. It's always heartwarming to know we are not alone in this battle. Just as it is also encouraging to see millions of us, who want to restore this great nation to its constitutional principles and Judeo-Christian values that made it great.

NUREMBERG TRIAL DOCKET

- Opening Statement from the Prosecution
- Witness List
  - Military Betrayal:
    - **Lt. Col. Theresa Long, MD**: What happens when you really fulfill your oath to defend your country against all enemies—both foreign and domestic?
    - **Lt. Col. Peter Chambers, MD**: The "Nuremberg Doctor" and special operator
    - **Major Samuel Sigoloff, MD**: When duty and honor are replaced by unconditional (and immoral) compliance
  - Health Care Betrayal:
    - **Scott Miller, PA**: Sanctioned for saving lives
    - **Anne Quiner**: Death by protocol
    - **Scott Schara**: The protocol from hell
    - **Dr. Mollie James, MD**: Are we sacrificing patients to accommodate the sacred shots?
    - **Bill Salier**: Survived active deployment in the Marines, only to then almost die because of his local pharmacy

OPENING STATEMENT

I t is an insurmountable task to fully quantify the depth and breadth of the damage COVID fascism has inflicted upon the entire human race.

Between the lockdowns, criminalization of human breathing without a Chinese face diaper, denial of lifesaving treatments, and distributing and then mandating what turned out to be shockingly dangerous shots—the physical, social, mental, and economic destruction is too vast to measure. It is quite possible modern existence will not fully recover from this tyrannical episode in our lifetimes, if at all, given the unfortunate precedents set.

However, it would constitute an equal crime against humanity to allow these stories to go untold, and thus allow these atrocities to go unanswered, without fundamental legal and political changes to ensure they never happen again. Including, but not limited to, investigations and then tribunals to hold accountable those most guilty of originating this crime against humanity, along with an immediate plan to erect an impervious legal firewall around those human rights that were breached.

We must not forget what they did to us in the name of "science." We must not join the clamoring to "move on" and "return to normal" when the "new normal" the perpetrators desire is anything but. Nor should we offer reconciliation with those guilty of this long train of abuses without them first recognizing their crimes, and then repenting publicly for them.

We must also never forget that the Holocaust was perpetrated not in some primitive corner of the world in medieval times, but in Western Europe in the twentieth century. Clearly, the firewalls of "never again" placed as an obstruction to future medical tyranny during the Nuremberg trials, and embodied throughout the Nuremberg Code, have been breached and deracinated from their foundation. It is the calling of our generation to reconstruct, fortify, and eternalize those legal and political firewalls as they relate to science, medicine, and control over human beings. Because, if we don't, the next time "that could never happen here" happens here, it will be even worse.

The justification for a renewed version of the Nuremberg Code in the wake of the COVID fascism democide in many respects is more vital than it was in the wake of the Third Reich. Today, we face a Fourth Reich, which is potentially much more dangerous and inescapable than the Third Reich, and therefore needs even greater firewalls to prevent its proliferation.

First, as strong as Hitler's regime was during the 1930s, it was just one country. At some point, the natural jealousy, competitiveness, and survival instinct of competing nation-states would have to fight back or rebel against the Third Reich. No single nation could dominate the globe forever. The Fourth Reich, on the other hand, induced by the Great Reset of COVID totalitarianism, was the first form of fascism that was instantly global in nature. There was nowhere to escape its tentacles because the ideology of globalism has embedded the fascists as the ruling class in every western [former] democracy. Although America is still the most influential player on the global scene, COVID fascism was not confined to any one country or even region of the world. Thus, one cannot count upon a country or group of countries rising up against it the way the United States neutralized the Third Reich during WWII.

Second, the Fourth Reich is directed by the most dangerous mix of public-private partnerships. Thus, not only is it synchronized by global elites ruling every country, but by every global corporation working in tandem with every country's government to enforce the edicts of the Fourth Reich through censorship, discrimination, denial of basic services, and medical apartheid. We were unable to play the public sector off the private sector, or the private sector off the public sector—for they were the *same sector*.

For example, private emails from June 2021 released via FOIA revealed that the CDC Foundation worked with Facebook, Merck, the WHO, and other pharma entities on an "Alliance for Advancing Health Online" initiative to control the narrative.[1] So whether it's issues of off-label early treatments, vaccine safety and efficacy, science about asymptomatic transmission, or the threat of COVID to children, every morsel of information propagated by the Department of Health and Human Services (HHS) agencies is influenced and controlled by pharma and Big Tech to steer a specific outcome that will always benefit Big Pharma and the global regime.

Leaked Department of Homeland Security documents in June 2022 revealed how DHS officials set up meetings with Twitter executives to work on combating what they called disinformation.[2] The Biden White House worked with the corporate world both on stifling dissent and on enforcing the COVID mandates upon the citizenry.[3]

Perforce, the danger of the Fourth Reich's public-private partnership is akin to a nuclear bomb to individual rights in the sense that government will chase you while their "private" partners will catch you fleeing the tyranny. Everything the government was restrained from doing in the past, thanks to constitutionally protected rights, the courts and politicians were able to assert were kosher for the "private" entities to do. But we all know that it wasn't a free and unfettered marketplace that was prompting these corporations to impose draconian mandates on the bodies of their workers: it was corporations' incestuous relationship with the government.

The public is therefore left with no options because they can't challenge the incumbent private corporations in the marketplace, given the fact that governments grant them an inveterate monopoly through existing contracts, subsidies, and regulatory capture. Nor could they challenge the policies of the government through elections because they artfully vested most of that legal, economic, and logistical power to enforce their will upon civilization with the "private sector."

Finally, there is the issue of technology, which again, is aggravated by the previous two factors undergirding the menace of the Fourth Reich—globalism and privatization of government tyranny. The Third Reich did not have access to self-spreading vaccines,[4] lipid nanoparticle technology, mRNA technology, or any of the digital tracking and tracing tools global governments have today to monitor every citizen, their entire health care profile, compliance with unethical regime mandates, and their most intimate activities.

CDC documents that *VICE* obtained via FOIA show that CDC bought from a shady data company access to location data harvested from tens of millions of phones in the United States to perform analysis of compliance with the lockdowns.[5] Specifically, the surveillance included neighbor-to-neighbor visits and visits to churches, schools, and pharmacies. Given the extent of digital and nanotechnology, let your mind run wild as to the extent the government is monitoring and possibly controlling us without our consent.

For example, World Economic Forum (WEF) oligarchs have held forums discussing "Mind Control Using Sound Waves."[6] Pfizer CEO Albert Bourla bragged in 2018 at the WEF about "electronic pills" and the ability for insurance companies, and presumably other elite actors, to know which medicines you take and when you've been taking them.[7] "Imagine the implications of that—the compliance," exclaimed Bourla excitedly.

Klaus Schwab's top confidante, Israeli history professor Yuval Harari, explained exactly how COVID will allow them to groom the population into this transhumanist agenda. "Covid is critical because this is what convinces people to accept to legitimize total biometric surveillance," admitted Harari at the WEF without any hint of shame. "We need to not just monitor people, we need to monitor what's happening under their skin."[8]

At the 2020 WEF meeting, Harari made it clear that nothing short of godlike powers over human beings is the end goal of the self-appointed global ruling class. "In the coming decades, artificial intelligence and biotechnology will give us God-like abilities to reengineer life and even to create completely create to new life forms."[9] In August 2021, the WEF put out a dystopian video full of masked humans and QR codes titled, "Take a Peek at the Future," in which it showcased technology invented by NASA that can identify you by your heartbeat. Then, after suggesting children permanently do schooling at home in front of a computer, the WEF asks, "What pandemic era changes would you like to become permanent?"[10]

Along with the dystopian transhumanist agenda to use technology to control us will be the suspension of all freedoms. At the May 2022 Davos meeting, Australian eSafety Commissioner Julie Inman Grant told the WEF that because of "increasingly polarization" (aka dissent from the oligarchs) we need a "recalibration" of freedom of speech.[11] During the 2016 meeting of the WEF, Ida Auken, a Danish member of parliament, opened her remarks by envisioning, "Welcome to 2030. I own nothing, have no privacy, and life has never been better."[12] These are echoes of the Orwellian slogan posted at the entrance of Auschwitz—"Arbeit macht frei" which is German for "work sets you free."

Welcome to the Fourth Reich! Can you imagine if the Third Reich had access to this technology? Well, now that we know about it, we need an updated Nuremberg Code that matches the expansiveness of this technological threat of tyranny—along with the will of its practitioners to use it against our bodies—with ironclad legal shackles of government restraint.

Ladies and gentlemen of the jury, we submit that what humanity endured during the era of COVID fascism was not a "noble lie" of exaggerations designed to get people to the proper state of alert, nor was it even governments caught flat-footed after being ambushed with a pandemic they didn't see coming. In this book, we intend to offer evidence and testimony that, at best, nefarious elements among societal elites salivated at the prospect of "never letting a good crisis go to waste."[13] And, at worst, preplanned this societal shift all along—with COVID-19 simply serving as the MacGuffin of the plot.

In March 2020, there was a new global disorder established: a "Great Reset," in the words of leading globalist Klaus Schwab, that not only vitiated the ethos of the Nuremberg Code, designed to ensure that "never again" could humans be slaughtered like animals, but one that expanded upon the principles of the Third Reich. A global principle was established that a human being simply walking in locomotion, living his life without any signs of disease, is a threat to another human being. Therefore, under this diabolical reset of the Nuremberg ethos, that individual must initiate a set of affirmative actions *against his own body* to protect others, and failure to do so means he forfeits his life, liberty, and property.

Oh, and all standards of safety, efficacy, evidence, prudence, compassion, due process, scientific debate, dissenting opinions, and legal authority go out the window when determining what those ever-changing actions are. Nothing that objectively determines what works and what doesn't, what is moral and what isn't, could remain. The only standard would be a subjective one of no standard at all, except to comply with the edicts or face public ostracization, loss of livelihood, and even denial of lifesaving medical care.

All things equal, one could chalk up the triple axis of evil—the lockdowns, masks, and shots—to ignorance, panic, and carelessness. However, there are two factors that demonstrate the global powers behind this travesty in government and the medical-industrial complex acted with malfeasance and willful intent to destroy human life:

1. The perpetuation of these policies long after they were incontestably proven anywhere from harmful to ineffective
2. The vicious and cruel denial of treatment options that could have saved millions of lives—options that were established as much safer and cheaper than the ones that were promoted, then mandated

These two factors will be explored thoroughly through the testimony of experts, witnesses, and victims of the COVID crimes throughout the chapters of this book. They will demonstrate, conclusively, that the culture of cruelty within the medical field and government was purposeful, planned, and has now become permanent—even after their colossal harms and counterproductive efficacy have been proven in plain sight.

That absent an equal and opposing force of good, motivated by preservation of basic human rights and bodily freedoms, the COVID regime beginning in early 2020 will become the "new normal" in government, law, medicine, and science.

With that in mind, let's confront the first factor demonstrating there is no innocent and benign explanation for the set of policies pursued by our government and the medical field. Namely, the duration and perpetuation of these human experimentations well beyond when any reasonable person would have aborted them.

Even if one believes that locking people down, shuttering schools, and forcibly masking human breathing is a necessary evil (assuming the enforcers are not indeed evil themselves), they will eventually recognize that these policies are indeed a *form of evil*—even if they believe they are (hopefully) temporarily necessary.

As such, even if they believed they had the moral and legal right to institute these policies initially, they would have enacted them in the least restrictive manner, for the shortest period of time necessary, and would have immediately rescinded them the minute there was a suspicion they were ineffective and/or damaging.

Instead, the leaders in politics and medicine doubled and tripled down on these demonic policies for months, and, in some realms, even years on end to the very days this was being written. Long after it was clear that masks absolutely did not affect the epidemiological outcome of the virus in any part of the world,[14] they continued to forcibly mask two-year-olds, deny medical care to people with disabilities who couldn't wear a mask,[15] and prevent rape victims who couldn't have their mouths covered from living a normal life.[16] Kids were forcibly masked for eight hours a day in most parts of the country for nearly two years, assuming they even had in-person learning for much of that time period.

Nowhere is this maleficence—a long-term and inexcusable disregard for human rights, basic science, and sane risk-benefit analysis, along with a refusal to change course regardless of the new information—more evident than with the tragic human experiment of closing schools. Like with all the other policies, there was nothing immutable about the decision to close schools for months and years on end. It was a forgivable sin to shut down the schools for a week or two in the face of the immediate panic. But the facts were clear from nearly the first few weeks that children were not at elevated risk from this virus beyond the typical risks they assume every day.

After just a few weeks, it became incontrovertibly clear that the school closures had no bearings on the trajectory of the pandemic, induced a calamitous mental health crisis, and inhibited the learning development of a generation of civilization. Within the first month of the lockdowns, data from Iceland,[17] U.K.,[18] Australia,[19] Switzerland,[20] Canada,[21] Netherlands,[22] France,[23] and Taiwan[24] showed that children were responsible for little to none of the transmission to adults.

Already on May 2, 2020, the CDC posted in its COVID View Summary, "For children (0-17 years), COVID-19 hospitalization rates are *much lower* than influenza hospitalization rates during recent influenza seasons."[25]

CDC and state departments of health, along with all of the state and federal election officials who went along with it, could have aborted this cruel experiment on children after only one month of the shutdown and could have avoided the calamitous *long-term* educational, social, mental, behavioral, and developmental damage we are now fully realizing. As the tenth precept of the Nuremberg Code states, "During the course of the experiment the scientist in charge must be prepared to terminate the experiment at any stage, if he has probable cause to believe...that a continuation of the experiment is likely to result in injury, disability, or death to the experimental subject."[26] Yet they continued...and continued...and continued to shut down schools.

Each day, the CDC and various state health and education departments could have decided to do the right thing and follow the undeniable science and data on school closures and masking of children. Even as the suicides increased and the grades from Zoom school plummeted, they continued these policies without any evidence they served a purpose.

These sort of polices were akin to the most vicious form of chemotherapy: something you would administer only as a last-ditch effort in the most minimal dose, not as the first-choice effort indiscriminately without any precision.

These were not wartime decisions where a military or political leader is often forced to make one sudden immutable decision that could determine who lives and who dies instantaneously. Every day, they could have opened their eyes to what was before them and realized that school closures, small business closures (while the big retailers were open), masking, and endless testing and spying (aka "contact tracing") violated human rights without any appreciable benefit—but did come with copious personal and societal side effects.

Unlike in war, this was not a zero-sum game beyond each day's decision. We could have mitigated the harm one day earlier by choosing to do the right thing the following day. After the initial "two weeks to flatten the curve," we had ample evidence that even the most favorable risk-benefit analysis of these policies revealed them as a net liability on humanity, unquestionably as they related to children who always had the most to lose and the least to gain from the "new normal."

Had we frozen those policies in April 2020, the harm from just two weeks would have been minimal. Instead, we continued them for two years in many parts of the country and the masking never stopped in some places. In fact, the policies failed so miserably that the more we enacted them, the more the virus got worse,[27] which should have been an obvious sign that the expressed need to perpetuate those policies beyond those first few weeks bore witness to the circuitous, convoluted, and even *evil* logic of continuing them. But the pleas for public debate fell on deaf ears for weeks, then months—and in many parts of the country and the world—for years and until this very day.

Then there were the COVID shots, originally advertised as just as safe and effective as traditional vaccines, albeit with a quicker timeline that will accelerate the future of vaccine development.[28] We intend to bring expert testimony attesting to the fact that the key players in government and Big Pharma knew about the risks of these shots from day one. But just like with school closures, each day was a new decision point. They could have administered them with proper informed consent, and only to the people who absolutely needed them. Then they could have pulled them from the market as soon as they realized that the shots did not stay in the shoulder muscle while creating an increasing litany of inflammatory maladies throughout the body, including permanent disability and death.

Yet, the more the evidence showed the shots were dangerous and ineffective—and then eventually made it *more likely* you would get the virus—the more they not only doubled down on the shots, but then began mandating them on every human being alive regardless of age, risk factors, and whether one already had natural immunity, which was about half the population at the time.

We know based on a court-released document that as early as February 28, 2021, which was before most people got their first dose (especially those under sixty), there were enough problems with these shots, pursuant to the Nuremberg Code, they should have been removed from the market. Instead, they were mandated and expanded to younger people and those with natural immunity. We typically pull a product off the market after a few dozen suspected deaths. The swine flu vaccine in 1976 was pulled from the market after only a few dozen deaths and was halted in nine states after just three reported deaths in Pittsburgh.[29]

Yet Pfizer disclosed to the FDA at the time, but unbeknownst to the public, the existence of 42,086 adverse event case reports containing 158,893 total events, including 1,227 deaths. 25,957 of the events were classified as "nervous system disorders."[30] During the 1976 rollout of the swine flu vaccine, there were a mere 362 cases of Guillain-Barré Syndrome (GBS), a condition in which the immune system attacks the nerves and causes forms of paralysis, reported before it was pulled from the market.[31] As of May 20, 2022, there were over 4,000 cases of GBS, and 15,568 cases of Bell's Palsy, reported to VAERS from the COVID shots.[32]

In the document that Pfizer and the FDA wanted to conceal for seventy-five years, Pfizer reveals that "due to the large numbers of spontaneous adverse event reports," staff were forced to prioritize "the processing of serious adverse events" and the company had to hire large numbers of staff to handle all the adverse side effects.

"To date, Pfizer has onboarded approximately six hundred additional fulltime employees (FTEs)," reveals Pfizer on page six of the confidential document. "More are joining each month with an expected total of more than eighteen hundred additional resources by the end of June 2021."

In other words, Pfizer was preemptively ramping up in preparation for an avalanche of adverse side effects the public wasn't warned about ahead of time.

Furthermore, Pfizer details nine pages of several thousand known categories of adverse effects, which reveals the massive scope of injuries that were being reported to Pfizer. Pfizer knew that these were just the self-reported and *immediate* effects for a vaccine that had undergone absolutely no long-term safety studies and for which all of the control groups were unblinded and vaccinated. Pfizer and the FDA had access to this information and never released it to the public at the time, but nevertheless pushed the vaccine on the public in the biggest mass vaccination campaign of all time. This included the eventual success in jabbing children and babies with the old, failed sequence of the shot, even as the virus had already muted multiple times.

Then there is Pfizer's own all-cause mortality data from very early on in the process. Amid all the studies thrown around the debate table, there is nothing so revealing as the all-cause mortality rates of those in the actual clinical trials after a few months—trial arm compared with placebo. Such a measure will factor in COVID deaths, natural deaths, and vaccine-related deaths. In Pfizer's very own biologics license application that was used by the FDA to grant it full licensure (for the Comirnaty shot), Pfizer reveals, "From Dose 1 [started on July 27, 2020] through the March 13, 2021 data cutoff date, there were a total of 38 deaths, 21 in the COMIRNATY [Pfizer's mRNA vaccine] group and 17 in the placebo group."[33]

Say again?! Pfizer knew from early on—before the children were jabbed—that there were more all-cause deaths in the trial group in the adult trial? How can that be? Pfizer claims without evidence that "None of the deaths were considered related to vaccination." But if the vaccines were so effective, how could we see negative efficacy in the measure of all-cause mortality? Yet, pursuant to that very document, the FDA granted Comirnaty—de facto Pfizer—full licensure, which greased the skids for the military mandate.

From day one, it was clear that after subjecting people to so much known and unknown short-term and long-term risk of severe adverse events, there was no all-cause mortality benefit—and very likely a detriment.

What about the claimed benefits against hospitalizations? An analysis of Pfizer's and Moderna's own clinical trial participants coauthored by Dr. Peter Doshi, editor of the world-renowned *British Medical Journal*, found clearly that the trial participants were more likely to be hospitalized from adverse events from both Pfizer and Moderna's shots than to benefit from reduced COVID hospitalizations.

Specifically, Dr. Doshi and his colleagues found that the Pfizer shot was associated with an increased risk of serious "adverse events of special interest" unrelated to COVID of 10.1 events per 10,000 vaccinated for Pfizer and 15.1 per 10,000 for Moderna. In absolute terms, they did find a small benefit in reduced COVID hospitalizations, but when weighed against the increased risk of hospitalizations from vaccine injury, there was a net *increase* in serious adverse events of 7.8 per 10,000 vaccinated with Pfizer and 8.7 per 10,000 vaccinated with Moderna *over the supposed protection against COVID hospitalizations*.[34]

Thus, from early on, before they jabbed most of the public, the manufacturers and the "regulators" knew that the shots caused more harm than good. And this was for the *original* strain when there was slight efficacy, but very few people were vaccinated when the Wuhan strain was still circulating. They continued to push the shots for the new strains and introduced them to children and eventually babies long after we saw not just a net liability, but an absolute liability because there was no discernible efficacy and growing evidence of negative efficacy against the new COVID strains.[35]

Accordingly, all along, as they were spending more money, time, effort, government control, and public shaming to promote these shots, they knew they were violating the sixth precept of the Nuremberg Code: "The degree of risk to be taken should never exceed that determined by the humanitarian importance of the problem to be solved by the experiment."

Fast-forward to early September 2021, and we already knew from weekly U.K. COVID case data that the vaccine had negative efficacy.[36] Furthermore, there were already 1,000 deaths and hundreds of thousands of injuries reported to VAERS at that time. Not only did the FDA decline to pull the shots off the market, but our government did three things in late summer of 2021:

1. Issued full licensure to the Pfizer shot (technically only Pfizer's sister vaccine, Comirnaty, which is still not available for use here in the U.S. at the time this book was being written).
2. Approved Pfizer booster shots, which is itself evidence of the waning efficacy of the original ones.[37]
3. Accelerated federal and state mandates on a good chunk of the American public, especially federal workers, health care staff, and the military.[38] And they did so knowing full well that the shot not only came

with an escalating number of potential side effects, but it was concocted for a version of the virus that had no longer been in circulation for months.

In doing so, the FDA acknowledged that despite months of safety problems with myocarditis, there was also a huge unknown risk of subclinical myocarditis, which was likely much more widespread.

In the Pharmacovigilance Plan Review Addendum for Comirnaty,[39] the FDA conceded, "Incidence of subclinical myocarditis and potential long-term sequelae following COMIRNATY are unknown." However, it did note that a previous study on a smallpox vaccine "suggested an incidence of possible subclinical myocarditis (based on cardiac troponin T elevations) sixty-times higher than the incidence rate of overt clinical myocarditis." That would bring up the one in 1,000 rate among young males that Pfizer acknowledged[40] to as high as one in seventeen for subclinical cardiac ticking time bombs!

The FDA reviewers flatly stated, "Based on review of available data, there are known risks for myocarditis and pericarditis and an unexpected serious risk for subclinical myocarditis, which warrant PMR safety studies to assess these serious risks." They called on Pfizer BioNTech to conduct studies but noted that the sponsor rebuffed them. In other words, we don't regulate Pfizer; Pfizer regulates us...while enjoying free taxpayer funding, marketing, distribution, mandating, and complete immunity from liability. Seven and a half months after Pfizer's full approval, we still have no studies on subclinical myocarditis, and they aren't due to be completed until July 2023!

Jab first, study the effects later became the modus operandi, the starkest violation of the Nuremberg Code imaginable. As late as January 25, 2022, CDC researchers published a paper in *JAMA* asserting their belief that the tens of thousands of myocarditis reports to VAERS were "likely" underreported, yet that did not change their policies.[41] Instead, the FDA went on to approve the shots for even younger cohorts of young children, including third doses in the ensuing months. At best, this isn't science whatsoever but cognitive dissonance. At worst, this is *The Island of Dr. Moreau.*

And again, the Biden administration pushed it on every population, despite the risk status or prior immunity, and despite the negative efficacy and the fact that the vaccine was for an obsolete strain of the virus. There is no benign or innocent explanation for this.

Nowhere was the Third Reich–era ethos of jab first and study consequences later more evident than with the push to pressure and, in some circumstances, mandate the shots upon pregnant women. In medicine, we are so careful *never* to give any substance to pregnant women that has not affirmatively been proven safe with numerous long-term studies that directly examined its effects on pregnant and nursing women.

Nevertheless, a copy of the Pfizer trial informed consent document made public through FOIA lawsuits from the Informed Consent Action Network stated unambiguously, "The effects of the COVID-19 vaccine on sperm, a pregnancy, a fetus, or a nursing child are not known."[42] Nonetheless, this shot was pushed upon pregnant and nursing women and women of childbearing age without informed consent to the public, regardless of their risk level and immunity status. This was particularly true for those in the military and the health care field.

Shockingly, this novel gene therapy, after the manufacturers and the FDA already knew of countless safety signals concerning hundreds of maladies, was pushed upon pregnant women, even *after* all the safety signals were blaring red and even after the FDA knew the proinflammatory lipid nanoparticles[43] deposited, to a large degree, in the ovaries. Already in 2018, a study published in the *International Journal of Nanomedicine* showed that nanoparticles can "detrimentally affect the reproductive systems of mice in vivo and in vitro. At the cellular level, NPs can induce infertility by altering the activity, morphology, quality, and quantity of sperm."[44]

In the FDA's "Summary Basis for Regulatory Action on Comirnaty"—published nearly a year after the shot had already been administered and, in some cases, mandated upon pregnant women—the drug regulator stated plainly that proper information for use for pregnant and nursing women was missing. "Missing information: Use in pregnancy and lactation; Vaccine effectiveness; Use in pediatric individuals <12 years of age," the FDA divulged.[45]

Indeed, in Comirnaty's (Pfizer BNT162b2) purple-cap package insert, the label states unmistakably that "available data on Comirnaty administered to pregnant women are insufficient to inform vaccine-associated risks in pregnancy."[46] However, this informed consent written in fine print was never divulged to patients by the government, media, and most doctors. In fact, they lied and asserted conclusively that it was safe. In the ultimate violation of medical ethics, it was quite commonplace for OBGYNs to expel women from their practice if they declined to take the shot.[47]

They did this all months *after* seeing so many VAERS reports of adverse reproductive issues. As of early May 2022, there were 4,690 miscarriages reported to VAERS, 10,575 instances of vaginal/uterine hemorrhaging, and ubiquitous reports of menstrual irregularities.[48] In fact, menstrual irregularities were so common that a University of Chicago survey sought to recruit 500 women with menstrual irregularities in order to study the cause and effect, and instead, researchers received 140,000 submissions.[49] One preprinted study found that 42 percent of women experienced heavier bleeding, while only 44 percent reported no changes to their menstrual cycles at all. A mind-boggling 66 percent of *postmenopausal* women experienced breakthrough bleeding sometime after receiving the shots.[50]

Then there is the issue of fertility among men, which will obviously take longer to detect. The lipid nanoparticles deposit in large quantities in the testes just like they do in the ovaries. In the same week that the FDA approved the COVID shots on babies and toddlers in June 2022, an Israeli study of sperm donors published in *Andrology* found a 15.4 percent decrease in sperm concentration between two and five months after donors got the shots. Considering the shots lose their efficacy after five to six months by even the most optimistic data out there, that begs the question of what the routine and frequent booster shots the elites are demanding do to the male reproductive system long-term. That is a question the study didn't explore.

Furthermore, "total motile count," which represents the number of sperm in a sample of ejaculated semen, decreased 22 percent from prevaccine baseline and barely recovered after five months.[51] None of this was even discussed during the barbaric approval of vaccines on children, even though this study was the first of its kind on this question of vital importance to all of humanity.

According to the Declaration of Helsinki on medical ethics, "Physicians may not be involved in a research study involving human subjects unless they are confident that the risks have been adequately assessed and can be satisfactorily managed."[52] This is not just any research study but one involving two billion human beings, with hundreds of thousands of pregnant women being used as lab rats before risks were adequately assessed and after some risks are already apparent. It's a new biomedical paradigm of mandate first, study never.

As abhorrent and detestable as the issues we've already discussed happen to be, it is the government's relentless war—joined by the entire medical establishment—on safe and effective treatments that best demonstrates an undeniable and particularly cruel form of malice we shudder to consider. This point will consume a large portion of the testimony laid out in this book.

The Rosetta Stone to understanding the nefarious motivations behind the government-medical complex's response to COVID—or perhaps involvement in it—is the war on early treatment. You see, logic would dictate that anyone who is truly motivated by his desire to combat COVID—perhaps naively and even to a fault, but nonetheless altruistically—would have embraced and even obsessed over early treatment options from day one. After all, if COVID is so deadly that you are going to treat someone with no symptoms as if they are afflicted, then you most certainly would move heaven and earth to treat someone who has the virus with that same supposed urgency of life and death.

At least you would if you still took the Hippocratic Oath seriously.

Consider the fact that the same medical officials who would kick a rape victim off a plane for not wearing a mask, or forcibly mask a healthy preschooler for eight hours out of an alleged "abundance of caution," would also tell an elderly patient with heart disease or diabetes upon testing positive for COVID to go home and wait until he can't breathe before coming to the hospital as the only available protocol treatment for COVID.

Not only did these medical officials eschew any evidence of effective treatment with cheap and safe medications, vitamins, and supplements, they went to war over them. They censored and even fired doctors who promoted such treatments. They got pharmacies to refuse prescriptions to patients for whom every hour counted. They refused even the safest treatments at all stages, including when the patient was on a ventilator. And in some cases, even called child protective services on parents who would treat these children with safe medications.

And they did so without ever offering alternatives.

They did so even long before the vaccines and the supposed wonder of Big Pharma's expensive and dubious new outpatient drugs, which didn't come out until late 2021. Thus, the same people who felt COVID was a big enough threat that it was worth risking the ruination of modern society suddenly ignored the threat of the virus when a person actually got it, and then worked tenaciously to block the treatments.

Despite long-standing evidence throughout the pandemic that there were numerous safe options to treat and even somewhat preempt the virus—including the inflammatory response, respiratory distress, and blood clotting—the entire medical establishment vociferously opposed any and every suggestion. To this very day, there is not a single cheap therapeutic the establishment has endorsed, even though everything it has used has failed in the real world, despite the establishment spending billions of taxpayer dollars on development and free distribution.

The list obviously includes hydroxychloroquine and ivermectin, but also many other suggestions. Off-label medications include nitazoxanide, metformin, aviptadil, budesonide, fluvoxamine, fenofibrate, famotidine, cyproheptadine, methylprednisolone, and dozens of other vitamins and supplements, such as vitamin C, vitamin C, selenium, black seed oil, NAC, zinc, quercetin, and melatonin—just to name a few.

Even venerable aspirin was attacked instead of promoted once it was known to prevent the blood clotting.[53]

Nasal and oral rinse with a betadine solution was possibly the simplest and most effective way to cut down the viral load and the ensuing commensurate inflammatory response,[54] yet it was mocked and panned by the media as a tool of "anti-vaxxers."[55]

Again, all *without providing any alternative solutions*—both before the vaccines came out and after it was clear they were not working.

Why was it that the people who claimed to fear COVID the most believed in treating it the least? There is no benign or innocent explanation for this.

Just vitamin D alone could have saved countless lives. Over a hundred studies, many of them conducted early in the pandemic, showed the near-perfect correlation between higher vitamin D levels and better outcomes in COVID patients. Most of the COVID deaths occurred well after six months into the pandemic, which could have given people ample time to bulk up their levels. An Israeli study showed 25 percent of hospitalized COVID patients with vitamin D deficiency died compared with just 3 percent among those without a deficiency.[56] And those with a deficiency were also fourteen times more likely to end up with a severe or critical condition. A meta-analysis of forty pooled studies found that vitamin D supplementation correlated with a 65 percent reduction of risk for ICU admission.[57]

Even Dr. Anthony Fauci, America's so-called "leading infectious disease expert," admitted in an interview with a Hollywood actress in 2020, long before we knew if/when we would have the alleged vaccines, that he takes ample doses of vitamin D daily to boost his immune system.[58] So then how come he didn't launch a national campaign to get his countrymen to do the same with the massive platform he had? There is no benign or innocent explanation for this.

Furthermore, such an approach also wouldn't have come with a sundry list of complications like the vaccines, and it would have bestowed immeasurable positive side effects upon the population to safeguard against an array of other health concerns such as cancer and heart disease.[59, 60]

How many COVID deaths could've been prevented with wide use of all these treatments? We will never know because the establishment instead attacked those few doctors who were saving lives, and even fired them and sometimes stripped them of their licenses.

Accordingly, there is no middle ground when ascertaining the motivations behind the COVID fascism pursued by our government and the medical profession. There is no benign or innocent explanation for what they did regarding the other policies as well.

We could have potentially saved millions of lives from COVID and avoided the ongoing mental health crisis, all of the damage from the COVID shots, trillions of dollars in spending and economic damage, and diminishing a generation of children's mental, behavioral, physical, and language development had we simply aggressively treated COVID with protocols we knew were working.

How did we know? There were doctors screaming from the rooftops from day one on how to treat the virus, such as Dr. Vladimir Zelenko who treated hundreds in the very first wave that hit New York, and they had remarkable results to show for it. On April 30, 2022, Brazilian daily newspaper *Folha de São Paulo* conducted an analysis of the clinical outcomes of nine doctors around the world known for treating COVID early, including a few in the United States. Out of roughly 25,000 patients treated, they had a 0.13 percent case fatality rate.[61]

That is about a 93 percent reduction in mortality from the cumulative case fatality rate in the U.S. throughout the pandemic.[62]

And remember, these actual doctors were overrun with patient demands because they had to do the jobs of thousands of other medical tyrant physicians who inexcusably ignored their own regular patients. Imagine if every doctor would have been instructed to aggressively treat early with some of these protocols, buttressed by government posting helpful information and actively researching even better concoctions and protocols throughout the pandemic?

Imagine if a fraction of the money spent on failed therapeutics, vaccines, lockdowns, and subsidizing people to vegetate at home would have been channeled into fine-tuning some of the protocols from people like Drs. Vladimir Zelenko, Brian Tyson, George Fareed, Pierre Kory, Paul Marik, Peter McCullough, Ryan Cole, and Richard Urso? Imagine if the system would've supported such healers, instead of vilifying, censoring, and threatening them?

The true malfeasance of our government and medical establishment can be proven from the powerful juxtaposition of the standards with which they used to judge cheap, FDA-approved, long-standing safe therapeutics to the ones they used for expensive, novel therapies with known safety problems that did not yet have full FDA approval.

After rejecting every single safe, common drug, what was the one standard of care they used in the hospital beginning in May 2020? The worst choice imaginable—antiviral remdesivir, which incidentally, was developed by Dr. Ralph Baric of the University of North Carolina–Chapel Hill—the same individual who dabbled in the coronavirus spike protein gain-of-function research.[63], [64]

On December 12, 2019, less than five months before Fauci and the FDA pushed approval of remdesivir without consulting with an outside panel of experts, the *New England Journal of Medicine* published a study on remdesivir use in Ebola that should have gotten the drug permanently banned for *any* use.[65] Over the preceding year, the researchers conducted a randomized controlled trial of four therapeutics for use against Ebola in the Democratic Republic of the Congo: remdesivir and three types of monoclonal antibodies, including Regeneron. Of the four drugs, remdesivir had the worst outcome with a 53.1 percent death rate, which is higher than the death rate from the virus. In fact, both remdesivir and ZMapp (death rate of 49.7 percent) were deemed to be so dangerous that they were pulled from the study on August 9, 2019.[66]

On April 29, Fauci announced that remdesivir would become the standard of care, and another study he cited was a March 2020 study by the drug's own maker, Gilead Sciences, (eventually published in the *NEJM* in June)[67] of fifty-three coronavirus patients in the U.S. Canada, Europe, and Japan who used remdesivir for ten days.[68] Sixty percent reported adverse events and 23 percent reported serious adverse events. The most common being "multiple-organ-dysfunction syndrome, septic shock, acute kidney injury, and hypotension." Furthermore, "Four patients (eight percent) discontinued remdesivir treatment prematurely: one because of worsening of preexisting renal failure, one because of multiple organ failure, and two because of elevated aminotransferases, including one patient with a maculopapular rash."

This is why the NIH to this day warns about renal failure and liver toxicity from the use of this drug that is bankrupting us and killing people in the hospitals.[69] The World Health Organization, hardly a bastion for medical freedom, even recommends against using it.[70] The WHO's Solidarity trial, which was conducted on 2,750 patients in 405 hospitals across thirty countries, found "little or no effect of remdesivir on mortality," even though "the proportion of lower-risk patients happened to be appreciably greater in the remdesivir group than in the placebo group."

Consider the fact that remdesivir was known to be so dangerous, had no anti-inflammatory qualities so it couldn't conceivably work at the hospitalization stage, and was $3,000 a course of treatment. Yet it remains the standard of care to this very day, while Nobel Prize–winning drugs and long-standing, broadly safe and beneficial therapeutics and supplements are repudiated.

Indeed, not a single officially approved inpatient COVID treatment did not contain a black box warning from the FDA. Not. A. Single. One.

The only other treatments approved throughout the pandemic for severely ill patients, at the time of this writing, were baricitinib and tofacitinib. Baricitinib has an FDA black box warning for blood clots, of all things, and was used to treat a disease that was prone to clotting! Tofacitinib has a black box warning for "serious infections and malignancy."[71], [72]

What about our government's choice drugs for outpatient treatment after going nearly two years without approving a single drug outside the hospital? Merck's molnupiravir was so widely panned even by the sympathetic corporate media that it was barely ever used.[73] Yet the same FDA committee that admitted that the drug was likely mutagenic, caused birth defects in rats, and never really worked wound up approving the drug anyway.[74] Merck received over a $1 billion for this toxic drug.[75]

Pfizer's Paxlovid wound up being the king of outpatient treatment because Pfizer is king. However, the drug is mixed with a dangerous AIDS medicine, ritonavir, contraindicated with numerous classes of common drugs used by vulnerable patients, and left a horrible metallic taste in people's mouths.[76] Then, it became clear, despite the "90% efficacy," that it never worked in vaccinated people, and that it caused a rebound of even worse symptoms several days later.[77]

If there is one story that emblematizes the level of absurdity and depravity of the past few years, it was the story of Dr. Fauci himself contracting COVID in June 2022 after receiving *four* doses of the vaccine. He then admitted that after taking Paxlovid, *he got a rebound of the virus that made him feel "much worse" than the original round.*[78]

You couldn't make this stuff up.

There is quite literally not a single pharmaceutical and nonpharmaceutical intervention implemented by our government that didn't make the virus worse and cause side effects. And to this day, we have no understanding of the long-term effects of Paxlovid, just like with the "vaccines." At the same time, hospitals would deny people with no options the Nobel Prize–winning drug ivermectin, which was dubbed "generally well tolerated" by the NIH,[79] listed among the most "essential medicines" by the WHO,[80] and regarded as providing "immeasurable" benefit to humanity by the Nobel Assembly.[81]

There is no benign, or innocent, explanation for this.

Coming full circle on the juxtaposition of the measures they pursued versus the ones they essentially criminalized, the entire COVID regime began with the justification of flattening the curve to ensure there would be no overrunning of the hospitals. However, these same people instituted a de facto embargo on outpatient treatment that ensured that anyone who gets a serious case of COVID would wind up *only* in the hospital.

Then they experimented on humans with therapeutics and shots that were known to be trouble long after their lack of safety and efficacy was proven, while they went to the mattresses to block proven safe therapeutics as the first- and last-ditch efforts to save lives.

It is for this reason we allocate a good chunk of this book to testimony from experts, doctors, witnesses, and victims of the war on treatment. Commensurate with one's view of the severity of COVID—and the immutably destructive policies they were willing to implement to combat it—is the culpability of those who denied the treatment for it. We need the world to hear the extent of the malfeasance so that we can resolve to never allow this to occur again.

Every one of the interviews you're about to read were conducted with the actual witness. There are no anonymous sources cited. Everyone is on the record making these claims as their individual selves. And we have also captured the actual audio of each interview to verify their authenticity if requested. Should anyone come forth to question the claims contained therein, we will enter into evidence those recordings so you can hear the witnesses testify in their own voices. Several of these interviews are already a matter of public record.

It should be noted, though, that there are so many more witnesses to and victims of horrific biomedical crimes who declined to participate in this trial for fear of reprisal. That alone demonstrates that we are no longer living in the dreamy Western democratic world in which we were born, and exposes the urgent need for a reformation of our government and medical system. We need a new Nuremberg trial and we need a new Nuremberg Code.

Although some of our witnesses in this book will attest to a growing form of medical kidnapping and even hospitals tying down patients and forcibly giving them dangerous treatments, we don't even need to focus on these most odious forms of biomedical terrorism. Just the mere notion that government and big medicine can collude to absolve themselves of all liability for their products, censor all reports of adverse events, discriminate in medical care and all forms of public accommodation on behalf of those who don't join the experiment, and destroy their livelihood is a clear violation of the Nuremberg Code.

That is the medical authoritarianism the Nuremberg doctors and lawyers sought to remove from the medical field and sovereign governments for the rest of time; sadly, seventy-five years later, it's quite obvious they weren't successful.

You will sadly see this for yourself as you are confronted with testimony from witness after witness of the indifference and brutality deployed by the COVID fascists. Rest assured, we forced ourselves to limit the number of witnesses we will soon call to the stand. We did so for two reasons.

First, for the sake of time, because tragically there is a seemingly endless stream of those who have suffered from this barbarism from which to draw. Second, for your sake, ladies and gentlemen of the jury, out of concern for your ability to handle hearing in one volume the sheer depths of depravity that were unleashed upon us. For it is the very people most prone to be provoked to prevent such a tragedy from ever reoccurring, such as yourselves, who are also the least able to tolerate prolonged exposure to it.

With that said, however, some descent into the mouth of madness is required here lest we unjustifiably sentence our children and grandchildren to something unspeakably worse still to come, and currently being conjured deep in the bowels of the depraved minds who conjured this.

Therefore, ladies and gentlemen of the jury, we ask you to consider the testimonies of the witnesses we are about to call with courage of conviction to both render the proper verdict at the end, as well as the righteous punishment that is called for.

Because we will prove, beyond a shadow of a doubt, there was no benign or innocent explanation *for any of this*. And that therefore, you must take this evidence and demand your elected representatives plunge this evil back to the depths of hell from whence it came, and never permit it to return to haunt us ever again.

CHAPTER 1

Theresa Long: What Happens When You Really Fulfill Your Oath to Defend Your Country Against All Enemies, Both Foreign and Domestic?

Consider the fact that, as of March 10, 2022, attorney Mat Staver of Liberty Counsel presented data in court showing 127 adverse effect-reported COVID vaccine–related deaths in the military in 2021.[82] That is more than the ninety-three reported COVID deaths in the military since early 2020.[83]

Keep this in mind, COVID deaths tend to be overestimated in a younger population, while Vaccine Adverse Event Reporting System (VAERS) deaths, especially in the military, are woefully underreported. How is that for a breach of the Nuremberg Code's dictate that "the risk must be weighed against the expected benefit" of an experimental medical treatment?

In many respects, Lt. Col. Theresa Long, MD, army doctor and aerospace medicine specialist, is the nation's foremost witness of the violation of the Nuremberg Code during the administration of the COVID shots. She witnessed firsthand the devastation of the shots, the censorship and coverup of their dangers, and the malevolent and immoral attacks against those who raised concerns.

This all happened within the population that was the most consequential to our national security, revealing the scope of this crime against humanity.

You see, the United States military is the prized asset of the most powerful nation on earth. If the country, and indeed the world, would be convinced to take these dangerous shots, it had to begin with the U.S. military. As such, every facet of the Nuremberg Code—indeed any code of ethics and regard for human life—was abrogated in order to achieve this sinister and unprecedented military "mission."

Moreover, there is nowhere in the country where you will witness a more accurate assessment of the scope of damage from these shots than in the military. The active-duty force is a very confined and defined universe. It is also a very young and extremely fit and healthy population. Thus, a sudden spate of heart attacks, strokes, blood clots, neurological disorders, and cancers in this population cannot be dismissed as circumstantial evidence like it can in the general population.

And indeed, a military doctor like Col. Long cannot somehow erroneously conceive such a precipitous and cataclysmic change in the health of America's fighting men and women, let alone look away from it.

Dr. Long knew no other professional life outside of her beloved army, which she joined at just seventeen years of age in the early nineties. In 2008, she graduated from medical school and then served the army as a field doctor for a decade. Shortly before the pandemic, she became board-certified in aerospace medicine. During this fateful time, Dr. Long served as the brigade surgeon for the 1st Aviation Brigade at Ft. Rucker, Alabama, tasked with certifying the health, mental and physical ability, and readiness for nearly 4,000 individuals on flight status.

Although the extent of vaccine injury and government coverup that she witnessed is confined to a unique population, it is perhaps more relevant—both medically and morally— to the over five billion people of the world who were jabbed with the COVID shots than what almost anyone on earth can attest to. For this reason, we call Dr. Lt. Col. Theresa Long to the stand to tell the world her story, so that humanity may never be treated as lab rats again.

· · · · · ·

QUESTION: Let's begin with the period of time you started seeing health anomalies. Obviously, you've had a ton of shots yourself as a physician in the military. You've administered countless shots. That was the norm. People didn't think twice about it. This new COVID shot came out around January 2021 for the military. When did you start seeing the shocking abnormalities?

LONG: The first troubling thing that occurred is that we got an email telling us they were going to start a clinical trial, and they had identified the locations. My clinic was not on that list and I anticipated it would be at least a year for the trial to be complete, and we wouldn't even have to worry about the vaccines. Then literally within maybe a week or two later, the vaccine showed up at the clinic and there was no subsequent email, and no one questioned it.

Then one of my colleagues, who is a doctor in her late thirties who never had kids and has never been married, took the vaccine almost immediately. She did have Lyme disease before that, which could have something to do with her reaction to the shot, but she clearly got horribly ill from this vaccine and was down for a week. She couldn't even her move her arm and lost complete range of motion. She was really freaked out because it was her dominant arm and she was wondering if she would ever get back its full functionality.

Then my sister's son, who was twenty-one years old and in the Navy, took it. She was told he lost all sensation in his legs and couldn't move them for almost two weeks, which seemed insane to me. That was the first time I went into the Vaccine Adverse Event Reporting System (VAERS) to see if her problem was common. I started seeing some really horrific information, and that was maybe only two months into the rollout for the military.

At the time, there were already more deaths associated with the COVID vaccine than all the previous years combined dating back ten years. Some other troubling observations were when I attended the Medical Management of Chemical and Biological Causalities course at Fort Detrick before this pandemic hit. At the course, they talked about COVID-19 and hydroxychloroquine as one of the top drugs to combat it. Some other doctors and I made a mental note of the kind of drugs we would want on hand for a biological attack.

I asked my boss after the pandemic hit why we don't offer hydroxy to everyone on our post who wants it, given that we could have easily gathered enough data among the 4,000 soldiers at our station to determine if it works or not and it wouldn't hurt anybody. Yet, they told me to shut up and my input wasn't welcomed.

Subsequently, in May 2021, I went to the American Occupational Health Conference, which was online because of the virus. Dr. Michael Osterholm, who was Biden's COVID advisor for a period of time, said we needed to get a needle in every arm down to six-month-old babies. And we needed to impress upon our patients that their quality of life was directly dependent on their obedience to our recommendations. That was the first time I had a full-stop moment like "what is going on here?"

A lot of the conference focused on how we as a society were going to punish the unvaxxed. Doctors talked about involuntary vaccination, where people would think they were getting the flu shot, but they were really getting the COVID vaccine. Then I went to the senior preventative medicine course online and it was horrific right out of the gate, when a lot of the main leaders who were running the course spent the better part of the first day telling us how amazing Dr. Fauci was, how flawlessly he had performed over the past year, and how we needed to emulate him. I asked a number of questions at the end, and the first was why they didn't consider COVID a biological weapon until proven otherwise? To which I was berated and told I was a conspiracy theorist—until I reminded them I was an army-trained doctor in biological and chemical warfare, and this was completely consistent with the way I was trained to think.

Then I asked about the faulty pandemic models. Given that we shut down our economy, closed businesses, and destroyed people's lives because we were told over two million were going to die but at that point it was actually 500,000, was our model in the military closer or further from the truth? Was our intelligence better or worse than on the civilian side?

The head preventative medicine doctor, a colonel, said the military was using the civilian model, which was absolutely abhorrent. Then I asked if we skipped two years of phase two trials and three years of phase three trials, and we only lost twelve soldiers across the Department of Defense to COVID at that time, were we really going to risk the lives of 1.4 million soldiers with an experimental vaccine? The colonel retorted, "You are damn right and you are going to get every soldier you can to take the vaccine so I can get enough data points to determine if the vaccine is safe."

They didn't like when I kept mentioning that the vaccine was experimental. They went around the room and asked where everyone's main source of information was to make these decisions over the past year. One hundred percent of the senior leaders said the CDC and Fauci were their guiding lights. So that's when I knew we were in trouble because there was an echo chamber, and groupthink is one of the deadliest things that can happen in the military.

Then I went out to Ft. Benning, Georgia, for an orthopedics rotation and I was pretty shocked at the level of harassment, intimidation, and threats lodged against these soldiers. Right out of the gate, when they first rolled out the vaccine there was a townhall meeting at which they propped up a young specialist for a question-and-answer session, where she sold everyone on how safe and effective the vaccine was.

People started typing in the chat group and asking very valid questions, such as, "How do you know it is safe with your limited data?" and "What happens if I get sick a year from now?" The doctor who was overseeing the townhall got very irritated and shut things down pretty quickly, even if it was a wife of a service member who asked the question. I know in one case, they went after the husband and all his wife did was ask a question about safety.

Junior enlisted soldiers are very vulnerable, and having just finished my master's and having done a yearlong research project in public health, I was very familiar with the medical ethics of conducting research and informed consent. It would be considered unethical for people above a prison population, let alone junior enlisted soldiers, to manipulate them into taking an experimental drug—which is what the military was doing.

So when I got to Ft. Benning, I saw this discriminatory mentality and zeal for coercion on a larger scale. For example, the general of the post would implement policies, such as that the people who were vaccinated got to go to the nice gyms on the post or go to the food court or get weekend passes, and people who weren't vaccinated could not and had all these extra restrictions.

I sat in a briefing with the general and there were probably twenty to thirty full bird colonels and command star majors from across the post. I was the only doctor there and I was the only one who was masked per policy because I hadn't been vaccinated. But it was very apparent from the badges on my chest and the patches on my shoulder that I was a doctor. I completely expected someone to come up to me after the briefing and ask me if I had reservation about the vaccine, but instead I had the command star major of the post glaring at me and saying that he couldn't wait until vaccines were mandatory so he could hold people down and vaccinate them.

You started realizing this was really out of control and quite vindictive.

In my time at Ft. Benning, I met a female soldier training for Ranger school who was the most physically fit woman I have ever seen in my thirty years in the army. It was a program in which we get a very unique baseline of a soldier's health and conduct a whole extensive list of labs. They go to Ranger school, and then sixty days later when they come back, we repeat those labs with the intent of optimizing how to get them back to normal as quickly as possible. If you've never seen anybody go through Ranger school, they are so messed up when they come back. They are surviving on thirty minutes to three hours of sleep every day for sixty days. They are starved to the point where most of them lose fifteen to twenty pounds. A lot of the men will wet themselves throughout the day for months when they come back from loss of bodily function, or they can't feel their hands or feet for months afterward.

It was literally my last day at Ft. Benning in May 2021, and I ran into her in the gym of the tactical athlete performance center, which is where the Rangers and soon-to-be Rangers train. They have NFL-level trainers and nutritionists. She got to telling me about her concerns that she was the only female in her Ranger school class, and she was the only one not vaccinated, and that everyone from the general all the way down the chain of command had threatened her career.

They told her if she didn't get vaccinated, she would have to quarantine fourteen days before Ranger school and that she would never get to lead soldiers. We talked for a long time and she was concerned about her future fertility. She hadn't had any children yet and she didn't want to put just anything into her healthy body. She said she felt it was divine intervention that we had met, so I went forward from there thinking she wasn't going to take it.

On my drive back from Ft. Benning, I was very frustrated with what was going on and I wondered to myself if I was being reasonable with my concerns. I heard a lecture by Texas cardiologist Dr. Peter McCullough, so I called him on my drive home and I was very surprised he answered my call. We talked for an hour or so, and I felt reassured that I was correct in my assessment of the vaccine. I went back to my residency and I had to give a morbidity/mortality report, which is generally when a doctor does something wrong and they go behind closed doors with other doctors to discuss it. It's a learning event and it's not for any legal purposes. Part of my requirement for my residency was to do a morbidity/mortality lecture and I decided on public health and drug safety, and what mistakes medical professionals have caused.

All the people in my program obtained their master's degrees in public health. I thought it was very applicable. I covered the top eighteen drug recalls in FDA history and how they disproportionately harmed women over men. I talked about the Nuremberg Code. I talked about aviation safety and the potential for mishaps. Toward the end of the lecture, I delved into the VAERS data and talked about how many deaths there were compared to the previous ten years. During the group discussion, I actually pulled some VAERS cases of teenagers and others thirty and younger, plus a breastfeeding mom whose baby died, and people got really angry at me for presenting that information.

I went around the room and I asked the doctor whose wife just had a baby if he had heard of the case of the breastfeeding mom whose baby died twenty-four hours after the mom got the shot, and I asked if he would have concerns and ask his wife not to breastfeed after vaccination. He said he would have absolutely no reservations. I asked if they thought it was unusual for a teenager to die within twenty-four to forty-eight hours of getting vaccinated.

I remember a female emergency medical doctor in the room whom I asked how many times she remembered seeing a teenager suffering a massive, unprovoked pulmonary embolism and die. Her response was, "All the time." That's when I realized this was kind of crazy. These people can't even acknowledge the obvious degree of vaccine safety issues that were undeniably clear at the time.

I finished the lecture and was walking out the door of my residency and it caused a massive upset. My senior leaders came back to me and said that I couldn't say anything negative about the vaccine. I was going against the policy and I was told negative action could be taken against me. I told them that they couldn't tell me what kind of medical opinion to have, and that there was no policy I had to endorse their opinions.

Morbidity/mortality conferences are normally very emotionally charged because a doctor says, for example, they cut off the wrong leg or something, and takes a verbal thrashing from colleagues admonishing them for not being safe. This was just the complete opposite.

At first, I kind of laughed about it. However, people wrote complaints against me and I found out later that some of the twenty doctors in the room went to the judge advocate general and tried to have charges brought against me for giving the presentation and presenting facts. These were senior leaders who should have known that what I did was within normal medical decorum.

I stayed in pretty regular communication with Dr. McCullough and he said they were starting to recognize pretty regular cases of postvaccine myocarditis, after people had been berating him for daring to comment on vaccines because he was just a cardiologist. He thought this was like the hand of God, so he invited me to be part of his COVID-19 group. I became pretty obsessed and read everything on this topic for seven to ten hours a day.

Something was so disturbed in my spirit about what was going on that I literally got down on my knees and prayed for wisdom. The Holy Spirit had so strongly convicted me that it was my duty to stand up against what was happening. It wasn't a whisper. It was more like a shout: "You won't get the vaccine. You won't give the vaccine. You won't promote the vaccine." And that was before I ever met Dr. McCullough.

The famed cardiologist called me before the CDC announced its emergency meeting concerning myocarditis and told me I needed to stay on top of this for the sake of my pilots. I immediately called the group that processes all the army flight physicals and grants the pilots waivers for any conditions or medications. We don't even let our pilots take Benadryl or Allegra, but we were letting them take this vaccine. We are neurotic about safety and drugs with unknown side effects when it comes to aviation. They can't use Visine for their eyes. They can't drink 5-Hour Energy or Red Bull.

As a rule of thumb, we don't let them take a drug unless it has been on the market for five years because we just don't know the side effect profile well enough. But for some reason, they signed off on this vaccine without any question or follow-up on a single known safety concern.

I let my chain of command know I was part of Peter McCullough's group of 450 doctors concerned about the vaccine and myocarditis. The colonel was really angry that I was bringing this up, but he had no choice but to email all the cardiology consultants for aerospace medicine. His top consultant came back and conceded that, yes, myocarditis was a risk with the shots and all the flight surgeons and pilots should be made aware of it. However, they still said that the benefit of the vaccine outweighed the risk of side effects.

And I was shocked that colonel didn't send out any information about the risk. Keep in mind, the FAA grounds pilots for forty-eight hours after they take the vaccine, but the army applied only a twelve hour no-fly rule following COVID shots, which doesn't make any sense since we are always far more restrictive than civilian aviation.

So why wouldn't we at least apply the FAA's standard? And when there is research that the average onset of myocarditis is within seven days, why wouldn't we, out of our legacy of abundance of caution, set the no-fly time at seven days? Nope, twelve hours was good enough for the military. But if you came in contact with a friend of a friend of a friend who had COVID, we would quarantine you for ten days, and that was $8,000 lost in training per day. Commanders thought that was a huge detriment, not because anyone was sick, but because somebody had created this completely asinine quarantine policy. It was because of asymptomatic testing that everyone kept testing positive for COVID.

I went into the clinic the day after the CDC had issued the emergency warning for the risk of myocarditis and I was mortified. I expected to see a sign that said "Vaccinations temporarily suspended" or something like that—as we typically see with other therapeutics following the discovery of such an adverse safety signal—but it was business as usual with at least thirty people in line who would've been in the at-risk group for an adverse event.

I wrote an email to ask why we weren't pausing the vaccines and if we weren't, could we at least improve our informed consent regime? The response I got just blew me off and said this could maybe be a future research project. I followed up with yet another email and I didn't even receive a response whatsoever to that correspondence.

At this point, I was transitioning from my residency to my position as first aviation brigade surgeon. Before I could take the position, I was contacted by the U.S. Army Center of Aviation Excellence surgeon, and she said General David Francis, commanding general at Fort Rucker, needed me to get behind the narrative that the vaccine is "safe and effective."

I said I was following the facts and science. The surgeon was also a consultant to the surgeon general on women's health, so I told her about my concerns regarding pregnancy and lactation. I also recorded the conversation.

She told me if I wouldn't get behind the narrative, I wouldn't be compatible with my future assignment. That was whistleblower reprisal because she indicated that she had gotten my emails I had sent about informed consent, and her threat to remove me was a direct result of those communications. She said her biggest concern was that the only people getting COVID were the unvaccinated, and I said we can solve that problem by offering all the unvaccinated people ivermectin for prophylaxis. This was before the mandate and

I said we can't make them get the vaccine, so if your goal is to mitigate the number of COVID cases, why not do that? Why not simply focus on proactive treatment?

She said it was because if we did that then *people wouldn't want to get the vaccine.* I literally begged her, saying that while I really wanted to get behind this, I needed someone to show me where my science was wrong. I told her Peter McCullough was happy to talk with them and we could sit down and figure things out and they just refused. I had many conversations with the military's medical legal ethics attorney, who had reassured me on multiple occasions that they could not in fact tell me to have a specific opinion about a certain medical treatment.

Nevertheless, I ended up taking over as the first aviation brigade surgeon after all, and the first or second week I was there, they sent out a memo that they were mandating the vaccine. And then they sent out a memo saying unit personnel would use only as much force as necessary to assist medical providers with involuntary immunization.

It is unusual to go into a new job and have heavy conversations with a boss who barely knows you, but I basically told him this was medical rape and that if I caught anybody doing this, I would be reporting them to their licensing group. I told him about the unpleasant optics of a bunch of white soldiers holding down a black soldier in the deep south and injecting them with an experimental drug, or a female being held down and penetrated with a needle and injected with a substance by a bunch of men. Someone had not thought this through at all.

They backed down and announced they were going to allow medical and religious exemptions, but on the same day they sent out an email saying to keep this one in your toolbox: the Emergency Use Authorization was approved from the heads of all the major religions at the Pentagon—Jews, Christians, and Muslims—stating there was no valid religious grounds for not taking the COVID vaccine.

I thought this was going to end in one of two ways. If there is nothing nefarious about this vaccine, then the military is going to be extremely liberal with granting medical and religious exemptions and then they will go back to the White House and say they vaccinated every eligible person. But if it is nefarious in nature and is in fact a bioweapon, then they won't take no for an answer and won't grant exemptions. The latter proved to be true.

QUESTION: What do you mean by the shot being a bioweapon and when did it ultimately click in your mind that this was a nefarious plot to use a bioweapon?

LONG: As someone who was MCBC (Medical Management of Chemical and Biological Casualties) trained at Ft. Detrick in 2012 and at Ft. Hood when the Ebola outbreak occurred in Dallas, it was completely different this time around. Ft. Hood has over 50,000 active-duty soldiers, and we had a lot of freaked-out service members who were on the flight with the guy who had Ebola. I called the people who trained me at Ft. Detrick and we were able to get to the truth.

Then when I retook the MCBC training in 2018, a lot had changed. There were all these new diseases that all these insane maniacs have tried to use, they explained, including how biological substances were being black-marketed from Russia. One of the things they pounded home was that biological weapons were the poor man's nuclear bomb. You didn't have to be a superpower to afford them, but the challenging thing was how to disperse them to enough people to have a strategic impact. You had to be able to disperse it quickly enough before people caught on to what was happening and it had to get them sick enough. So, in my mind, when COVID came out, it met all the criteria that they trained us for in a biological weapons scenario. The thing that finally sealed the deal for me was watching the seamless choreography of the Italian ventilator stories; MCBC training taught me that if you see terror like that in people in response to illness, it's likely a biological weapon because the terror causes people to do anything to comply.

As a doctor, I know that one of the things that terrifies patients the most is the thought of being put on a ventilator. So, when I saw the news from Italy, I saw propaganda. The thought of being put on a ventilator and struggling for every breath was terrifying for people. I was also aware of the Wuhan lab being at the epicenter of all of this, which is why this all made sense as a bioweapon. But that was a first step.

Then, in order to get people to inject the other bioweapon into their bodies—the vaccine—you have to create a new technology, which in this case was mRNA, and you mandate that everybody take the bioweapon and they take it by a very fast timeline. That met all the checkmarks I had been trained to look for. You had to get people vaccinated quickly before the cat got out of the bag that these things were going to kill you. Sure enough, I learned from the clinical research study agreement between the Department of Defense and Pfizer, which involved 44,000 active-duty service members, that all their clinical data was processed through Israel and then given back to Pfizer.

It was mind-blowing that we would give this kind of sensitive data to a foreign country—even an ally. If you look at the clinical timeline for that study, what you start to recognize is that the timelines for the military getting everyone vaccinated by a certain date line up with the deadlines that Pfizer had to meet to get their Emergency Use Authorization (EUA). You start realizing that our military deadlines for vaccination had nothing to do with the health of the force and everything to do with ensuring Pfizer got the EUA quickly.

We were on somebody else's timeline, but it wasn't Russia or China's; it was Pfizer's. Then it made sense to me why that senior preventative medicine physician said you were damn right that you were going to get him as many data points as you could, because that's all soldiers really were—data points. There was some kind of contractual agreement and there were people in high positions whose sole purpose was to ensure Pfizer got that approval.

As I took over my position at Fort Rucker, I took my concerns to the director of immunization for the Defense Health Agency. That's the new, huge, and overarching healthcare system to take us from regional health care commands, where we had two-star generals that you would go to, and all of that was taken away and replaced by something they're still rolling out. If you were planning this whole pandemic, having your medical command in this complete upheaval and eliminating critical generals is a brilliant strategic move. I think a lot of this would never have happened if we had generals with whom you could interact at the local command the way we used to reach out to them.

The Defense Health Agency removed any kind of local decision-making from even the smallest military training facility. All that independent command, such as the hospital commander being the one who made decisions about how that hospital is going to be run, ended up being removed. Iron-fisted central planning and control was clearly put into place for a central goal that was not about the health of our military.

QUESTION: Is that consolidation of authority how they reached a critical mass of groupthink to overwhelm the opposition before it could get off the ground?

LONG: One of the other odd things from the get-go was how the CDC got inserted into the chain of command. We would receive random CDC emails that somebody forwards and there weren't any conversations about the military's unique mission and how the CDC recommendations might be irrelevant or downright stupid for us. There was just "the CDC says, so do." It was extremely unusual for the military.

Here's an ironic example of how much the military outsources our health protocols and planning to the CDC. In the initial phases, there wasn't a single N-95 mask in our clinic. The general was telling everyone we were ready, but we didn't have any. I have heart failure, so initially I was concerned. Getting N-95s was hard so they were regarded as gold. When I tried to hand them out when I got them, I got eye rolls. They told me the CDC didn't recommend them and Fauci says there was no point. And then a few weeks later, when Fauci said everyone needed a mask, these same people became militant little Nazis getting in your face and yelling at you if your mask came down a little bit. It baffled me that really intelligent doctors just became so dumb, and how military doctors completely lost their independence.

QUESTION: Can you tell us more about specific inter-actions you had within the military infrastructure about your concerns?

LONG: I talked to the director of immunizations and I laid out my concerns and what we were covering in Dr. McCullough's group. She came back to me and told me not to worry about all these other people because "we just need to get you taken care of." So she wrote me a one-year medical exemption, and on it she wrote out and detailed my safety concerns, which seemed really odd if my concerns were irrational.

At that point they were concerned about the ethics and that they had already received a gag order: they could not discuss the vaccine with any soldiers. But they reached out to me to say they were going to choke soldiers off from any legal information so that they could corner them into getting the vaccine and threaten them with dishonorable discharges. I had nuclear commanders contact me. I had people in the most critical positions call and tell me they thought this was a coup. This isn't just poor decision-making. This is a huge problem. The thing I realized, from a strategic perspective, is that there is no higher endorsement for product safety than for the DOD to mandate that every single service member take a drug into their body.

If you can imagine what would have happened if I had been sitting at the Pentagon, when all these decisions were made, and someone asked me about reacting to a total of thirty service members dying from COVID by giving 2.4 million people an experiment vaccine to prevent that, I would have said hell no. And I have to tell you I probably would have said that if they told me 5,000 or 10,000 died. You don't throw good money after bad money. Just because something is potentially deadly doesn't make another thing safe.

Let's say someone at the Pentagon reacted to me by saying it's too risky and we will wait another year; there is no way civilians would have jumped on board if they saw the military balk at it. And even more so globally. For the whole rest of the world to see the U.S. military mandate it, our prize fighting force, well then it had to be safe.

That's an endorsement I guarantee you money bought somewhere along the line because without a military mandate, this BS would have stopped.

QUESTION: You ended up being a key witness at Senator Ron Johnson's hearing in October 2021, and again through your lawyer at another roundtable he hosted in January 2022. Did you receive any backlash for that?

LONG: I ended up testifying before Senator Johnson because if I talked with a senator, it was protected communication, and he organized the roundtable to provide a forum in which I would be protected for speaking out.

My commander had called me in after the affidavit and gave me a counselling statement suggesting that I could not discuss the affidavit with anyone and basically my whole virtual identity on the internet got erased. People couldn't even find pictures of me. Most of the people emailing me in the military were asking me two questions: Was I real, and did I write the affidavit?

The military went so far as to change my rank to make me hard to find. When people called my unit, they told them I didn't work there or could not confirm or deny that I existed.

If they called the health clinic where I worked, they said I didn't work there. When my family tried to get a hold of me through work, they became terrified and concerned. They asked how hard it would be for the military to kill me because they were setting people up to believe that I was a figment of someone's imagination.

QUESTION: Can you discuss, without giving away private medical information, some of the unusual serious injuries you saw among those under your care?

LONG: Before I saw Senator Johnson, I had seen five pilots one morning; two had chest pains after the vaccination and one had brain fog. The two with chest pains said they came to the clinic specifically because they had read my affidavit online in late September 2021, and that was the first time they realized a cardiac complication could occur from the vaccine.

Pilots notoriously want to underreport health concerns. They want to fly. They don't want to be grounded. So, to put it bluntly, they tend to lie all the time. That's how they are. So, I ended up grounding these three pilots and talked about it with Senator Johnson. Shockingly, when I got back from Washington, I was told by a surgeon that I did not diagnose the pilots appropriately.

I went back and looked at the medical records. One of the pilots they pulled back in and told him to stop taking the medication I had put him on, and they put him right back on flight service without any further testing. They tried to do the same with the other pilot, but he refused and said he was going to follow what I said. He took the medication and by the time he saw the cardiologist, his pericarditis was resolved.

I had ordered a cardiac MRI the same day I treated him, and that order was cancelled. The cardiologist did a stress test and an echo and an EKG and all those were totally normal, and they wanted the kid to go back to flying. I said I'm not allowing it until we had completed the cardiac MRI. We went round and round and the cardiologist finally did it.

Here it was six months later when the results came back and it was devastating. He had several areas of scarring in his heart, and it ended not only his flying career but his career in the army as he has been given a poor prognosis. Can you believe that, left to their own devices, they would have placed him back on flight service?

I'll admit before the cardiac MRI came back, I had kind of started to doubt myself. Personally, I had never seen a case of myocarditis. I had seen pericarditis but never myocarditis. Yes, that's how rare it was before the vaccines. Not only did the cardiac MRI shock me because I had been so gaslit I thought I might be crazy, but the physician's assistant I was working with said that *this entire time*, we've had pilots we've been working with who have had chest pains and they've had all these negative EKGs, echoes, and stress tests and we sent them back to flying.

And she said she herself had experienced intermittent chest pains since taking the vaccine as well, but every time we sent them back flying, she was reassured that she didn't need to do anything. She recently had a baby not too long ago, and she was telling me she was sick or was experiencing chest pain and bad brain fog all the time. Would you want a pilot flying like that?

Another staff member told me the number of referrals to cardiologists for chest pain had skyrocketed. She told me I wasn't wrong and that they were treating me like I was crazy while they were constantly having to refer people off post.

QUESTION: What did you see the further you investigated?

LONG: I pulled records of health issues for the last two years at my post before the vaccine and something like 85 percent of them were muscular/skeletal/orthopedic injuries or behavioral health. Then when I started looking at records from the time we were rolling out the vaccine, it changed to where the primary problem was now medical and not muscular/skeletal and not behavior health.

It was cancers, chest pains, and cardiac workups. It was neurologic dysfunction and thyroid dysfunction. It was blood clots and strokes. It was things I did not see in my entire medical career in the army.

I have never seen so many bad medical ailments plague such a small population of young and healthy people. I started to take all the unique medical cases and ask them if they were vaccinated and, if they were, when did their symptoms start? A very troubling picture started to emerge almost immediately; I started to see all these guys who started vomiting blood or had blood in their stools and they got vaccinated about three months earlier. I saw a natural progression of when different organ systems take the hit from the vaccine.

At Fort Rucker there are only five people who would know the totality of medical events among our 4,000 at the training center, and only one of them—me—who is qualified to understand we were seeing highly unusual patterns emerging. That's where I repeatedly tried to engage my brigade commander and tell him none of this was normal, but he kept calling it bad luck. There was a lot of passive-aggressive behavior at the clinic, where they did not want any of the sick soldiers to see me, even though the injured soldiers were intentionally seeking medical care from me. There were days I would sit there with all of these open appointment spots and they wouldn't fill them with anyone.

It was kind of a catch-22. In some ways, I didn't want to see patients because I knew that because of my recommendations, the higher-ups would take retaliatory actions against a pilot due to their negative feelings toward me. One day, I was sitting there without patients and I thought, you know, when I got my master's in public health I got access to the Defense Medical Epidemiology Database (DMED), and I was required back then to do a year of research. It is the most comprehensive medical epidemiological database for the military, and you could look over ten-year periods to see whether males or females have more disease.

After months of asking everyone about the number of adverse events transpiring, I thought I could see where we were trending with myocarditis and other things. I sat there for eight hours straight on January 10, 2022, pulling diagnostic codes for every unusual thing I had seen in my population. I was trying see if it was a one-off or if it had been occurring across the DOD. The data was so horrific. I sat in my office retching over the garbage can and crying. I couldn't believe what I was seeing.

The numbers were so bad that it indicated one of two things: either treason was happening at the highest level or it was gross incompetence.

QUESTION: You were subpoenaed by Mat Staver of Liberty Counsel to testify in one of his legal cases representing military personnel fighting the jab mandate. How did the brass respond?

LONG: I told pretty much everybody in my brigade headquarters meeting that I had been subpoenaed to testify, and I put on my leave calendar that I would be at a court case. I got to Florida and my brigade commander called me one night and said he heard my brother had a stroke and then that he really didn't, and I just used that to sneak down to Tampa to testify in a federal court case. So which was it?

I told him I didn't make a habit of lying. My brother did have a stroke and I was going to go to Minnesota to see him but then I got subpoenaed. The next night, we were getting ready for the court case and I got a message from my XO telling me that I needed to be available to be counselled over the phone by my commanding officer. They sent over the counselling statement that told me that I couldn't discuss anything from the DOD or that was in the stored possession of the DOD. They basically told me I couldn't testify and if I did, I would face adverse action.

When my commander called back to actually issue me the counselling statement, I told him that I felt threatened and intimidated, and that I felt he was witness tampering. He told me it didn't originate with him and that he was just passing along information, which means there was undue command influence. I went back into the conference room with the attorneys and I broke down. I was incredibly angry and frustrated. The opportunity comes to go down to Florida and testify in *Navy SEAL 1 v. Austin* and get it all off my chest to maybe stop the damage that is being done, and then the very people who should be concerned about the soldiers getting hurt were more concerned about covering their own ass.

I got pretty upset. Staver told me he understood and that I didn't have to testify. I told him I would pray that night about it. I had already arranged for my husband and kids to drive or fly down to be there because I wanted them to be in the courtroom where I could look at them and know they were safe while I was testifying.

I woke up the next day at three or four in the morning with Leviticus 5:1 on my mind: *"And if a soul sin, and hear the voice of swearing, and is a witness, whether he hath seen or known of it; if he do not utter it, then he shall bear his iniquity."*

Although I read the Bible, Leviticus is not a place I spend much time in so I didn't even know what Leviticus 5:1 said. I got on my phone and read it and it said that if you are called to testify about something you have seen or that you know about, it is sinful not to testify and you will be punished for your sin. I felt that was a really clear answer to my prayer. I told Staver it was a go and that I had to testify.

I got up there to testify and we went through all of my credentials, and then they started asking me about the DMED data and I told them I was sorry but they told me not to answer your questions about that. The judge, Steven Douglas Merryday, said, "Excuse me, what did you just say? Who ordered you not to testify?"

I said it was my commanding officer. The judge wanted to know exactly what happened and I told him about the phone call the night before. It was a pretty emotional moment because I looked at my kids and my husband, and I knew that if I testified, I could go to Leavenworth. I could go to jail. But

I also recognized that if I didn't testify, more of my soldiers could get hurt or killed from the vaccine and I would be disobeying God. I got a little emotional and told the judge I was willing to accept the consequences.

It was appalling that at one point in my testimony, when I was discussing the Pfizer documents and I was laying out for the judge that 88 percent of all women who got vaccinated end up with a quote "dead baby," the opposing counsel started laughing and high fiving. It was a very surreal moment. The judge had to admonish them on two separate occasions for their behavior.

At one point, the opposing council asked whether I had read the investigation about the DMED data that was published. I asked where it was published. They handed me a Word document that said there was a glitch, and the glitch occurred only in the months I pulled the data for only the diagnosis that I pulled. There was no official crest or signature saying who did the investigation. It was unbelievably absurd.

I've done many investigations for the military. You have sworn statements. You have specific forms. You have appointment orders about who is doing the investigation, what the scope is, and the questions you have to answer. This had nothing. It literally looked like the opposing counsel whipped it up the night before.

Then the opposing counsel started attacking my information about VAERS that I requested from the CDC. I asked for all the VAERS reports on military service members because the military wouldn't give it to me. It showed that 8,853 reports had been filed on service members and that included 119 deaths. The young attorney started yelling and saying, "Isn't it a fact that all 25,000 deaths reported in VAERS have been fully investigated and that only nine of them are from the vaccine?"

I said I would love to see that report, and she walked over and handed me a printout from the CDC website and it said "a review of the reports indicates the causal relationship between J & J COVID vaccine and TTS (Thrombosis with thrombocytopenia syndrome). Continued monitoring has revealed nine deaths causally associated with J & J COVID vaccination. CDC and FDA continue to review reports of deaths following COVID 19 vaccination and update information as it becomes available."

I told her that does not say what you just said it says, because those were the only ones they affirmatively confirmed but they did not discount the others, which were still under investigation. She asked if I believed in peer-reviewed journal articles. The judge said, "I got this one" and asked her, "Young lady, you don't really believe that the CDC's website is a peer-reviewed journal article, do you?"

Opposing counsel were then given three opportunities to present expert witnesses to counter my testimony and they could not.

CHAPTER 2

Lt. Col. Peter Chambers: The "Nuremberg Doctor" and Special Operator

Like Dr. Theresa Long, Lt. Col. Peter Chambers was a military doctor who cared deeply about the health of the troops under his command. What makes him unique is that he himself was seriously injured by the COVID shot as a result of trusting the military he so faithfully served for over three decades.

Chambers is quite the rare breed of soldier. He is one of the few people in military history to earn a Green Beret at the same time he was a medical doctor. One would think the military would take to heart the concerns of a warrior doctor regarding a novel therapeutic that was mass distributed, and eventually mandated upon, the military—especially when Chambers himself was so seriously injured.

Although the shots weren't quite mandated at the time, Chambers gave into initial pressure and trusted his government and military like a loyal soldier. He received a dose of the Moderna shot in January and another in March of 2021. Shortly afterward, he experienced numerous neurological symptoms, including severe vertigo. Suddenly, this super health doctor and special operator was diagnosed with a demyelination, which essentially causes damage to the myelin sheath that surrounds nerve fibers in the brain.

It is the equivalent of stripping the insulation off a wire, except the live wire is in a human brain. The injury forced him to medically retire from the military in 2022. Our nation needlessly lost the vital talent of many seasoned warriors due to injury from the shot or due to refusal to risk injury from the shot, which resulted in being discharged on account of the mandate.

Given that Chambers himself was a doctor, he was able to discover that others in the military suffered a similar ailment, which is quite rare for healthy young soldiers. He was also one of the top public health officials in the Texas National Guard initially tasked with coordinating the Guard's response to COVID.

Yet, this revelation of his own injury and those around him, like every other safety signal, did not budge the military command. It was self-evident from day one that no number of safety concerns would deter them from the mass vaccination program for a virus that posed very little threat to healthy soldiers.

In fact, as early as April, even before Chambers attempted unsuccessfully to open the hearts of military commanders and army health officials, it was clear they were fully aware of the myocarditis problem.[84] Emails obtained by the *Epoch Times* in June 2022 showed that military health officials were never concerned about the damage of the shots to the troops, but they were concerned that the damage would get out to the public and force a shutdown of the program.

According to the FOIA emails, Lt. Col. Harry Chang corresponded with military and California health officials on April 27, a day after the *Military Times* reported the Pentagon was aware of the issue of myocarditis among the soldiers, dismissing the concern about needlessly ruining the hearts of young, healthy soldiers.

"A pause of the Pfizer/Moderna administration (much like the J&J blood clot pause) will have an adverse impact on US/CA vaccination rates; assessed as unlikely due to causes of myocarditis can come from multiple sources (e.g. COVID, other conditions, other vaccines/prescriptions, etc.)," Chang wrote in an email to Tricia Blocher, an official at the California Department of Public Health.

Yes; in Chang's view, it was totally normal for soldiers to get myocarditis, even though few doctors ever dealt with it. What was his real concern? That the news would cause a pause in the shots. "However, increased reported #s & media attention is likely to trigger a safety review pause by ACIP/FDA," he added.

To understand just how pervasive this utter disregard for the lives of our troops was among the military leaders, we call Lt. Col. Peter Chambers—the modern-day Nuremberg doctor—to the stand to tell his story of personal injury, sacrifice for the military, and unsuccessful attempt to get them to abide by the Nuremberg Code:

· · · · · ·

QUESTION: You have a fairly extensive and impressive background in the U.S. Army. Can you lay it out for us?

CHAMBERS: I came into the army in 1983 right after high school and joined the infantry, did my first stint, and got my honorable discharge in 1990. Then I went to the inactive reserves, went to college, and then to medical school with the intent of being a small-town doctor like my dad. Then 9/11 happened, and I got back into the army with Special Forces as a battalion surgeon to support Green Berets in combat.

By summer of 2012, I had been in a lot of combat, and decided I wanted to go through the Special Forces qualification course. At forty-five, I was about twenty years older than the typical enlistee, but I made it through selection as the first doctor who was allowed to do that because I resigned my commission to allow me to go. I became battalion surgeon at Third Special Forces Group and I was a flight surgeon, so I had two areas of specialty: I supported combat operations in theater and training stateside.

In 2015, I left active duty again and went into the Texas National Guard. I was deployed to Jordan, Syria, and even did a stint in Guantanamo Bay. Then, by the time I came back to Texas, the COVID thing kicked off in 2020. I was asked to be the liaison for the Texas National Guard to Governor Greg Abbott's COVID task force. My primary job was to help the public health docs with any support from the Guard regarding testing, procurement of personal protection equipment, and coordinating tens of thousands of soldiers for the COVID response.

So to sum up my qualifications, I'm a primary care doc—family practice, emergency medicine, and flight surgeon trained—and I jumped out of planes with Green Berets and did combat trauma. I have some medical school classes in immunology and virology under my belt, and I've dealt with some viruses downrange, particularly some pretty bad ones in Africa. But I got up to speed pretty quickly on what COVID was from a pathophysiological standpoint, as the tip of the spear while treating people in the Guard.

QUESTION: That's an incredible resume of service to your country, for which we wish to thank you. But you've brought us now to the beginning of your time observing and participating in U.S. Army policy as it relates to COVID. Can you pick it up from there to describe when things went awry?

CHAMBERS: I was in the Texas National Guard at the time; a border mission came along in February of 2021. Col. Peter Coldwell, the Texas state surgeon, came to me and said I couldn't go down to the border and take care of soldiers if I didn't take the COVID shot. It wasn't mandated at the time, but we had our own self-imposed mandate for providers in order to work. There was no adverse side effects reporting feature out yet, and I didn't know anything about mRNA therapy yet. Not to mention the fact that I'd been taking shots in the military since 1983 and never batted an eye, including multiple hits of the infamous anthrax vaccine. I trusted the military brass 100 percent that the COVID vaccine was going to be safe and effective, especially given that we always had informed consent with everything before.

STEVE DEACE AND DANIEL HOROWITZ

So, in January of 2021 I took Moderna's COVID vaccine to go to the border. Somewhere along the way came the mandate, and if you did not have the shots by January 2022, you were out of the National Guard. Unfortunately, I had already started to notice vaccine reaction symptoms in myself about forty days or so after the shot.

I started developing brain fog and had two pretty significant cases of vertigo. The second one happened when I was jumping out of a plane at night while doing a recertification. At about 9,000 feet, I realized I couldn't see my altimeter while tumbling through the sky at terminal velocity and decided to pop my chute. I landed about two miles from the drop zone instead of being squashed out on the pavement somewhere.

I went in to get checked out and the CT scan found demyelination. You find that with multiple sclerosis, but it is also what we are seeing now from Pfizer data showing well over 1,000 adverse reactions.

With that sort of neurological malady, you feel like a lightning rod. I don't run a 5G device anymore or put it to my ear. Radio and microwave frequency can wreak havoc with somebody with demyelination. The treatment is stuff like resting the brain and antioxidants.

QUESTION: **Did you see other neurological injuries or adverse side effects on the border mission as the jab mandate came about? Obviously, the number of soldiers getting jabbed would've greatly increased during that time.**

CHAMBERS: We were seeing specific groupings of injuries based upon vaccine lot numbers that you can look up in the VAERS database. For example, we had six younger guys who got cases of myocarditis over a five-month period of time. Here's the problem with the Guard—they aren't on active duty, so they end up going to a civilian hospital. As such, workman's comp covers for injuries, but maladies like chest pain don't get covered since they are not on TRICARE. Also, nobody in the Guard was ordering the cardiac MRI that was required because they wouldn't touch it for obvious reasons.

I would try to interpose with my medical command, and even with the task force commanding general, General Tracy Norris, for a meeting but she refused. So after two attempts to have office calls with the senior ranking officer in the state of Texas, the only thing I could do as a soldier was go up the chain to members of Congress.

The first one I hit was Rep. Dan Crenshaw, who of course is a veteran. I waited a few months and nothing happened. So I went to Rep. Van Taylor from Plano and spoke to him personally on the phone for an hour or so. Nothing happened. Finally, Wisconsin's Sen. Ron Johnson reached out to me because he was actually someone looking into this issue, and I talk to or email him directly at least once a week.

QUESTION: Was this almost like a "don't ask, don't tell" policy regarding the COVID vaccine? Were they even interested in putting in the surveillance to monitor the shot?

CHAMBERS: I had a two-star division commanding general, Charles Aris, do one of his walkthroughs at the base camp. I had a whiteboard full of information I wanted to talk about. He had a one-star and a colonel behind him who agreed with me but wouldn't speak out because of fear of reprisal. I said 78 percent of my guys were testing positive for COVID using

PCR testing and were asymptomatic. Seventy-eight percent of them were double-vaxxed and 15 percent had had no vax. All he told me in response was to get the numbers up on the shots.

I told him that wasn't the science. He said he didn't care about the science; he cared about the policy, and that was to get the numbers of shots up. I told him I had to tell him per regulations about the six people who had been to the hospital. Two of them had been to the ICU, one because of bleeding in his brain, and the other one had a stroke that required speech rehab. That's not exactly a normal occurrence for soldiers so young. He just made a joke at my expense and walked on.

QUESTION: What is the benign, innocent explanation for why the army wouldn't want to follow up on the health concerns of its most precious resource—its enlisted men?

CHAMBERS: The simplest answer is apathy and cognitive dissonance, but not mass formation psychosis. They know this is going on. This is how I know they know. The state surgeon, Col. Peter Coldwell, who fired me off the border for offering informed consent for the COVID vaccine, just retired. He sent me an email that said he was sorry for the way things went down, but now that he was retired, he could tell me the truth. He agreed with me all along but couldn't say anything because it was a political situation. I don't think that is benign. I think it was cowardice.

QUESTION: What would be of greater political interest to the military brass than the health of their soldiers?

CHAMBERS: The mission. For them, the mission was to make their vaccination numbers look good and my men were only 28 percent vaccinated at the time, while the other units around the country were 80 percent vaccinated. That's all they cared about.

QUESTION: A Green Beret such as yourself, who is also an MD, in other words the rarest of the rare even among the elite soldiers, is bringing his concerns about the vaccine to the brass and they don't care?

CHAMBERS: It goes even higher than the military brass. When I went to the office of Congressman Crenshaw, a SEAL team buddy, there was crickets. His chief of staff finally called me the day before I was going to testify before Senator Johnson and asked if there was any way to help me now. They only did that because they knew I was about to testify and would bring up their names.

I bring up Crenshaw's name every time I get asked about how I met Sen. Johnson because I originally filled out a whistleblower's complaint on Crenshaw's website. I thought he'd listen, but I heard nothing from his office. I even had a SEAL buddy of his place a call for me, but the congressman wanted nothing to do with me. It was only an hour before I was going to meet with Sen. Johnson that a staffer for Crenshaw finally called and said he wanted to help.

If you are a congressman, these are the sons and daughters of your state and you should be concerned. Now I go around the state to raise money for a foundation that gives it to the vaccine-injured soldiers because he didn't. Being rebuffed by a congressman who was a fellow special operator really broke my heart.

QUESTION: So, the mission is really just to inject as many of the enlistees as possible with an experimental substance, regardless of the consequences?

CHAMBERS: With these generals, it's numbers and what makes them look good because they are just looking to add another star. One of them, Tracy Norris, said during an audio conference brief while we were on the border that if we didn't get her the numbers she needed, she wouldn't get a three-star job in Washington, D.C. She said that out loud and we all just sat there with our mouths open like, "Are you kidding me?"

I had twelve soldiers come off the border mission, and I believe it's from the shots. Those with cardiac issues usually showed symptoms within a week of the shots while neuro deficits were typically more insidious in onset, with a month or two passing before they felt really bad. Specifically, we had two males in their thirties with stroke-like symptoms that ended up in the hospital. One underwent surgery for subarachnoid bleed.

That's not at all normal and statistically extremely improbable, a point I tried to impress upon the generals all the time. If I was downrange and we were in Afghanistan, and there were this many people who I had to send home with non–combat-related injuries, we would have a problem.

Well, here at the border is a mission, too. We are on the border dealing with an invasion of our country. We have to double up on shifts because we don't have enough soldiers to fill them when people suddenly disappear. I remember when

South Dakota sent us some troops to help out over the summer, and I had to send a twenty-eight-year-old back on the plane with Governor Kristi Noem because he had myocarditis. That soldier had just received his vaccine before he left South Dakota to join the border mission. When he arrived and stood his post, he developed chest pain within a week, and was later diagnosed with myocarditis at McAllen Heart Hospital.

QUESTION: And they didn't even put in a surveillance or treatment regime for those injured?

CHAMBERS: Army regulation 40-562, chapter eight, specifically talks about the need for surveillance postvaccination, and you have to follow it all the way out. You can't just say "good luck" and leave the soldiers on their own. We have to take care of our folks, but it's not happening. So, when I entered some of their injuries into VAERS on the military vax side, now they at least have some documentation. Maybe one day, when our heads are out of our butts, they can go to the VA and get some help. But for now, they don't have anything in their medical records in their military file, and that's where the ball is being dropped. The argument they use is that if we don't get everybody vaxxed, then our military readiness numbers won't be up to par. Well, actually the military readiness among the double-vaxxed is tanking.

QUESTION: Is there at least an effort to treat or help the vaccine injured within the military?

CHAMBERS: There's the official medical system and then there's the shadow medical system, and that is people like us.

For example, when I was down at the border and I was not allowed to have ivermectin in my inventory, I had people go buy me some. I would put it in a stock bottle, I treated people with it, and people got well.

QUESTION: What is your current state of health?

CHAMBERS: The vertigo is gone. The brain fog still comes and goes. I'm taking vitamin D and Zinc. I'm also taking ivermectin and hydroxychloroquine once a week to bind the spike proteins that are still in my system.

QUESTION: They eventually fired you from the border mission for daring to hold them to their own regulations. Was it officially because your vaccination numbers were too low or they didn't like what you were telling your enlisted patients?

CHAMBERS: They called to ask me why only six people out of 3,000 had taken the shots. They wanted to know what I was doing or saying to them. I said two words: "informed consent." I created a sixty-page PowerPoint presentation and I used data from the CDC, the NIH, the FDA, the WHO, and VAERS to refute the argument that it is even necessary.

When that happened, the state surgeon requested my presentation, told me never to show it again, and that if I couldn't convince soldiers to take the vaccine then I should pack my bags.

CHAPTER 3

Sam Sigoloff: When Duty and Honor Are Replaced by Unconditional (and Immoral) Compliance

Pfizer's shot contains 208 ingredients from nineteen different countries.[85] Every member of the military is coerced to get that shot, despite the fact that to this day we don't know most of those ingredients. Pfizer is completely absolved from liability, it can have its shot mandated on every member of the military, and it successfully fought to keep ingredients secret.[86]

What happens, then, if you are a military doctor?

Like Drs. Theresa Long and Peter Chambers, Major Samuel N. Sigoloff is a military doctor who saw the damage from the shots firsthand. He had a slightly different purview as a family doctor taking care of the families of soldiers; he was involved in writing medical exemptions for those with medical conditions or allergies that were a clear red flag for this vaccine. He was formally reprimanded for speaking out against the shots, with his commander claiming he made a comment in a gym unbecoming of an officer simply for abiding by his Hippocratic Oath and offering his professional medical opinion on the dangers of the shots.

To understand the scope and severity of the malice to punish those who raised concerns about this experimental product in the military, we call Dr. Sam Sigoloff to the stand so that the world knows what has happened to the United States military during the era of COVID fascism:

. . . . . .

QUESTION: You deal primarily with the families of enlisted military. Can you give us an example of what you saw clinically among those who have gotten the COVID modRNA vaccine?

SIGOLOFF: One example is an elderly retiree wife came in and she had a rash on her leg shortly after she got the Moderna vaccine. Rashes will usually blanch. You push on it and the redness goes away and then it comes back, but this was a non-blanchable rash. Petechiae, pinpoint bleeding underneath the skin. Sometimes that can be benign; sometimes that can be the harbinger of death.

QUESTION: The military data indicated there were issues with nursing women. What did you see among that group?

SIGOLOFF: When women breastfeed, the proteins in their bloodstream are concentrated in their breast milk. So, when you breastfeed your child after you put direction on how to make unlimited amounts of spike protein in your body, the life-giving breast milk is now a harmful liquid filled with spike protein. We now know the spike protein is the dangerous part of the virus. Then there's lipid nanoparticles, which are fat-soluble, and there is a lot of fat in breast milk. Do those lipid nanoparticles transfer in the breast milk? I don't know. I do know that in a Pfizer cumulative report, it says they've seen problems like irritability, rashes, weight loss, and fever with 14 percent of breastfeeding babies.[87]

I know one of the infants I saw had a fever every single day for four months. All the symptoms the infant had begun about a week or two after the mom got the second shot of Moderna. If you know anything about medicine, a child who has a fever for an extended period of time needs to be evaluated for Kawasaki disease. My workup for that was negative on the child with the persistent fever. The most tragic part of this infant is that the mother was unable to comprehend that it was actually her breast milk that could be causing her infant's illness.

QUESTION: Is it true you got suspended for practicing medicine by the military for offering and signing off on medical exemptions for the COVID vaccine?

SIGOLOFF: Yes, and until I get my privileges back, which we are in the process of negotiating, I am prohibited by the military to practice medicine anywhere. This also happened to another military physician when some service members were referred to a civilian immunologist. That immunologist wrote those service members a medical exemption for the jab because the patients were determined to be allergic to its contents. This other military doctor put the report and exemption into the patients' chart and sent it forward. That military physician is now in summary suspension, even though he had already happily taken the shot himself.

In my case, I wrote my medical exemptions based on the toxic lipid nanoparticles. If you look at the material safety data sheet made by the manufacturer, they say they are not for medical use nor veterinary use. They are for research use only and all safety relies on the end user. These toxic lipid nanoparticles may be a state-of-the-art weapon system; how else can any justify that the toxicology reports in those safety data sheets are classified? Who can classify them?

QUESTION: We do use lipid nanoparticles to distribute various cancer drugs through the body. What is different about this?

SIGOLOFF: When I first saw the ingredient list of Pfizer and Moderna, I saw some compounds I didn't recognize and looked them up. DSPC and DSPE are in both of them. They are both patented (US Patent 9,737,528) for the purpose of delivering drugs through the blood barrier into the brain.

They assured physicians that the shot would go into your arm and stay in your arm. If that's the case, then why would they add these compounds that were designed to take it to the brain? There is a patent from 2014, U.S. Patent 8,785,505, that discusses the side effects of lipid nanoparticles. Side effects like suppressed immune response and disseminated intravascular coagulation, or bleeding (often to death). They don't even know how long the lipid nanoparticles stay in the human body because it's a fat-soluble molecule, meaning it can go into and stay in every cell membrane of the human body because every cell membrane is made of fat.

QUESTION: When you shared all of this with your commander, who is not a doctor, what was the reaction?

SIGOLOFF: I was summarily suspended and my patients' medical exemptions were revoked by my commander, who, by the way, is not a doctor. In the United States, it's a felony to practice medicine without a license. I got in trouble and threatened for trying to report it as a serious crime to the authorities. There is an army regulation or law, DA PAM 40-502, 7-1b, that says if a commander disagrees with a doctor's opinion, the commander must order a "fit for duty" examination, where you get a second, medical opinion on the service member. Unfortunately, my commander continued to disobey such laws and regulations and I continued to get punished.

QUESTION: What did they do then when people got COVID? What was the treatment regimen?

SIGOLOFF: It originally was "go home and hope you don't die." Soon I learned about ivermectin, because there is a lot of good evidence behind it and it was very safe. TRICARE covered the cost of this medicine, so I didn't need to have a prior authorization for the patient to get the medication. My commander, a registered nurse, then took it upon herself to ban the off-label use of lifesaving medications to ill patients.

This commander was withholding a congressionally-approved TRICARE benefit from ill patients. Now TRICARE requires prior authorization before it will cover the cost of ivermectin. Most people don't understand that if an insurance company doesn't cover a treatment, the patient can still get the treatment. This is a topic that most nonmedical people don't seem to understand at all. Just because insurance won't pay for a treatment doesn't mean a doctor can't prescribe the treatment.

QUESTION: Don't you deal with off-label medication all the time?

SIGOLOFF: All the time. And I've never been given an order outlining what I am allowed nor not allowed to prescribe in my nine years of clinical experience.

QUESTION: You're facing double jeopardy here aren't you? Your military career is in hot water, and because of that, your ability to practice medicine even as a civilian is jeopardized?

SIGOLOFF: It's not good enough that they want to get me out of the military. My fellow military physicians want to destroy my life and everything I've worked hard for. If I don't do exactly what *they* say and do what *they* want, I won't be able to provide for my family. That's what it means to take the medical license from a physician.

QUESTION: Part of your reprimand claims you were overheard raising concerns about the COVID vaccines, so it was also how you counseled patients as well. Is there any precedent for that?

SIGOLOFF: I was talking with a company commander to explain how I believe it was an unlawful order to tell service members to take an experimental vaccine. As officers, we are duty bound to disobey unlawful orders. That company commander wasted no time to report in a sworn statement what I said.

A brigadier general then wrote a letter of reprimand and offered me the opportunity to have it not go into my permanent file. In my response, I told him that my permanent file is not on this earth but it is with my *Lord.*

QUESTION: The picture you're painting is that of course most of the doctors are all saying the same thing about taking the vaccine because if you don't toe the line, look what happens. Do you get the sense a lot of the doctors in the military see the problems with the vaccine, but they view opposing it as a career suicide mission?

SIGOLOFF: I think a lot of the doctors will never see it because they are too spiritually blind to ever see it. In a chat group I was in, I actually had a pediatric cardiologist say, "A little myocarditis is no big deal."

There is no such thing as a mild case of myocarditis for a child. It seems like this shot is the god of our time. Fauci claims that he is the science. Is he the chief priest? If you try to go against it, they will try to destroy you and leave you with nothing. But I would rather tell the truth and go into the fire for it than bow down to their false god.

QUESTION: Does what you've seen and what you're going through change your opinion on whether people should join the military moving forward?

SIGOLOFF: My son is about six years old and he sees Daddy come home in uniform and he likes to wear a camo shirt to be like me. But when he is old enough to understand, I will tell him about the evil I was fighting from within my own ranks. He will never join the military. That trust is completely broken.

CHAPTER 4

Scott Miller: Sanctioned
for Saving Lives

Self-righteous doctors and scientists were allowed to discriminate, stigmatize, and suppress alternative viewpoints in the media and academia throughout the pandemic. No matter how many times they were proven wrong, how destructive their suggestions turned out to be, or the vast numbers of innocent lives they failed to save, they were exalted as "the heroes of the pandemic," even though almost all of the people with alphabet soup degrees after their names never treated a single COVID patient.

Contrast that with Scott Miller, a modest and God-fearing physician assistant who treated pediatric patients in his small but very busy clinic in Washougal, Washington. He was beloved by his patients, and regarded as a smart diagnostician and clinician who would give his child patients all the time they needed—often for physical and behavioral ailments that vexed doctors who had more credentials than he did.

The last thing Miller needed was to insert himself into the COVID pandemic. He could have been like all the other "compassionate" practitioners, who told people who were suffering from the impact of the virus that there were no treatments, and he would still be respected today by the Washington State medical governing body—like countless hordes of other doctors and PAs in Washington who chose to let their patients suffer or die without treatment.

Instead, he dedicated himself to daily studying and researching, and sacrificing his for-profit clinic for a year and a half to treat several thousand people who weren't even his regular patients. Because of his commitment to truth and his willingness to act, he was able to treat thousands of people, and saved many hundreds of lives. His anecdotal experiences and the actual science had proven that providing early, aggressive treatment was imperative to keeping people out of the hospital. He also dedicated his time to serve as a patient advocate for those admitted to the hospital, locked away, isolated, scared, and alone.

Not only did the state government successfully block virtually all patients seeking treatment and encourage doctors not to treat anyone early for the virus, but they also punished the providers who were actually saving lives. Although he had only the title of physician assistant, Miller's knowledge of the pathophysiology of how this bioweapon hurt us, as well as an understanding of how to treat and heal people at every level of disease state regardless of comorbidity, made a greater impact on his patients than all the handpicked cable TV "experts" put together.

Rather than learning from his example, local doctors who were jealous or enraged about his commitment to saving individual lives lodged complaints against him to the medical board. Pursuant to these complaints, none of which were from patients Miller treated, the Washington Medical Board enacted an emergency suspension of his medical license based mainly on a perfunctory review from the Washington Medical Commission's "expert witness"—Dr. Leslie Enzian. She did not even take the time to speak with Mr. Miller. She apparently had the unequivocal stance, based on treating zero COVID patients, that any information outside of the CDC guidelines was dangerous.

It was her "conclusion" that led the medical commission to enact an emergency suspension of Miller's medical license, which ensured the medical commission would face no dissent and provide no way for COVID patients to obtain competent treatment. For saving so many lives during the pandemic, the state of Washington drove Miller to bankruptcy.

Miller's story represents a critical breakdown in our health care system. Currently, there are over 1.4 million clinicians licensed to practice medicine in America. Unfortunately, only a small handful across the country took the time to do the research and had the courage to not only treat, but also speak out against the atrocities taking place in our hospitals. The few who have sacrificed to stand up to the COVID genocide and abide by the Hippocratic Oath have been relentlessly investigated, fired, or lost their licenses to practice medicine for doing their jobs. It is the doctors, the members of medical commissions facilitating these attacks, who belong before a tribunal for the crimes against humanity they committed, just like those who did similar things during the Third Reich.

How do we ensure that doctors are never prevented from properly treating patients again?

It is for this reason we call Scott Miller to the stand to tell the world his story witnessing medical malpractice with deadly consequences.

. . . .

QUESTION: How did you end up becoming the only one treating COVID in southwestern Washington State?

MILLER: I guess I lack the gene for self-preservation. In all seriousness, I kept hearing Tony Fauci say, "There are no treatments." I just fundamentally rejected his premise that symptoms cannot be treated. I began sharing information with colleagues early on, and the frequent response was "there just isn't enough data." I am sure there were several other providers treating, they just weren't speaking out.

And I have to clarify, it wasn't just me handling all those patients/families. My front office worker/biller, Christy, and my office manager, Kerry, took this on as well and they were heroic. They were very scared early on, taking phone calls from people who could barely speak, worried they were going to die. But we would follow up daily, and they would hear the gratitude for choosing to help after patients' symptoms rapidly improved. They saw that the treatments worked, which gave them reassurance to trust me, and we never looked back.

Later on, an ICU nurse, Megan, who lost her job for refusing the jab, joined our crusade for treatment. She said it was an easy decision after seeing the damage it was causing to coworkers. One of the first cases she helped us with was an overweight man with diabetes. His wife contacted us after being told by his doctor's office to take him to the ER because his oxygen level had dropped into the seventies. She knew that if she called 911, he would likely die in the hospital.

Christy reassured her, telling her we had seen worse. Kerry ordered supplemental oxygen, I prescribed medications, and within an hour and a half, he had supplemental oxygen and medications. Plus, Megan arrived to administer further IV therapies. That's how we made this work, to treat and to help pull as many people from the depths as we could.

Also, unlike other clinicians, I never closed during the lockdown. I was one of the only clinics that stayed open for in-person care. I made a commitment in March of 2020 that I wasn't going to be more afraid of this than anything else. I've been around some of the sickest people, and I wasn't about to stop when people needed medical help the most.

QUESTION: Where did you get the initial clinical infor mation on the pathophysiology of the virus, which gave you the confidence necessary to buck the trend and go ahead and start treating COVID?

MILLER: It was a total God thing. It was March 15, 2020, and I was actually researching pediatric sleep issues and melatonin, and came across an article from Italy explaining the COVID situation. It had a fascinating breakdown of the virus, its pathways, its impact on the immune system, and the things we can do to inhibit or mitigate or decrease inflammatory responses. I also saw a study from Australia about ivermectin inhibiting viral replication within forty-eight hours. For all the ignorant doctors who never heard of ivermectin, I had been using it for years for kids with scabies and lice, and it has a virtual zero side effect profile. It's also dirt cheap and

I figured if I gave it to kids, why wouldn't I try it on adults? That's just a couple of examples of the news and data that was actually readily available.

One of my first chances to test this was on a father of one of my patients. I offered him a treatment for persistent coughing. I got a nebulizer and gave him a round of albuterol and it didn't do anything even though he was an asthmatic. So, I got some budesonide nebulized steroid solution to put in the nebulizer and he said within a couple minutes he was feeling better. It didn't make sense to me that it happened that quick because that is a maintenance medication.

I was intrigued, so I sent in a prescription for Singulair/montelukast and cyproheptadine and gave him samples of N-acetylcysteine (NAC), and recommended higher-dose vitamins D and C, zinc, and melatonin, because of the mechanisms in the literature I was reading out of Italy. He called two or three days later and said he felt much better—almost two weeks of crippling cough, congestion, and fatigue were gone in a couple of days.

My mind was blown.

That was right around mid-March as we were hearing more about COVID. At this point, it wasn't illegal to prescribe and we weren't banned from practicing medicine. It's not like I was using medications that had high side-effect profiles, where we would have to get lab work to monitor liver enzymes or things like that. These are safe medications, so I felt very comfortable experimenting. I am also a fan of anecdotal evidence in the absence of any other guidance from expert doctors apart from "do nothing."

QUESTION: You aren't a medical doctor, but you do have the qualifications to treat patients and prescribe medications, and from day one you were studying the pathophysiology of the virus to be able to help save lives. At what point did you become the community COVID treater in lieu of all the physicians/specialists in your area?

MILLER: I honestly didn't know, at first. I thought everyone was doing the research, trying to figure out how treat people and save lives. In April 2020, I had already been going through the information, the research from around the world, and sharing it with the families in my clinic. I would write down the list of vitamins/supplements and tell families to tell their parents what to take as a regimen. I told my mom to share the information with everyone in her bridge group, her Bible study, church, and everywhere else. I was desperate to get information to people but also cautious, knowing that what I was saying was going against the death mandates.

Then, there ended up being a rally in Olympia at the capital and I was asked if I would speak on medical freedom. My wife, Shelly, was very concerned and didn't want me to have anything to do with speaking out or becoming a target. Now you have to understand what was at stake for us. I built my practice from nothing, started off doing home visits, then worked in a garage that was converted into an office for almost a year as I waited for the build out of my medical office. At this point, we were finally viable. For the first time, Shelly didn't feel like she had to check the bank account just to pay bills or go to the grocery store. We were financially doing pretty well.

So, the night before the rally Shelly and I were talking, she was sharing her concerns, running through the possibilities, and started crying, asking why I would do this and risk everything. Why couldn't I just keep helping people quietly and flying under the radar?

I asked her if she was afraid of COVID. She said no. I asked her why. She said, "Because you know how to treat it." I told her that every day I had families for whom the "cure" is worse than the disease. It was destroying families, the well-being of children, and my job was to advocate for them. Also, I was ticked at the lies and fear being perpetuated on our citizens.

Shelly went to bed and I paced around the backyard late into the night, consumed in prayer. I felt like I was trying to bargain, wondering why I felt so convicted, yet trying to get out of it. I was like, "Okay God, I have been working a lot of hours and I'm not going to drive to the rally, so if you want me there somebody else would have to take me."

Then, I heard a knock at my door at 5:15 a.m.

Two women showed up at my door and offered me a ride, which was apparently my sign and call to duty, so I went and spoke. As our community and the country were becoming more aware of the damage being inflicted on our children and the detriment of distance learning and isolation, a local parent group started a Reopen Camas School Facebook page. I was invited to join and began sharing information, research, and some of the heartbreaking things that kids/teenagers would share with me privately.

I have heard people say that we won't know the true negative impact of this plandemic on our children for years. I was already seeing/hearing tragedies on a daily basis, inundated by stories of the devastating, crippling impact that social isolation and fearmongering was having on our children.

After a couple months of sharing information and answering questions parents had, one of the mothers in the group contacted a local reporter, John Ley. He reached out to me, asking if I would be willing to do an interview regarding whether it was "safe" for kids to return to school. During the interview, I spent a couple minutes discussing the lies spread by "top health officials" and government-controlled news media about kids being "super-spreaders."

The rest of the time was spent sharing information I had been studying. I told him about the science, the data, the treatments, and the successes I had seen. His article ended up being about prophylaxis and early treatment management. It got posted on a Monday, and on Tuesday our phones started ringing and it never stopped. That was the fall of 2020.

Throughout the first year, none of the people calling for help were from my practice. I would like to think that it was a testament to the efficacy of prophylaxis and having protocols/medications previously prescribed. The people that were sick were all adults, had gone to their primary care, urgent care, or the hospital, and they had all been turned away, being told that there were no outpatient treatments. They were merely told to come back to the hospital when they had trouble breathing.

This scenario finally ended up happening to a good friend of mine in November 2020 and she almost died. She called me on day nine of symptoms, informed me she has a history of asthma, and so I sent multiple prescriptions to the pharmacy. I had missed another call from her, and she unfortunately reached out to her primary care who directed her to call 9-1-1. The ambulance took her away before her daughter could even get back from the pharmacy. I spoke to her multiple times while in the hospital, and she was rightfully scared and said that her treatment was awful. She was right; I found out she was on a protocol less aggressive than I would recommend for a child with croup.

I told her husband to take all of the medications to the hospital, have her leave AMA (against medical advice), and if needed, go back into the hospital for further care. She decided to get in the car and go home because nothing could be worse than the hospital. Two days later, she was out of bed and did a mile walk around her neighborhood. She was asthmatic with some underlying conditions and told me she thought she was going to die in that hospital. I told her I had sadly already heard other stories like hers.

Around that time, I was asked if I would be willing to call a doctor at Mayo Clinic to advocate for a patient's brother-in-law. I had recently treated her and she asked me if I would share that information with the doctor. It was so surreal. The doctor refused to invest any time looking at the research or provide any treatment outside of the "NIH protocol," and the patient died. This was at the prestigious Mayo Clinic!

They should have treated him, done something, anything. That is when I realized their protocol *was a protocol of nontreatment*. The CDC nontreatment protocol had been unleashed across the country. This was evil. They stopped practicing medicine. They let people get to the point where they had to be put on a ventilator and they often just died. These doctors let hundreds of thousands of innocent people die.

QUESTION: **How did the local media react when they found out about what you were doing to treat COVID?**

MILLER: We didn't receive any backlash for a long time, which was weird. I thought that I would have a very negative spotlight on me after the article discussing treatments. That all changed in May of 2021 when I went to a school board meeting and wasn't forced to wear a mask because I had an exemption. Another local "reporter" wrote an article about a local pediatric PA who called the school board members either ignorant or pure evil, and claimed to be able to cure COVID—which, of course, was me. I simply replied, "I know there are treatments, because I treated over ninety people this month."

From that point on, things escalated. There was a previous frivolous complaint accusing me of lying on my initial application for a medical license in Washington, which is complete idiocy and they knew it. I had addressed the issue in November 2020 and provided proof that the claim was false. A month after the article ran, I received a stipulation of disposition from the medical commission, telling me that if I confess to lying on my initial application and sign their order, I could be treated like a criminal for three years.

A week after the stipulation, I received a package from the state medical commission with thirteen complaints about my comments to the school board from a group that was literally just pulling off complaints from that reporter's hit job. They were calling for an emergency suspension of my license because I was advocating for kids not to have to wear masks while playing outside on the playground. I had written exemptions for my pediatric patients, and they begrudged me for standing for science and against child abuse.

As 2021 wore on, I became increasingly more involved in my community and was sharing more information, which led to more and more people who were reaching out for help. I eventually began receiving calls from families asking if I would be willing to advocate for their loved ones in the hospital. The first incident locally was pretty crazy.

I had been to an event celebrating a local husband/wife dentist team, and that night he found out that his brother was transferred to the ICU and was about to be put on a ventilator. He had me speak with his sister-in-law. After the event, the patient's brother, sister-in-law, mother, and I sat in their car, had the wife on speaker phone, and called the hospital. After multiple phone calls to the hospital, repeatedly begging the ICU nurse to connect us with the on-call doctor, we were finally able to speak with her.

The patient was about to be put on a ventilator, with horrible bilateral pneumonia that the doctors simply labeled "COVID pneumonia." He was on remdesivir, lisinopril (blood pressure meds), and six milligrams of dexamethasone. I told her that she was a gifted doctor who has used her knowledge and expertise to save many lives, and that tonight she could be his hero if she would just treat his pneumonia. Please put him on antibiotics, switch his dexamethasone to high-dose methylprednisolone, and discontinue his lisinopril—which she did.

The next day, the patient was sitting up eating, and after only two days on this regimen he was up and walking around. At that point, the daytime doctor was trying to take him off the methylprednisolone and put him back on dexamethasone, which seems to always happens. Here's the thing I started to notice. Anytime a patient started to improve in the hospital, whatever beneficial treatments that were given, the subsequent doctors tried to undo it rather than double down and copy it. Anyway, that man—who was also a husband, father, brother, and son—walked out of the hospital a week later.

I know it sounds crazy, and people ask me why the doctors would do that, but it happened almost every single time. They typically defend their actions by suggesting that they can't be sure my protocol or suggestions are what helped them get better, even though it's the only thing they did differently. People are dying and they won't change anything, because they claim they don't have any large studies. Well, what about the results right in front of your face?

QUESTION: What was it like when the delta variant arrived in late spring 2021 and things were supposed to be getting better with the vaccines, but they actually started showing signs of getting worse?

MILLER: It was pretty bad! I would see my pediatric patients all day, while my staff was answering a never-ending stream of phone calls from people who tested positive for COVID. We had a big whiteboard with a list of their names and there would be an asterisk next the most acutely ill. I would call my wife really quick to check-in, and then I would start my evening with the adults around 5:30 p.m.

Remember, it wasn't simply sending some medications and everything would be fine. Ivermectin worked really well almost as a standalone medication in 2020, but after the roll-out of the inoculations, things changed, and I had to figure out the added variables that certain powers were using to try and kill us. On the nights that I did sleep, I would often go to bed around 3–5 a.m., after running my pediatric practice all day and handling the onslaught of new COVID patients from dinner until I got through the list.

If I wasn't advocating for families with a loved one in the hospital, I usually started follow-up texts around 1 a.m. and wouldn't finish until the sun was coming up. There was no pause button; there were no days off, because we were their last hope for care. It was a never-ending stream of need.

I remember one night I miraculously got home around 8 p.m. and I just broke down. I looked at my wife and told her I needed this to stop. I would go three days without sleep. My son said, "Daddy, if I got COVID would you at least pay attention to me?" I felt like I was falling apart on so many levels.

I was on the phone all night long with people suffering in multiple times zones. Pharmacies were withholding meds, and it wasn't just ivermectin. By July 2021, they were even withholding budesonide and Singulair. They were even withholding basic medications that were known to treat multiple issues, but the pharmacy boards were pressuring them to not dispense anything by me if there was a suspicion that it would be used for treating COVID.

I guess it made them feel like heroes if they suspected a request had anything to do with COVID and they denied the request. It was shocking to me. It got to the point that I just started buying medications myself with my own money. That way I could give at least two or three days' worth of dosing while we fought with the pharmacists because time was so critical. The elderly with comorbidities, who were the most vulnerable to COVID, had such a narrow window to keep them out of the hospital.

QUESTION: Did you find it ironic that you were willing to meet in-person with patients that weren't even yours, but the doctors who complained about you often weren't willing to meet in-person with their own patients?

MILLER: Some of these poor folks didn't have family members to help them, or they and their family were all so sick that they couldn't take care of each other. I would walk into these homes and see how sick these people were. I knew that merely dropping off prescriptions wouldn't be enough. With delta, people had extreme brain fog or would get these very dark thoughts and feelings of impending doom. I would walk into their homes without any PPE and give them a hug and I would hold them.

Many people were shocked, and I would tell them that I would be fine and that they were going to be fine too. I would assure them that we were going to get them better, together, and I would help them push through this. Then I would just hang out and talk with them to pull their minds away from the lies of the twenty-four-hour news cycle of death on TV.

QUESTION: When was the first time you were contacted by the Washington State medical board?

MILLER: In August 2020, I received a letter from Adam Calica, medical investigator for the Washington Medical Commission, about an anonymous complaint regarding an incident in 2012. The complaint stated that, "Miller was informed of a complaint filed against him in 2012 that had serious consequences for him criminally and professionally in California. Once he knew that criminal charges may follow and that he was being disciplined in California, he **immediately** applied for a medical license in Washington State."

The complainant claimed I had lied on my application for a medical license in Washington State. With a little effort, Calica could have seen that the felonies were for a *different* Scott Miller and that my "fleeing" was the slowest and most transparent "escape" ever! Taking thirteen months to apply for a license does not equate to "an escape."

Then, the hospitals started filing complaints. More and more families started reaching out to me asking if I would advocate for a family member in the hospital. They were barred from being able to go into the hospital, and often found it virtually impossible to get the treating doctor to speak with them. I would simply have the family call the hospital and ask permission for an advocate to be on the call. I had some success getting the doctors to change. Eventually, they would ask my name. I had an ICU nurse share with me how angry the doctors would get because I was asking them questions.

Then in June of 2021, the Washington Medical Commission sent me a packet they wanted me to sign saying I needed to take ethics classes and pay fines for the time it took to investigate me. I also needed to write an essay and send in my last three years of continuing medical education. When my office manager tried to pull that information up, she said that all records of my continuing education were gone.

Where did they all go?

I was just standing there thinking that this is way bigger than just me. That's when I contacted an attorney, and a week later the madness really began. I received a batch of thirteen complaints from a local group citing unprofessional conduct. In each of the complaints, they stated that they had read the newspaper article I mentioned earlier. None of their complaints were from anybody I had treated, just an apparent hatred for someone willing to go against the narrative and save lives.

QUESTION: When did the state board go in for the kill?

MILLER: I had sent a patient to the hospital for imaging and labs. The hospital convinced her to stay for "observation" and she never came home. Her son and I advocated for appropriate treatment every day, but it was refused. I think something snapped in me; a part of my heart broke when I found out she had been killed. I made a social media post about it, calling out her doctors, calling out the hospital, naming the people directly involved with murdering her. About twenty minutes after I posted it, I took it down after receiving a call from a doctor friend of mine who said that wouldn't help my cause.

The problem was that I had also been speaking out at events and was the keynote speaker at a public health forum where I shared what was really happening in our hospitals and the methods they were using to kill people. On October 15, 2021, I arrived at work to find a large packet on my desk, and inside was the summary emergency suspension of my license. It stated that I was a direct threat to my patients and the community, that I was treating people below the standard of care, and I was spreading misinformation about unproven therapies.

QUESTION: Some providers can barely count on one hand the people they helped that survived, but you can count on one hand the people that didn't, out of thousands you treated.

How has your experience changed your view of our health care system?

MILLER: I don't think I considered there to be a centralized bureaucratic control that prevented physicians from using their education, their clinical experience, their knowledge base, and their intuition prior to this. I thought ours was the best health care system in the world.

If you were sick with anything, you wanted to be here in America. Apart from that, sure, we all understood the pharmaceutical companies rule everything and keep you from looking at actual underlying causes for what is going on and pursuing preventative care. However, in terms of being able to medicate things away or mask symptoms, I always thought we were top-notch.

Then COVID broke my heart. We had people going into the hospitals, and if they weren't vaccinated, doctors would say they need to put them in a tent and it needs to be set on fire—or that they can just go home and die. These were human beings. We've lost the slightest hint of compassion. It was criminal. It was evil.

QUESTION: Did any other health care professionals come to you during COVID after seeing people on death's door be rescued, or who had heard about your success, to ask for more information about how you were enjoying so much success?

MILLER: Three naturopathic doctors, one DO, and one NP. Each of them has played a vital role in helping us continue our mission! Not a single MD, though.

QUESTION: What was the reaction of the community when they heard you had been suspended for helping them?

MILLER: It was very humbling. Letters poured in from across the country. A mom I had helped got a rally together at the clinic. There were so many people there, the families from my pediatric practice, and even COVID patients I had helped over the phone and never got to meet in-person. Some of the most beautiful prayers were emailed and texted to us. And of course, there was the financial support, without which there is no way I could have kept fighting.

Also, none of this would've happened if my staff hadn't been on board. Kerry and Christy, my goodness, those two women helped saved more people through their actions than every single doctor in a hospital setting in Washington State combined—guaranteed.

QUESTION: You mentioned that early on your wife was justifiably afraid of reprisal when you first started to take a stand. Was there a turning point for her that throughout this whole ordeal she has stood by you?

MILLER: It was August of 2020 when we were fishing on the Columbia River. Shelly got a call from a childhood friend who said her dad was sick. He was on day eleven with COVID and his wife put him on the phone and he clearly wasn't doing well. I got his information and told him I would send him what he needs, but it was a Sunday and the small-town pharmacy where they lived was closed. They called 911 the next morning and he went to the hospital and never came home.

Shelly got the call that he died, the second such call in the prior two months. We were sitting on the couch; she was crying and asked what would have happened if they called me last week. I said he would be home right now, because it would've been early enough for the treatment protocol to save him. That's when Shelly told me she didn't know how I was going to win this, but I needed to do what I could to help as many as I can, and she would support me. With her encouragement, this has been my mindset:

> The risk to my soul is too great for having truth, the ability to heal, but doing nothing out of fear. I will have to answer to my children one day, and hopefully, many years from now, my Creator. I want our children, and our Creator, to see that I buried no talents. That the gifts granted to me were used to serve a much higher purpose. I am not okay with being afraid and living in fear. I am not okay with my family being afraid and living in fear, and I am not okay with my community and our country being afraid and living in fear. My goal will be to bring light, truth, and healing.

CHAPTER 5

Anne Quiner–Death by Protocol

How did we get to the point where a year and a half into the pandemic—with all the modern medicine and billions of dollars spent—we still had healthy middle-aged people walking into hospitals with pneumonia, yet leaving in a casket? How is that hundreds of thousands of people wasted away for months on end with no update to any of the protocols the doctors knew were causing harm and making patients deteriorate rapidly?

Anne Quiner's testimony is the story of so many widows who lost loved ones prematurely from what should have been an eminently treatable ailment, especially after months of endless research and resources thrown at the virus. Likes so many Americans, her husband, Scott, caught the virus during the fall of 2021 (long after the vaccines were supposed to end the pandemic, not strengthen it). Within a period of a few days at the hospital, like so many others, he went from a healthy middle-aged man who just had to kick a form of pneumonia to a ventilated vegetable.

STEVE DEACE AND DANIEL HOROWITZ

What so many Americans experienced in the hospitals was a circuitous cycle of denial of care, denial of science-based treatment, and administration of dangerous protocols. The standard hospital death protocol exacerbated the respiratory distress, which created a self-fulfilling prophecy of clinical deterioration and further need for more risky and harmful intervention. They would isolate them from their families and advocates, as well as starve and scare them to leave them helpless and hopeless, thereby inducing high blood pressure and anxiety, which further aggravated their respiratory distress. In that case, they would proceed to give them antianxiety medications and sedatives, which would further intensify their breathing problems. Then, at each stage, the doctors would immediately seek "palliative care" and give up on the patient, even if they had decades to live.

Who, or what, is really behind this curtain of evil?

Scott Quiner's story is the embodiment of what countless suffered at the hands of a medical system that was incentivized to place "public health protocols" over the principle of the individual patient care. So the world can fully comprehend what transpired in American hospitals, we call Scott's widow, Anne, to the stand to tell her story:

· · · · · · ·

QUESTION: Before October 2021, you and your husband, Scott, were living in Minnesota. Would you describe him as a healthy middle-aged man?

QUINER: Yes. He was fifty-five years old, wasn't on any medications, ate healthy, stayed active, and was pretty muscular in body range.

QUESTION: What brought him to the hospital in October of 2021?

QUINER: Scott started feeling ill and coughing a lot. He thought it was bronchitis but coworkers of his tested positive for COVID. He had to do a test for his employment and the saliva test came back positive. We contacted a naturopathic doctor who prescribed ivermectin and steroids, and he started on them right away. A friend had a portable oxygen machine that he began using because we were trying everything to keep him from going to a hospital.

After a couple days when he was still not catching his breath, I took him to Ridgeview Hospital in Watertown Minnesota. I thought it was an independent hospital that wasn't doing Dr Fauci's protocols, so I dropped him off at the front desk, explained the situation, and went back to park the car. By the time I returned, they had already brought him to the backroom.

Oddly, the administrator getting Scott registered asked me what religion he is. I said "Christian." She replied "Christian" in a weird way, which got me wondering what that had to do with his care.

Scott later texted me a picture with a message that said: "It's a good thing I came in because my oxygen levels are up and I'm feeling better." But then mysteriously, the next day or two, I didn't hear from him. I was in contact with the doctors at this time requesting the Front Line doctors' MATH protocols like an IV of vitamin C, thiamine, vitamin D3, iver-mectin, hydroxychloroquine, zinc, melatonin, and Regeneron monoclonal antibodies. To which the doctors responded, "We will comply on some of these but not others."

That's how I learned that even if I have the health directive and power of attorney signed by my husband, that doesn't give me any rights to his wishes. He was never given the iver-mectin or the steroids he took with him to the hospital; I later found those items still in his bag.

Instead of the proper steroids backed by the most data (methylprednisolone) he was on before, the hospital replaced it with another steroid called dexamethasone (Decadron). A very low-dose IV Decadron was administered, but the steroid I requested per the MATH protocol was denied, as well as IV vitamin C, thiamine, and vitamin D. They only wanted to give him remdesivir, which doesn't help anyway.

When the doctor first called me about Scott's update, she asked me, "Why wasn't Scott vaccinated?" to which I was responded, "What does that have to do with his treatment? Are the patients who are vaccinated and unvaccinated being treated and cared for differently?" That's the way it sounded, especially since almost every clinical note starts out with "A 55-year-old male, *unvaccinated...*" (Emphasis added.)

Unfortunately, this wasn't just the sentiment of one hospital. Later on, after Scott was transferred to Mercy Hospital in Minnesota, on the first call I received about Scott, the doctor again asked me, "Why wasn't he vaccinated?" My response was, "It's an experimental gene therapy and it takes years for it to be approved; we will not put something in our bodies that is against our personal beliefs."

QUESTION: Why did Scott go to the second hospital, Mercy in Coon Rapids, after about a week?

QUINER: Ridgeview staff told me he needed to go because they did not have the "supplies" and he needed a higher level of care. He was on a waiting list from the hospital and if I didn't transfer him ASAP, they asserted, he would drop to the bottom of the list and would probably never make it out of there.

QUESTION: At any point, did they inform you of a diagnosis or a plan of action for your husband's treatment?

QUINER: Scott was intubated on November 4 at Ridgeview, then transferred to Mercy Hospital on November 6, 2021. I know now it's not ideal to transfer a patient on a weekend, which can foul up the patient's medications (which happened in our case as well). I requested that Scott start immediately on the Front Line doctors' MATH protocol after he was transferred to Mercy Hospital. The doctor complied only with a 1000mg oral dose of vitamin C daily, 5000mg vitamin D, thiamine, and melatonin. I was finally able to see him at Mercy hospital around November 10. They never complied with my requests for simple, safe nutrients to be administered to Scott. I would only hear the nurse, say, "I'll ask the doctor and they may approve one but not two of these basic nutrients or none at all since we have our own protocols."

The hospital was an hour away, and given it was a Minnesota winter, suffering from lack of sleep by checking his progress notes and labs nightly, I was praying for this nightmare to be over. My daughter and I had access to Scott's charts online and were up nightly reading the doctor's notes, looking at his labs, and praying fervently with many sleepless nights in complete frustration and anger. I would sometimes be driving there and back so I could take care of my kids at home. I had to rely on my faith and strength from God in the darkest hours!

The first time I arrived at Mercy and saw the COVID unit, my first reaction after seeing other patients in their rooms is that Scott didn't seem as bad as others. The patients probably were in their later stages, which I didn't understand until later. But as the days progressed, being there daily at his bedside, I was quickly observing a lack of staff. His care and meds changed all the time depending on the nurses and doctors, to which the nurses would say that they were just following orders from the doctor that day.

After the transfer, and days of me complaining about his suspicious regimen of meds, the doctor on call said, "I'll be right back." She goes to the pharmacy and states in her own words, "I am so sorry we screwed up. When Scott was transferred, we didn't catch the medications he was on. I'll fix it." That's when I learned you need to be vigilant of a transfer on the weekends.

Around December 4, the staff began telling me they were going to give Scott a tracheostomy. Now at this point and multiple times before, I was constantly asking, "When are you going to wean him off the medications and the ventilator?" But the answer depended on the doctor on call that day. On one occasion in mid-December, he was at 40 percent on the ventilator, so I told the doctor, "You could have removed him from the ventilator yesterday." He replied, "I know that." But they didn't do it; I was so furious!

Doctors were all over the map on when to remove him from a ventilator. One doctor wanted him at 60 percent, another 45, and still another at 40, so each time, the staff would say, "Tomorrow, it might happen." Then tomorrow came, and it was another doctor who moved the goalpost again. It was a constant barrage of confusion and it changed daily, sometimes even hourly.

On December 6, Scott was put on a tracheal tube, and his sedation and paralytics were dramatically increased. A couple days before the tracheostomy, I called the nurse, Jake, in the evening to see how Scott was doing. He replied, "You know they're planning on a trach tube and there are complications. If you take him home after and decide you don't want to deal with it anymore, don't clean it; he'll die of pneumonia and you won't have to deal with it anymore."

I felt paralyzed and literally didn't know what to say as I couldn't believe he told me how to murder my husband!

There was never a coherent plan for care. He only saw PT/OT twice in two and a half months. I would ask about a respiratory therapist coming in, but for a large hospital, there frequently wasn't one around. Especially around Christmas, there were not many staff members available, only those on call.

Later in December, the doctor did a CT scan, and said his lungs were so bad but the rest of his body was stable. His labs weren't bad, but his carbon dioxide levels were beginning to elevate. However, the doctors pretty much decided based on his stiff fibrous lungs he was going to expire. The doctor requested I sign a "Do Not Resuscitate (comfort care)" order, but I suggested again they try alternatives, such as glutathione, budesonide, and the MATH protocol. The doctor repeatedly said, "He's going to expire!"

When I asked about a lung transplant (given that the rest of his body was okay and he had so much life to live), after much delay, the pulmonologist called the University of Minnesota to inquire about a transplant at the end of December. The university coldly responded, "He's not vaccinated and too ill." (Well, they had him on a paralytic most of the time.)

QUESTION: Can you describe what it was like when he was on a ventilator? How conscious was he?

QUINER: It was torment, grief, sadness, and beyond anything, feeling utterly helpless. Watching him have coughing fits and running out of his room trying to find someone because his alarms were going off, as Scott lay at the mercy of whatever doctor or nurse he had that day, was horrific.

He was medicated heavily at different times and sometimes altogether (Ativan, fentanyl, Versed, Seroquel, Precedex, Haldol, Tylenol and oxycodone), but never given enough doses of vitamins and nutrition for a critically ill person to recover. I looked into his face more than once and said, "I am so sorry what they did to you and I regret ever bringing you to these hospitals knowing they could have given you the proper treatment and I was refused on almost everything I requested."

During the day when I was there, the nurse would ask him to respond to commands by opening his eyes, blinking, and squeezing my hand—and he did. But delays and the boluses of the sedation meds would put him right back on paralytics, which seemed to be the common theme with the lack of staff and no real plan of care.

QUESTION: Can you describe the feeding regime while he was on a ventilator, how he deteriorated, and when you realized you had to get him out of there?

QUINER: After two to three weeks at Mercy, I had heard of Dr. Joseph Varon in Houston, Texas, was using the MATH protocols and having results. At this point, I was exhausted beyond belief, so I had other friends trying to find me a lawyer and a patient advocate. My cell phone was going off constantly—everyone wanted to hear how Scott was doing. I requested for Scott to be transferred to anywhere outside of Mercy. The doctor at Mercy told me he couldn't be transferred to another local hospital. They had no beds and since Scott had a bed, he wasn't able to get another one nearby.

Now it was the end of December. While others are celebrating Christmas, our daughter, Andrea, flew in from Denver to see her dad. I requested if we both could see him since it was a one visitor only policy and Christmas. They denied it. Andrea went by herself and the staff barraged her with questions like "Have you talked to your mom about putting him in palliative care or comfort care?"

On another occasion, my in-laws came down to see their son. They got the same barrage of questions about when the "difficult wife" was going to sign the DNR and put him in "comfort care." I will add Andrea was with him on December 24 and said, "Dad! I'm here," to which he responded by opening his eyes and a tear came down. She was so thrilled and emotional!

This began another ordeal with the one-visitor policy and hospital staff. My pastor, Calvin Woods, came in to pray for Scott on several occasions, but one day my three pastors Calvin

Woods, Brian Holley, and George Gibson all came together. When you get off the elevator on the COVID floor, the nurses station is right there. They were immediately stopped and told only one was allowed in the room as a clergy.

Pastor Holley asked, "Is there a waiting room down the hall where we can go, while one of us prays for Scott?" They were very adamant in refusing. We decided to have Pastor Brian go to the room to pray for Scott while the rest of us went down to the chapel to pray, too. While we were there, an armed security guard came in and had us removed. When we asked why, he replied that he was only following orders, per the charge nurse we just talked to earlier. We then left and went to the waiting room and waited until Brian came back.

The nutrition Scott was being fed was an IV osmolyte drip and two to three packets of protein supplements. I looked at the label and informed the staff that it wasn't adequate. I even asked if I could bring my own nutrition to give through the IV, which they again emphatically refused. I hired a patient advocate with Graith Care LLC, Priscilla Romans, who has an ICU medical background. There was an ethics consultation at Mercy and I brought Pastor Calvin for support and Priscilla was on the line listening in.

Matt from the hospital risk management team let me know that the current meds and treatments were no longer beneficial and wanted me to sign the DNR. To which I responded fervently that I had a prescription for glutathione to administer in his ventilator, along with letter releasing them from any liability for pursuing that treatment. When the doctor asked me where I got the prescription, I said the doctor is a retired obstetrician-gynecologist, to which she responded mockingly, "An OBYGYN doctor is prescribing glutathione."

I brought with me some research about glutathione, but she refused to read it.

As an aside, throughout the ordeal, I brought in lots of research and left it for the staff in Scott's room, but they would only dismiss it because "it's just clinical trials." Ironically, these same doctors asked me to do a clinical trial of baricitinib for Scott early on, which is a drug that has an FDA black box warning for increased risk of serious heart-related events such as heart attack or stroke, cancer, and blood clots.

Anyway, at the meeting, Priscilla chimed in very professionally suggesting to the doctor protocols that worked with other patients. The doctor was getting very mad when I stated that I wanted to exercise my "right to try," which happens to be the law in the state of Minnesota. To which the doctor responded, "When you and Calvin came into the room everything was fine, but when you put your advocate on the phone the atmosphere changed. I want you turn that phone off," as she pushed my phone back towards me.

I left it there and said, "No. She's my advocate, I hired her and will keep her on." At this point, I wouldn't sign any DNR because I was requesting to bring him out of sedation so I could talk to him. The doctor just wanted the DNR signed, so that ended the meeting.

QUESTION: What did you do as last-ditch effort to save Scott's life?

QUINER: Already in mid-December, I was trying tirelessly to transfer him but never seemed to get anywhere as he deteriorated from lack of nutrition. On January 10, after days of grinding pressure, I was at the hospital and the nurse told me

STEVE DEACE AND DANIEL HOROWITZ

the ethics committee wanted to schedule another meeting. Naturally, I refused, knowing what they wanted already. The nurse actually said, "No, they just want to talk to you." I still refused and said, "They can call me at home." The pressure of me being there was getting very tense by now.

In the meantime, I called the nurse in the evening and asked her if there were any doctors at the hospital who would work with me on alternative remedies. The nurse, after mentioning she was scrolling and scrolling through her screen, finally was able to give me three doctors' names. So, I picked out a doctor who happened to be one of those assigned to Scott. On Tuesday, I'm thinking I was finally getting to meet a decent doctor who might give me my "right to try."

However, shockingly, the next morning, the chaplain and a rep from the ethics committee called me at home (I legally recorded the conversation) saying they were really sorry but the committee had decided Scott was too sick to ever recover, and that they were going to turn off his ventilator on January 13 at noon whether I was there or not.

At that point, my only thought was that I needed time to get him out of there! The staff had hoped that we would be there to watch him be executed while we felt helpless. I also said I needed more time to fly my daughter Andrea home and get my elderly in-laws down from Northern Minnesota. They said they'd call me back in a day or two. They hoped my family would be there, but either way they were proceeding with their plans. They would give me a couple days to contact my family to schedule his execution.

That day, January 11, I received a call at home from the doctor I thought was supposedly decent, and all she did was lament, "If we could only go back in time and Scott was vaccinated, we wouldn't be having this conversation." I told her, "There's people dying in hospitals that are vaxxed and unvaxxed." To which she retorted, "Not in this hospital under my care."

At that point, I called Shane Mekeland (my state representative), asked him for help, and forwarded the recordings of these threatening conversations to him and Priscilla (my patient advocate). They forwarded the audio to talk show host Stew Peters. At this moment, time was desperately running out, so I went on *The Stew Peters Show* live and my story went viral.

The next day, just one day before the scheduled execution, Shane called attorney Marjorie Holsten, who first tried to solicit help from other attorneys, but met with me later in the afternoon and we drafted up an ex parte motion for a temporary restraining order. Final documents were filed by 4:30 p.m., close to the court's closing time. Close to midnight on January 12, Marjorie received an email from Mercy hospital's attorneys at a high-powered law firm, requesting that the ex parte motion be denied. The judge assigned to my case required Mercy hospital lawyers to file a response by 10 a.m. on the 13th, the very morning they were planning to execute my husband.

Mercy lawyers filed their response with one striking sentence: "Plaintiff's position is not supported by medical science or Minnesota law, and as a result, Mercy will ask the Court to issue and Order that Mercy has the authority to discontinue Mr. Quiner's ventilator and proceed with his medical care plan." (An earlier filed document stated that the medical care plan was termination of life.)

In Minnesota, the law does not support the hospital's right to terminate a patient as part of the care plan without the patient's or family's consent. Thankfully, an hour later, the judge issued an ex parte temporary restraining order enjoining Mercy Hospital from turning off life support at noon on January 13, which would have been just an hour later.

QUESTION: Describe the process and emotions of evacuating Scott from Mercy hospital.

QUINER: Many calls were made to make the arrangements to have Scott medevacked via Life Link to Houston United Medical, where Dr. Varon agreed to accept him as a patient. This was a roller-coaster event. Mercy was unable to fax 600 pages (couldn't email at first) and then someone at the Texas hospital said they had no beds. Then, there were concerns that Scott wasn't healthy enough to fly. Mercy was dragging their feet on the transfer almost to the point we had to warn them we would file an order to have Scott removed from the hospital if they failed to cooperate. Note that on his chart they had set a date for Scott to be discharged on January 15. At this time, though, he had no discharge date set, so it was very suspicious.

Meanwhile, back at the Texas hospital, they originally said they had no beds, but my advocate, Glen Hopkins, told them the situation and through that contact, I received a call from the hospital's president. He graciously agreed to accept Scott despite his condition. Then Mercy had to set up the Life Link transfer and my state senator, Bruce Anderson, had a backup plane ready just in case Mercy didn't follow through.

On the morning of January 15, I was at the hospital with my suitcase to fly to Texas with Scott and still unsure if Life Link's EMTs would allow me to go. I was told by Glen to be calm and stay out of their way because they didn't want a hysterical woman causing them more stress. I was taking pictures of Scott and Mercy's risk manager Matt pulled me aside and said, "I'm hearing from my staff that you're taking videos of them." I responded, "No, I'm taking videos and pictures of Scott," and walked away.

After a couple hours of the flight crew going through procedures, they said I could come on the flight. But if I came, we would have to refuel halfway. In-flight, everything seemed to go smoothly. I told them I didn't want any more meds administered to Scott, only as needed. We refueled pretty quickly in north Texas, and about fifteen minutes from landing, I started to notice they were looking worried. I found out later the EMTs were only given two oxygen tanks for that entire trip! They were running out of oxygen, and I was desperately praying and getting nervous as we were approaching the runway.

We were completely out of oxygen when we landed and there were odd noises coming out of Scott's tracheostomy. We couldn't hear it in-flight with the headphones on, but the EMTs quickly determined there was a leak in his cuff. It was evident to me that Mercy never notified the EMTs that he did have a leak when they were going through the transfer. I knew that he had a leak because I already addressed that with Mercy prior to leaving, but the staff just blew me off as they usually did.

We landed and were completely out of oxygen in the two tanks. The EMTs were throwing things out of the way to get a better reach to help Scott. I'm reaching for the other oxygen tank, as they asked me to see if there was any last bit in there to use. To make matters worse, the pilot was notified that the ambulance was delayed a half an hour. The EMTs were yelling to the people on the ground they needed oxygen, and it was super windy outside, which didn't help the situation.

At that moment, the EMTs were getting out the LUCAS Device for CPR as Scott was flatlining. I was in the front of the plane crying and praying on my knees while this was all happening. A second ambulance showed up with oxygen, and they were able to get Scott in the ambulance. I was in the front seat and the EMTs told me they got his oxygen back up to the nineties, which was amazing. The ambulance was flying through traffic, honking the horn and barely anyone seemed to care or move out of the way. The EMTs were in the back yelling for the driver to slow down a bit but still move quickly.

We finally made it to Houston United Medical Center and they quickly rushed Scott to the room they had reserved for him. Initially, the president of the hospital had to call a congresswoman to release a bed for Scott. She came to the hospital to meet me personally, along with my brother Joe and his wife Kathleen as well. I was so shaken up when she arrived, I really didn't know what to say but "Thank you!"

Dr. Varon came quickly to the hospital when Scott arrived. I briefly talked to him and he said he wanted to go spend some time with him and get to know him. Dr. Varon was with Scott a couple of hours. When he came back, he said Scott was critically ill but he would do whatever he could to save his life.

Dr. Varon mentioned he was ordering a lot of tests. I asked, "You mean like tomorrow?" To which he responded, "No, we're doing them now," and stated, "This is a hospital." That brought me to tears. *Dr. Varon posted on his record that*

Scott was the most malnourished patient he had seen in his entire career. After treating COVID patients nonstop for almost two years and being a doctor since the eighties, that's quite a statement.

The staff quickly started the IV of vitamin C, ivermectin, sodium bicarbonate and glutathione—all the things I asked for at Mercy for weeks. Dr. Varon said he knew how hard I tried to get Scott there earlier, but this system just makes people sicker.

In Minnesota, Mercy said Scott had stiff lungs but they wouldn't do anything about it except more meds and lots of scans, x-rays, and labs. In Houston, they tried very hard to save my husband, but he passed about a week later.

Scott was a previously healthy man who came down with COVID-induced pneumonia and ended up dying despite all our modern medical care. I know they are doing it all for big payouts. The longer I delayed their system by not signing the DNR, the more they lost money because they wanted his bed for somebody else. They wanted him out of there. I wouldn't give Mercy Hospital the honor of that after what I had experienced there. All they cared for was their money and protocols that weren't working and they knew it, but they refused to try anything else. Dr. Varon later said that if Scott would have been there a couple weeks earlier, he would have had a better chance of survival.

QUESTION: So you believe the hospital protocol murdered your husband?

QUINER: Scott didn't die from COVID pneumonia; he would have recovered from that. He died from the hospital protocol and malnourishment. Scott will forever be in the hearts of those who knew and loved him. Knowing that Scott is with his Lord and Savior Jesus Christ brings a peace that surpasses all understanding. We celebrated thirty-five years of marriage and had three wonderful children together—Andrea, Jesse, and Nathan.

I would like to thank everyone who tried to help us: special thanks to my family, my in-laws, Free Life Family church, Priscilla Romans, Glen Hopkins, Stew Peters and his followers, Shane Mekeland, Bruce Anderson, Marion O'Neill, Dr. Varon and his team, Marjorie Holsten, Thomas Renz, Dr. Eric Hensen, Pastor David Agyepong, and Kimberly Nelson.

I can't remember everybody but I'm so thankful for all the amazing people who prayed for me and my family during this tragedy. Thank you, Jesus, for your hand of protection and comfort over my family during this entire time.

CHAPTER 6

Scott Schara: The Protocol from Hell

J ust when you thought you have heard everything, something comes along and jolts you even more. Scott Schara of Freedom, Wisconsin, has a very tragic story. Grace, his nineteen-year-old daughter with Down Syndrome, died of COVID in the hospital in October of 2021.

Or did she?

Aside from the denial of proper care in the hospitals during the pandemic, there is mounting evidence that some doctors may have actually administered dangerous care that flew in the face of basic science and medicine. Then there is the culture of cruelty and the disregard for human life, especially those deemed unworthy of living, reminiscent of the last time we saw a breach in medical ethics—which is what inspired the push for the Nuremberg Code.

Unlike most other victims of medical malfeasance during the pandemic, Scott Schara researched and documented the details of his daughter's care. They reveal a horrific pattern of mal-intent from day one, which begs the question: how ubiquitous was this culture of death in the minds of so many medical professionals throughout the past few years?

How does a teenager with moderate respiratory issues from a virus wind up dead a few days later? How did people wind up dead hours later after their blood oxygen levels were sufficient and stable on noninvasive oxygenation?

Scott's story demonstrates the same hospitals that refused to administer fully FDA-approved drugs targeting the respiratory distress also had protocols to liberally use sedatives, opioids, and antianxiety meds that were contraindicated with each other.

These medications collectively induce further respiratory distress, which is like treating a fire with gasoline. Rather than offering drugs like ivermectin and methylprednisolone, or supplements like NAC, they needlessly sedated people to further slow their breathing. This created a self-fulfilling cycle of respiratory distress and the need for mechanical ventilation. Throw the starvation protocol into the mix, and you have the perfect storm that if systemically utilized, could have led to thousands upon thousands of young and middle-aged people winding up dead a few days after low oxygen levels.

Even more disturbing is the evidence he is willing to present demonstrating that his daughter's Down Syndrome placed a target on her back to sadly never leave the hospital alive. One study from the U.K. showed that "people with severe mental illness and learning disability" had the highest death rate in hospitals. But given that the virus targeted people with physical inflammatory ailments for the highest death rates, why would those with mental illnesses most often leave the hospital in a body bag?

Let us not forget that one of the reasons for the crafting of the original Nuremberg Code was the understanding of the logical outcome when a society and the medical profession view those with mental impairments as less than human and more expendable.

To understand more about the war on the mentally ill, we call Scott Schara, Grace's dad, to the witness stand:

· · · · · · ·

QUESTION: How long after Grace contracted the virus did your daughter go to the hospital?

SCHARA: We estimate she contracted the virus on September 28, 2021, because she had a sniffle that resembled allergy symptoms. The delta variant was running rampant at that time, so we started her on the Front Line doctors' protocol that day. She had been on a vitamin regime for several months before then. We tested her on October 1 with a home test and she was positive. We took her to urgent care on the morning of October 6 after her regular doctor refused to see her because we told her Grace had COVID. As I see it now, this is all part of the control and scare tactics being used.

We were motivated to take Grace to urgent care because of Front Line doctors emphasizing concerns with oxygen saturations lower than 94 percent. We were monitoring Grace's oxygen with a pulse oximeter at home and that morning she was not able to maintain oxygen saturation above 90 percent. Interestingly, the urgent care nurse didn't start Grace on oxygen right away and only did so after I pressed her, following a text from my wife.

This should have been a signal to me that oxygen was not as big of a concern as we thought. Instead, they focused on blood chemistry. The blood work done at the urgent care facility showed a high D-dimer, which they convinced us was an emergency. Grace and I then rode in an ambulance to the hospital on October 6 to get a CT scan to determine if she had clots. We subsequently found out that COVID often produces the symptom of a high D-dimer. The CT scan confirmed that Grace had no clots, which is the typical result relative to COVID. They also did a chest x-ray and diagnosed Grace with COVID pneumonia. This diagnosis is a play on words, as COVID pneumonia does not resemble regular pneumonia—at no time did Grace have any trouble breathing and she had no chest congestion. I see this situation as another piece of the manipulation narrative used to scare people.

QUESTION: You took her to the hospital with a blood oxygen level in the high eighties. Why did you bring her there? Can you share the progression of the viral symptoms in the ensuing days, and what the hospital did and did not do?

SCHARA: Our working assumption, like most Americans, was that a hospital is there to help people, not to kill somebody. So, we let its substandard care go because we did not think they could do what they actually did. The ER doctor convinced us to admit Grace to the hospital for oxygen and a steroid and suggested that she was going to be three or four days in the hospital at most.

The first day was normal until they put a high-flow cannula on Grace, and I was none the wiser. After all, I thought she needed it to get oxygen. I perceived the oxygen situation as an emergency and the hospital staff played off that fear.

Grace was pretty irritated by the oxygen device. It was shooting air up her nose at forty miles per hour. Because of that irritation, they switched her to a BiPAP mask after my suggestion since Grace used a CPAP for sleep apnea. Research subsequent to Grace's death showed that both the BiPAP and high-flow cannula were not necessary, but tools used as part of the mandated COVID protocol. They did an excellent job fitting it and everything was fine. Then the next morning the pulmonary medicine doctor came in and suddenly asserted that they must place our daughter on a ventilator in the next two hours.

I asked what that recommendation was based on. He said they did a blood gas draw late the previous night, which was when Grace was pretty frustrated. Her blood pressure was 235/135mmHg, and her heart rate was 150 beats per minute. Because of that fact, I told him I didn't think the blood gas draw was accurate, and I asked him to recheck her numbers.

They did a new draw and she was fine. I asked him what the prognosis was if Grace went on a ventilator, and he said only 20 percent of people walk out alive once they are on a ventilator. The attending nurse started crying. I spoke to her and found out that she also had a daughter named Grace, and she knew if I made that decision our Grace would die.

Before this incident, I thought ventilators were a tool used to treat COVID, believing what President Trump unknowingly told the country at the beginning of the plandemic about how vital they were. I immediately began researching and found out that only 15 percent of COVID patients walk out alive once they are on a ventilator, and the majority of them die in the first year of related complications.

QUESTION: If her blood levels were fine, then what was her actual diagnosis?

SCHARA: As mentioned earlier, the diagnosis was COVID pneumonia, but the communication was so poor I couldn't get my arms around it and I was just left with fear. With COVID pneumonia, the symptoms are treatable with steroids. It's really not a big deal, but they make it into one, so you really don't know what to do without more information and they don't give it to you.

QUESTION: Did they force the ventilator?

SCHARA: After the first attempt, it never got forced, yet they asked four more times for a preauthorization "just in case." They told us the need for these things often "happens in the middle of the night when we can't get a hold of family."

QUESTION: Do you remember what her oxygen saturation level was in the first day she was in the hospital with the BiPAP on?

SCHARA: That's a fantastic question because it opens up quite a can of worms. On October 9, Grace was pretty hungry after resting for most of the previous day. I ordered food and helped feed her because of the BiPAP mask, and the nurse came running in and said, "You can't do that!" She said the oxygen saturation was only at 85 percent. I thought about that statement for fifteen minutes and I thought that can't be. When we were in the emergency room and she was just on a regular cannula she was in the high nineties.

I had my own COVID materials and supplements in the room, because I suspected I would be getting COVID, too. The materials included my own pulse oximeter. I put the oxygen finger meter on Grace and it read 95 percent, so I called the nurse back in. After she confirmed the pulse oximeter reading was accurate, I asked, "Why is my fifty-dollar meter more accurate than your fifty-thousand-dollar meter?" She said, "Because the leads get sweaty." I asked why she wasn't more attentive since this statistic was the primary marker being used to monitor my daughter's care. She snottily responded that I was just lucky I caught this.

After the fact, I requested the bill the hospital sent to Medicaid after Grace died. I found out that in the seven days Grace was in the hospital, they only changed out those leads three times despite my challenge, and the cost they billed Medicaid was only seventy-eight dollars a lead. At such a minor cost, why wasn't this situation a priority?

Bigger picture, we've learned an awful lot since Grace died. Grace was malnourished because of the lies about oxygen saturation. The fact is that Grace should have been fed the entire hospital stay, and them starving her contributed to her death. They chose to sedate Grace instead of feeding her. Even if Grace's oxygen were temporarily in the eighties, it would not prevent feeding her. You can clearly see the agenda through the eyes of this oxygen situation.

QUESTION: Are you saying they were using fake numbers to try and get your daughter on a ventilator?

SCHARA: It's worse than that—*she never needed a ventilator*. The faulty oxygen numbers continued all the way into Grace's last day. Ninety minutes before Grace died, her sister Jessica recorded her oxygen saturation at 93 percent, while the hospital recorded it at 44 percent! These numbers I'm certain were used as the justification to kill Grace. The experienced ICU nurse commented to Jessica, "Sorry, there is nothing more we can do for your sister."

QUESTION: Your last answer leads to quite a claim. Do you believe the hospital killed Grace, or was it just a series of mistakes made in the fog of a pandemic?

SCHARA: Since Grace died, I have invested almost every waking hour researching, investigating, and getting the word out. Almost everyone who looked at this case said it was murder, but I wasn't convinced. After seven months of research, I have come to the belief that Grace's death was indeed a premeditated murder, ultimately caused by our government's agenda and facilitated by purchasing hospital cooperation with huge financial incentives. I'll walk through the evidence to support my claim and let you be the judge.

At approximately 8 a.m. on Grace's last day, October 13, the doctor called Cindy and me at home. I had been kicked out of the hospital on October 10 by an armed guard for challenging Grace's care, so our older daughter Jessica was now in the room since my wife was home sick with COVID. His call was the fourth request for a preauthorization for the ventilator.

We said, "No." He said, "Grace had such a good day yesterday that we should work on nutrition." He even discussed Grace sitting up in a chair. He framed this feeding discussion as the next step for getting Grace on the path out of the hospital and recommended we approve a feeding tube. Even though Grace could have been fed total parenteral nutrition (TPN) through her peripherally inserted central catheter (PICC) line, the doctor led us to the feeding tube decision. He told us a feeding tube would be better because it would get Grace's organs working versus TPN going into the bloodstream. He also told us there was a risk of infection with the PICC line.

We foolishly approved that recommendation. I say "foolishly" in hindsight now that I see Grace's malnourished status in the right context, as well has how his "recommendation" fed into the overall narrative. As I mentioned before, Grace needed this alternative only because they chose to not feed her conventionally, which they could have easily done.

There was a fourteen-year veteran ICU nurse on Grace's case that day, the same nurse as the day before. About 8:30 a.m., Jessica said to this nurse that she was going to take a shower. The ICU nurse insisted Jessica go home to take a shower. Jessica explained that I was able to shower in the room. The ICU nurse told Jessica she didn't care what I was allowed to do; Jessica was *not* to shower in Grace's room.

Jessica, a bit fearful of being kicked out because of what happened to me, went home to take a shower. Not coincidently, this nurse was overly nice to Jessica the day before and now had a completely different attitude. Before Jessica left, she hugged and confirmed with Grace if it was okay to leave and shower. Grace nodded her head in approval, acknowledging what Jessica was saying.

When she got back, she overheard two doctors and this ICU nurse in the hallway say, "The family is not going to like this."

They had strapped Grace down to the bed while Jessica was gone because Grace wanted to go to the bathroom. I later found out from examining the twenty-two doctor's reports, which were based on the twenty-two times a doctor had visited Grace during those seven days, that they referenced *thirty-six different times* that Grace had Down Syndrome. My opinion is they strapped her down because they could get away with it, and they used it as an excuse to rachet up the sedation medication being used on Grace.

They illegally had Grace on the sedative Precedex four full days before her last day, without our knowledge. When she was without an advocate for forty-four hours, they increased the dosage *seven times*. I say "illegally" because the package insert says it is not supposed to be used for more than twenty-four hours.

Precedex is an anesthesia drug used to knock people out before surgery. Nurses who use this drug will tell you it is to be used for only three hours. The hospitals are now using it to set up the goal of a ventilator. As soon as the patient is put on Precedex, the amount of money the hospital receives increases because the room is now classified as an ICU. In Grace's case, she never switched rooms and the care didn't change.

More importantly, if you want to get out of the hospital, by your own free will, you are not allowed to do so as that choice is considered AMA—against medical advice. The medical malpractice nurse, who reviewed the detailed records, concluded the hospital "chemically restrained" Grace with Precedex. The package insert for Precedex states, "Adverse reactions associated with infusions greater than twenty-four hours in duration include ARDS, respiratory failure, and agitation."

Grace's death certificate states the immediate cause of death as "Acute Respiratory Failure with Hypoxemia." Is that enough proof? Hypoxemia is another side effect of Precedex. Not surprising, her second cause of death is listed as "COVID-19 Pneumonia"—to facilitate the government death bonus payment to the hospital.

Interestingly, this cause of death also facilitates a funeral reimbursement to the family—the government who just killed your loved one wants to "help," an obvious tactic to take your focus off the crime. My wife said, "We don't want their dirty money," and we have not fallen for this trap.

After unstrapping Grace, they didn't wait for Grace's numbers to rebound. They went right to the feeding tube, so now Grace was scared. She asked Jessica for help. Jessica witnessed the attending nurse challenging the ICU nurse to wait. She refused and treated Grace inhumanely and proceeded with the feeding tube.

The feeding tube was inserted at 11:37 a.m. but it was not confirmed through x-ray that it was placed properly until 1:59 p.m. This fact lends itself to the idea of the feeding tube recommendation being used as another tool used to take Grace out.

They used this self-fulfilling deterioration in health as an excuse to rachet up the Precedex to near-max dose at 10:48 in the morning. Remember that at 8 a.m.—just a few hours prior—the doctor called and said Grace had such a good day the previous day. He had us approve the feeding tube based

STEVE DEACE AND DANIEL HOROWITZ

on this fact, and further referenced Grace moving to a chair because she was doing so well. Jess hugged Grace just two hours earlier and gave Jess a head nod regarding her leaving for an hour to shower.

Now she was out of it for the rest of the day, which is just insane—literally knocked out starting early afternoon. But they didn't stop. At 11:25 a.m. they gave her a dose of lorazepam, and then followed up with a second dose at 5:46 p.m.

Remember, Precedex is what they use to put you out before surgery. Lorazepam is used to stop anxiety. Why did she need that when she was already knocked out? Then they gave her a third dose of lorazepam three minutes later (5:49 p.m.). And to top it off, at 6:15 p.m. they gave her a two-milligram dose of morphine as an IV push.

That combination of meds in twenty-nine minutes would have taken anybody out, much less someone with COVID pneumonia who needs anti-inflammatories, not sedatives that slow your breathing all the more.

We have 100 medical professionals who agree with the conclusion of the med combination as cause of death. One intensivist wrote and told me, "I agree the medications killed your daughter." Even more substantial, the doctor who helped review the records last November, concluded: "Each of these meds (Precedex, lorazepam, and morphine), on their own, have an increased risk of serious or life-threatening breathing problems and cardiac arrest, and there's an additive effect when used in combination. *To use them like they did in a person with a diagnosis of acute respiratory distress is beyond believable as to intention.*" (7 mphasis added.)

But it gets even worse. For this combination to happen, not only did the doctor have to order the contraindicated meds in violation of the morphine package insert, a pharmacist had to sign off on the order, the hospital medication alarm had to be overridden, and the fourteen-year experienced ICU nurse had to inject the meds!

Jessica was in the room when these meds were injected and was told nothing. Shortly after the morphine injection, she thought Grace was getting cold, so she asked the ICU nurse to take a temperature on Grace. This nurse refused to take a temperature and told Jessica to just cover Grace with a blanket.

Jessica asked if this was normal with what they did to/gave Grace and was told yes, this is normal. In spite of the morphine package insert requiring the monitoring of the patient, no doctor or nurse entered Grace's room from the time the morphine was injected until she died. There's nothing normal about any of this.

· · · · · · ·

Jessica started to panic and called my wife and me to tell us that Grace's vitals were dropping like crazy. I told her to get the nurses and she said she had been and was trying, but they wouldn't even come in the room. We started hollering to the nurses via FaceTime to help save our daughter. They hollered back that she was DNR: do not resuscitate. It was the first we knew she was labeled DNR. We screamed back, "She's not DNR; save our daughter." They could have easily done so, as the morphine package insert requires they have the reversal drug bedside.

QUESTION: Wait, are you telling us that this is how you discovered a DNR had been illegally placed on Grace?

SCHARA: Our attorney hired a medical malpractice nurse to review our records after the fact. I thought we had everything, but she said we were missing at least 1,000 pages. She wrote up a second request and received another 948 pages. On page 853, we found out the doctor put a DNR order on Grace eight minutes after the near-max dose of Precedex was administered that morning of October 13. But at the time, we hollered to the nurses that she wasn't approved for a DNR, and that to the contrary, we wanted them to save our daughter; the nurses used the doctor-ordered DNR as the excuse to not save Grace. One nurse read this fact to Jessica from her computer screen at approximately 7:22 p.m. The doctors or nurses would not come in the room all while this was going on.

We watched Grace die at 7:27 p.m. on FaceTime.

This whole thing with the DNR violates several Wisconsin state statutes. Our family has the details related to the illegal DNR on the website we've created in Grace's honor (the website address can be found at the end of this chapter).

In hindsight, I believe Grace's fate was sealed on October 13 when we denied the preauthorization request for a ventilator the fourth time. Specifically, they finally realized we were not falling for the ventilator push. Why else would the doctor discuss a conceptual DNR with us when we are expecting Grace to get out of the hospital after her nutrition level improved?

The circumstantial evidence supporting this conclusion is based on the fact that the hospital and the ER were both at 100 percent capacity on Grace's last day. The hospital was making only $1,680 per day because we didn't authorize the ventilator, but the hospital did receive a $13,000 COVID death bonus. As my wife put it, "Grace was worth more dead than alive."

QUESTION: Are there any other facts you'd like to add about why you believe this was medical malfeasance, not just malpractice, and are you sure she wasn't just one of the unfortunate victims of COVID pneumonia itself?

SCHARA: It is important to frame our beautiful daughter Grace's last day in light of how well she was doing. I have already referenced the doctor's comments on the morning of Grace's last day. The night before, she was talking and FaceTiming, even though she was sedated. We had no idea she was sedated. We just thought she was sleepy from the hospital protocol keeping her up all night, and Jessica being told Grace was using all of her energy to breathe.

In spite of being sedated, her oxygen saturation was at 98 or 99 percent all night on October 12. The morning of her death, she watched a recorded video from her nephews telling her to get well, gave Jessica a head nod when Jess left to take a shower, and was still communicating with Jessica.

After Grace died, I took my wife to the hospital to be with Jessica and see Grace. I had to stay in the truck because I had COVID. Our pastor also met us there. Two important facts help illuminate the tragedy just explained.

First, after the funeral director left, our pastor walked my wife out in a wheelchair. Additionally, a nurse who had Grace's belongings on a cart walked next to her. The nurse leaned down and said to my wife, "Me and several other nurses don't believe Grace should have died today."

Second, Jessica told us there was an armed guard posted outside the room during the time we were screaming to save Grace. Furthermore, she crawled in bed with Grace after she died just to lay down with her, and she said the armed guard just watched her through the nurse's window for about twenty minutes until my wife arrived.

QUESTION: Since your daughter's death, you've done a lot of medical research on your own. Can you describe what you've found in terms of the use of Precedex, lorazepam, and morphine together?

SCHARA: The morphine black box warning says specifically not to combine those meds because it can cause death, and the first page of the package insert says you are supposed to have a reversal drug readily available and monitor the patient. But once they administered morphine, a nurse did not enter that room until after Grace died. No such monitoring ever occurred. Those three drugs should never be combined! The goal should have been to help Grace, not suppress her breathing and oxygen—the result of using "end-of-life" medications on her.

QUESTION: Where has your research led you as to the reason behind Grace's death?

SCHARA: I have well over one hundred hours of research into her death. We had reviewed the records the first week of November and realized she was killed. However, we had no idea where things would lead. In fact, at that time we saw our Biblical responsibility to meet with the hospital and show them our research so they could repent and not have it happen again.

After they refused to meet, the research intensified. At the beginning, I thought all of this had to do with the money. In Grace's case, as mentioned earlier, because we wouldn't approve a ventilator, they made far less treating her daily than they were going to make if she was a COVID death. The hospital was at 100 percent capacity and so was the emergency room. "So, let's take her out for a higher-paying patient," was probably their modus operandi, right?

But then I read about attenuated care and rationed care and how that has led to genocide. The end-of-life medications, like those used on Grace, and DNRs are already a state sanctioned standard of care in the U.K. Grace's case shines a light on what is on the horizon in the U.S.

What is really going on is pretty clear. They want to take out the disabled and the elderly as an end to itself, not just for money. Money is certainly a motivation but a secondary one. One of the most direct pieces of evidence for my allegation of willful misconduct is that I sent complaints against the doctor and the hospital to the regulatory departments with the state of Wisconsin.

Both did investigations and both said the doctor and the hospital did nothing wrong. That's telling you the hospitals are owned by the government. The government can't convict itself, so it gives them a free pass, and that is sickening.

QUESTION: Do you believe Grace's Down Syndrome played a role in this from day one?

SCHARA: I've become convinced of that. When you start putting facts together, conspiracies become truth. Disabled women are eleven times more likely to die with COVID in a hospital than nondisabled.[88] The mainstream press will say that's because they had some condition that made death more vulnerable to COVID, but that wasn't the case for Grace because she was never acutely ill and was young and otherwise healthy before they starved, sedated, and euthanized her.

QUESTION: Are you pursuing legal action?

SCHARA: We've already said we aren't looking for any money. In the end, we'd like one thing to happen. We'd like Grace's death certificate to be changed to the truth. I'd like the doctors and nurses who did this to repent. That's the best justice you could ever have because they are looking at spending eternity in hell, and I wouldn't wish that on my worst enemy. We have a legal team headed up by Tom Renz, who has convinced us that using the legal system is the fastest way to stop the hospital killings. We believe God is leading our efforts.

QUESTION: What is your goal from telling your story?

SCHARA: Our hearts ache for Grace and we know nothing will bring her back. I have never missed someone this much. We are sad the healthcare system didn't get to know our precious Grace. She brought joy to everyone she met. Grace was the best gift God every gave to our family. We had an angel walking around with us for nineteen years. She called me "earthly dad" and called my wife "earthly mom." She was my best buddy and my wife's best friend. We've been asked what we miss most…the answer is "everything." I don't know why God picked our family to bless with such a wonderful child. They didn't just take one of ours; they took one of His.

Genesis 50:20 says: "You intended to harm me, but God intended it for good to accomplish what is now being done, *the saving of many lives* [emphasis added]." Through God's grace, our Grace can be used to save many lives, both physically and spiritually. He is certainly using Grace's death for good. She knew Jesus and we hope others come to the saving knowledge of Jesus through the work He has us doing now. God has opened so many doors since Grace died that it is hard to fathom.

God is sovereign and He has a purpose.

More details about Grace's murder and how to help with the family's cause can be found at OurAmazingGrace.net.

CHAPTER 7

Mollie James: Are We Sacrificing Patients to Accommodate the Sacred Shots?

We clapped for them meekly, cowering behind the curtains of our homes in March 2020 as the ambulances slowly rolled down the streets of New York City. They were our heroes and national treasure. So much so that we indulged their goofy and often creepy TikTok videos relieving their stress in the hospitals with black humor and cheesy dances, after supposedly being inundated with patients consuming every second of their time. They could do no wrong. Except...for what they actually swore an oath to do. Those were American doctors during the pandemic.

Few people in the world witnessed the violation of the modern Hippocratic Oath more intimately at every stage of the pandemic than Iowa-based ICU specialist and surgeon Dr. Mollie James. Indeed, unlike most other outpatient and hospital doctors who were an accomplice to the therapeutic nihilism dictated by the spirit of the age, Dr. James took the modern Hippocratic Oath seriously: "I will apply, for the benefit of the sick, all measures [that] are required, avoiding those twin traps of overtreatment and therapeutic nihilism."[89] Her superiors did not and worked to prevent her from proving the right medicine and eschewing harmful treatment options.

Dr. James is board-certified in general surgery and critical care medicine, with a separate expertise in functional medicine. Although the virus had not made much of an appearance in her part of flyover country, she rushed to volunteer her expertise as a critical care doctor in some of the hardest hit areas of Queens, New York, in March of 2020. She hoped to bring her innovative touch and calm demeanor to hospitals that were in full-scale panic confronted by a novel virus for which there was no blueprint of treatment from the government and the Master of Medicine. She continued to work for eighteen months in the ICU, traveling between the Midwest and NYC.

What she witnessed instead was a shocking display of therapeutic nihilism—with the hospitals promoting dangerous treatments and vociferously blocking commonsense approaches to treatment using safe therapeutics and supplements, even when all else failed and the halls of the ICU were littered with the bodies of people cut down too early. Between her frustration with the therapeutic nihilism, discriminatory behavior against unjabbed patients, and a mandate that she herself get the shot despite having already recovered from COVID, Dr. James quit her work in both hospitals and flew back to the Midwest in late 2021 to help people from the outside.

One of the most seasoned special operators in the fight against COVID was taken off the battlefield because she didn't accede to the spirit of the age.

Dr. James established a telehealth service to treat hundreds of COVID patients early in the disease. She figured if her hands would be tied treating people in the hospitals, she as may as well be free to treat them at home unrestricted by greedy and capricious treatment protocols, and free to follow her scientific and clinical instincts and her compassionate ethos.

Moreover, after seeing hundreds of people die in the ICU, she understood as well as anyone else that almost none of them would have died had they gotten early outpatient treatment. So she established a telehealth clinic designed to get people treatment as quickly as possible for a virus for which every hour matters.

Yet, her altruistic commitment to treat patients was matched by the long arm of the malevolent medical cartel's zealotry to deny treatment. Like other heroic doctors prescribing outpatient treatments, she was stymied by an inability to fill prescriptions as the same forces behind the nihilistic hospital treatment wanted to ensure patients didn't fare better at home. She had to waste so much time and effort fighting with pharmacists who, for the first time in history, blocked safe FDA-approved drugs, and had to devise numerous subterfuges to get her patients the right medications. Despite her best efforts, this cost patients their lives and she can still see their faces in her mind.

Dr. James's testimony is particularly important because she originally defended the New York hospitals from early allegations of malfeasance. She gave them every benefit of doubt one would accord to those beleaguered by a sudden pandemic with no blueprint to follow. But she came to realize that eventually a blueprint was created and was indeed followed. It just wasn't one motivated by healing but by following a nefarious plot.

For this reason, the prosecution calls Dr. Mollie James to the witness stand:

· · · · · · ·

QUESTION: In 2020, Americans were very and deservedly sympathetic to the health care system/professionals. But from a system standpoint, at least, there seemed to be a transition from "We are just overwhelmed and confused" to "We have an agenda here." Or is that unfair? You served on the front lines; what did you see?

JAMES: I would say that transition started in the spring of 2021 when the vaccines came out. Toward the end of the spring, when everyone had a chance to get the vaccine, that is when I would hear doctors and nurses whisper to each other when patients came in, "I bet they aren't vaccinated."

There was just an increasing attitude about that, and then toward the end of summer of 2021, there was downright hostility. Health care workers were posting online that if you get sick and you don't have the vaccine then you deserve to die, you shouldn't get care, and you shouldn't take up hospital beds.

Back in April of 2020, during the height of the initial peak, no one knew what was going on and we were flying blind. I was trying to give everyone the benefit of the doubt when I was in New York. They were so traumatized by what happened in March and April of 2020 that they resigned themselves to the fact that everybody dies. I have to say I kind of fell into that mindset as well. When you try everything you know and everybody dies, it is like a dagger in the heart and I think what happened is that they just gave up. I don't know what happened in the rest of the country, but I suspect they heard about the New York disaster and just gave up too before they even felt the trauma. It just became about getting the vaccine once it came out.

Interestingly, though, I didn't see much better treatment of patients even if they did get the vaccine. I mean, there was hate if you didn't get it, but there wasn't love for people who did.

We knew the patients weren't responding to the ventilators like we thought they would and we knew no one was getting better while intubated. If you look at the guidelines back then in the early days of the spring, they were never quite sure what to do, but they adamantly opposed obvious treatment options. Antibiotics? Maybe, maybe not. Remdesivir? Maybe, maybe not. Fluids? Maybe, maybe not. But they all said don't give steroids because it's a viral infection and you will suppress the immune system.

Then, by early summer, they said this is an inflammatory condition and we need to give steroids. Then we started getting autopsy reports that there was microclotting and we needed to give blood thinners. Doctors were on a sliding spectrum regarding the scope of their treatment choices, but a small percentage of patients started getting better once we gave them low-dose steroids and full-dose blood thinners. That was phase one of the treatment.

Why didn't we use tried and trusted commonsense protocols we've always used for those in respiratory distress? We abandoned our basic assumptions regarding respiratory infections for several reasons, not the least of which was fear.

Nurses at home, where the surge hadn't even hit, were often in tears. The escalation and sensationalism of the situation made the anticipation unbearable. They would break down and say, "I have a family and I don't want to die." There was almost an end-of-days vibe.

At that time, we didn't realize it was mainly an inflammatory condition of the lungs. They were calling it COVID pneumonia even though it's not a pneumonia at all—it's a pneumonitis. Most doctors and professionals treating COVID still don't understand the mechanism for why people get sick. The lungs fill up with inflammation and blood clots and people tell you that they can't breathe, but what they are really saying is they can't take a deep breath.

So, when you look at the mechanics of the lungs, the volume (or depth of breath) people could breathe in and out was dropping because of capacity issues in the lungs. Just like a balloon expands and contracts, the lungs do the same thing, but in the case of COVID patients, their lungs were stuck. They couldn't go any bigger, so the respiratory rate went up to compensate for the small breath (low tidal volumes). Those rates would go up and up and up, and at the last second, those patients would "fall off a cliff," decompensate rapidly, and go into cardiac arrest.

One of the biggest mistakes by doctors is that they were focused on a patient's oxygen saturation and not considering how fast the patient was breathing. High respiratory rate is one of our warning signs of critical illness, and it got completely overlooked. So, they were really getting the mechanism of why people were getting sick wrong from the beginning. This was a critical failure, as the oxygen level is one of the late signs, and by that point, often we have missed the window for earlier and more effective treatments.

You can't properly treat something you misdiagnose, and two years into the virus, the medical profession still seemed to refuse to study the virus from a clinical treatment standpoint. And as recently as winter of 2022, I testified in a court hearing in which the patient was informed by the hospital that from the last positive test, he would be in isolation for twenty-eight days!

Hospital administrators were just making up policy out of thin air. There was no basis or justification for isolating patients such a prolonged period. These hospitals just do whatever they want to and take their incentive checks for the remdesivir and ventilators.

QUESTION: What sort of things did you try to implement when really nothing was working and what was the response?

JAMES: Singulair, which is an asthma medication that blocks inflammation of the lungs, was one obvious choice I tried as early as May 2020. Also, high-dose Omega 3s, which can be difficult to get in the hospital. In December 2020, when I heard Dr. Pierre Kory's testimony about ivermectin, I wanted to immediately try that. But the minute I started ordering it, the medical doctors would block it and cancel my order. Then there is nebulized budesonide. The respiratory therapists wouldn't give nebulizers. They said if it was a COVID patient they wouldn't give it, even though it is standard of care for people with inflammation in the lungs.

We had one patient admitted during the summer of 2021 to the cardiac ICU that needed the heart-lung bypass machine, or ECMO (extracorporeal membrane oxygenation). She worked in a medical office and had received the Pfizer shot in December 2020. Almost six months to the day after her Pfizer shots, she came in with COVID ARDS (acute respiratory distress syndrome). She was placed on ECMO and I discussed and recommended to the surgeon to give her ivermectin. I hadn't seen it used in ECMO, but it could help and had a low risk of harm.

I was given the green light. I ordered it right away, but then the pharmacy blocked it, stating it was a restricted drug that needed approval from an infectious disease specialist. I did so, and he ordered it the same evening. He was then called by the pharmacy and told the "COVID committee" had not approved it. That's an example in which three doctors agreed about how to take care of a patient, and some blind committee and a pharmacist put the brakes on it. Doctors now worked for pharmacists who illegally practiced medicine.

Also, the minute I would leave the hospital, my colleagues would come in and stop all the vitamin D and vitamin C that I had prescribed.

QUESTION: For the first six months of the pandemic at least, the COVID treatment protocol seemed to be isolate for ten to fourteen days after a positive test, and if you don't have symptoms and test negative, return to daily life. But if you do have symptoms, stay home until you can't breathe, because there's nothing we can do until then. And if that happens, come to the ER and maybe you'll end up in the ICU on a ventilator. When people progressed to the ICU, how many of them did you eventually see walk out?

JAMES: I would say more than three-quarters didn't make it.

QUESTION: When did this sort of corporate medical culture you are describing prevail? Did COVID provoke this or was it already there?

JAMES: It was already there. Years ago, I had orthopedic surgeon colleagues who told me they were reprimanded for "not operating on a high enough percentage of patients they saw in clinic" by a hospital administrator. I experienced a similar conversation when I was the general surgeon at my hometown hospital. Only surgeons can make operative decisions. We know the entire story of the patient, the facility, the support team. We have a responsibility to act in the patient's best interest. There is no administrator, nurse, or medical physician qualified to make those decisions. These are two very clear examples of hospital administrators putting profits over patients due to the corporatization of medicine. So, major issues were already there; it's just that COVID amplified the problem and highlighted many more patient safety issues.

Here's the progression of how promising early treatments were set up to fail and eventually became denigrated. It started with hydroxychloroquine in the spring of 2020. I have consistently reported that as early as April 2020, we gave every COVID patient HCQ and I saw no clinical benefit.

Over the summer, we had a number of patients with cardiac arrests (which isn't uncommon with the high percentage of patients in salvage therapy), and then *The Lancet* article came out claiming HCQ caused arrhythmias. As an abundance of precaution, we stopped using it. Again, basic risk/

benefit: it wasn't helping and *may have been* hurting, so we got rid of it.

By the time they got to the ICU, though, it didn't help because HCQ inhibits viral replication. It's powerful when given up front at the onset of symptoms, but offers minimal benefit to patients weeks into a cytokine storm like we were seeing. Then when ivermectin came on the scene, many docs felt like they got burned with hydroxychloroquine, so they didn't want to go down that road again. I truly don't believe most doctors in hospitals are evil, but I think they were very closed-minded and a little too trusting of the government.

The majority of time I was working in the hospital during COVID, vaccines were not available. So, it was just a horrible situation, it was no one's fault, and we just did what we had to do to survive the day.

Once the vaccines became available, the entire attitude of the doctors, hospitals, and whole world changed in an instant. Now, you were evil and a morally corrupt person if you had questions or concerns about a rushed, experimental shot. Now, it was *your* fault if you got sick. You did something wrong—you didn't wear a mask, you didn't lock down hard enough, you were irresponsible, or you didn't get your shot. The blame game started and it has been truly awful ever since.

QUESTION: Can you talk about some of the stories of maltreatment you witnessed when people hired you as an outside clinician to get prescriptions and get guidance about the hospital process?

JAMES: There is one really sad case of a twenty-seven-year-old man from Minnesota. He was ten days into illness and he had been seen twice in the local emergency rooms for 103 and 104 fever, but had been sent home without any kind of treatment. He got to me when he couldn't take it anymore. I consulted with his family at 9:30 p.m. on a Thursday. I arranged for IV fluids at 8 a.m. the next day. He died at 2 a.m. So why does a twenty-seven-year-old die without treatment after twice being in the ER? Apparently, he told his mom he wouldn't go back to the ER again because they turned him away without doing anything the other times. That is pathetic care. There is something we can do to help everybody.

Another case is a lady in her fifties in the hospital. She was on five liters of oxygen, then the next day she was on eight liters and I said, "Get out so we can help you immediately." Her family wasn't comfortable with her walking to the front door and wanted her to use a wheelchair. The hospital refused to let them use their wheelchair to leave, so the family said they would bring one themselves and take her out. They were threatened that they would be arrested if they set foot on hospital property with a wheelchair, and a pulmonologist told the patient if she left, she would die of low oxygen levels and that would be on her family's hands. So, they treated her with standard crappy treatment and she died in the hospital.

QUESTION: **Wait, just to clarify, you were seeing what amounted to medical kidnappings? As in a refusal to let patients leave?**

JAMES: Almost every patient we talked to would have enormous pressure put on them. They were told that insurance would not pay for the hospital stay if the patient left against medical advice, they were told they would die if they left, they were told they had to stay to finish their remdesivir therapy, or if they left AMA (against medical advice) they could then not be readmitted if they got worse at home.

None of those things are true.

Those of us trying to help patients from the outside spent a lot of time giving patients pep talks and very clear instructions to overcome the pressure they felt when preparing to leave. We told patients, "You need to put your shoes on and walk toward the door," otherwise they were ignored. We explained it was wholly up to them, but if they couldn't overcome the resistance and do that part, they would be in the hands of people who were not treating them appropriately. Of course, the patients were sick, they were exhausted, they had brain fog, and they were extremely scared, so it is quite a lift to get them up and out of the hospital.

Another case with seventy-eight-year-old gentlemen. The family called us and said he was leaving. He was on 80 to 100 percent oxygen. I did a video visit with the family to evaluate him prior to offering our services and he was lying on his stomach on a high-flow nasal cannula. He was drinking orange juice and he and the family were talking to me. The nurse came in to push Ativan and the family wanted to know what that was. I said it was for anxiety and they said he wasn't anxious. The nurse said the doctor ordered it. They asked their dad if he was anxious and he said he was fine. They told the nurse not to give him the drug. If they had, he could have aspirated while drinking his orange juice and died.

We got him out of the hospital and into hospice and somehow arranged a high-flow cannula, and he went down from 80 percent to 30 percent oxygen. By treating him, he's now off oxygen and he's fine and he's back playing with his grandkids.

We'd find ways to get patients in the hospital the treatments they needed the hospital wouldn't give them. There are some pretty creative ways we got around the senseless and mean-spirited hospital searches of patient belongings to get ivermectin into hospitals. So, we started experiencing what we were calling "miraculous healings." Since the hospital wasn't used to COVID patients rapidly improving, they really didn't know how to respond. Eventually, they suspected meds were being smuggled inside, so instead of asking how we could help every patient get better, they blocked visitors and confiscated personal belongings.

This is the point at which the saturation of evil thoughts began to translate to evil actions. I had a patient who was drinking a smoothie that had vitamins in it, and the nurse ripped it out of the patient's hands. Patients would ask for vitamin C, vitamin D, and steroids and they would be denied. If you came into the hospital and called it an asthma attack, they would give high-dose steroids and proper treatment. For COVID, they would refuse these meds used daily for other conditions.

QUESTION: What is the benign, innocent explanation for a doctor's disappointment that a patient was getting better, to the point that they tried to snuff out what actually did make them better instead of prescribing it to other people?

JAMES: There isn't one. I had a patient who was about seventy, in the hospital, and who was starting to get better one day. When he first went to the hospital, he was put on remdesivir after a day or two and the daughter found out and told her dad to refuse it. So what did the hospital do? They cut off his phone privileges as if he was a prisoner in jail. When he started to get better, the wife could no longer see her husband by herself, but had to have a chaperone in the room and had to be searched every time she entered. But he's home now and doing okay. That was one of the few better endings.

QUESTION: How about outpatient care? When did this business begin with pharmacists practicing medicine? Have you ever had off-label prescriptions blocked before?

JAMES: Never! I actually grew up working in pharmacies. My first job was working in our hometown pharmacy. I started out in pharmacy school. I worked in them throughout high school, college, and medical school, so I've never had a contentious relationship with the pharmacy profession.

The very first COVID prescription I had blocked was for my mom and dad in Iowa, and the pharmacist told me she didn't like the data I had so she wasn't filling it. Every month, fewer and fewer places would fill them. They would have filled it three weeks early but suddenly would stop. From Walmart to Walmart, the erratic denials would be for all different reasons. One said it was corporate policy, another said they weren't comfortable filling it, and another said it was because of the FDA. It was always different so you knew it was all made up.

A pharmacist can block something if it can cause a dangerous interaction with another prescribed drug, for a dangerous dose, or if he has a conscientious objection to the drug, such as with an abortion pill. When it comes to challenging a diagnosis, that is not any of those three things. They are not trained to do that. That is practicing medicine without a license.

QUESTION: Did you ever ask the pharmacist who blocked you what they would give the patient instead?

JAMES: The first prescription I had bounced was for my parents. They were higher risk and I wanted them to have meds on hand in case they got it. The pharmacist flatly refused to fill it. I asked questions. I tried to understand the logic. I offered resources. I offered published studies for my dosing and treatment plans. They rejected those offers and became belligerent. Some would hang up on me. It was really quite unprofessional. During fall of 2021 to spring of 2022, we had team members in tears almost daily when they realized how hospitals, doctors, pharmacists and nurses were complicit in blocking care and creating obstacles for our patients.

This is especially infuriating when you know they are twenty-four to forty-eight hours away from clinical improvement on the correct treatment plan. There are several incidences of pharmacists creating roadblocks and then trying to create issues for treating physicians with the medical boards.

I had one patient in critical condition and the pharmacists repeatedly lied to me about the reason they weren't filling my prescription. The patient had filled a few tablets at one place, but they couldn't fill the entire prescription.

The next pharmacist told me:

1. They didn't want the patient to get a "double fill" of the meds.

2. It was against state law—which I countered with the fact that their colleague in the same chain filled it down the street.
3. It's not FDA-approved, thus we had to review what FDA approval and off-label prescribing looks like. We are talking about ivermectin, a Nobel Prize–winning drug here; of course it is FDA-approved.

QUESTION: How many total patients did you treat with ivermectin and other off-label drugs and supplements, and how many of them did you treat successfully?

JAMES: Over eighteen months in the ICU, I treated about 2,000 patients with the prevailing NIH/CDC/hospital guidance. Approximately three-fourths of them died from undertreatment. From September 2021 to now, our James Clinic team has treated nearly 4,000 patients, and I think we have had maybe twenty deaths. And those were in high-risk patients with several comorbidities who sought care after ten days of symptoms and/or had strokes from their COVID disease.

We had many patients who were high risk with comorbidities who saw us late and did well. The availability of our office to give IV fluids and steroids, blood thinners, and hyperbaric oxygen made a huge difference in patients who presented with critical illness. My work represents one of the largest comparisons of in-hospital versus early treatment experiences, and strongly supports treating early.

This is really hard to reflect on when you consider I took care of 1,500 people who died but didn't have to. That continues to weigh heavily on me, and that's why I have become an activist in their honor.

CHAPTER 8

Bill Salier: He Survived Deployment in the Marines Only to Almost Die Because of His Local Pharmacy

They lied about the origins of the virus, blocked the ability to get proper treatment in hospitals, dissuaded doctors from prescribing effective treatments outpatient, and forced upon people dangerous "cures." But perhaps one can still avoid the death trap by finding a doctor willing to prescribe outpatient to avoid the hospital's so-called (and dreaded) "protocol," right?

Sadly, no, because they thought of everything.

To the point they even got the pharmacists to ensure that even if you could find a doctor to prescribe you the right medication, for the first time in history, the dispensers of the drug would deny you that lifeline. And boy was it a lifeline. With a gain-of-function virus for which every hour counts once someone's blood oxygen level drops, they cruelly caused thousands of people to scramble to find medication from alternative sources. For some, it was a death sentence.

Once again, the Fourth Reich trumped the rule of law and the ethos of morality. One such man ensnared in this illegal and immoral pharmacy embargo on lifesaving drugs was Bill Salier of Minnesota. Bill ultimately enjoyed a happy outcome, but only thanks to his knowledge of farming, which led him to use veterinary ivermectin during his time of dire need. So many others weren't as fortunate.

Bill Salier is an American's American. He's a retired marine who saw action in Somalia, and was also charged with protecting President George H. W. Bush at Camp David. He then took over his father's family farm and worked that land for a quarter century. In between, he even ran for the U.S. Senate and did spot duty as a local talk show host. Service and patriotism are at the heart of who Salier is, and he's even from the heartland. We now call him to the witness stand to share his testimony.

· · · · · ·

QUESTION: You're a retired marine and farmer, two professions that are obviously very physically demanding. Were you still in good health heading into contracting COVID-19?

SALIER: Yes, and I had considered that when COVID was first starting to flare up. I weighed the pros and cons when it came to the COVID vaccine, and thought at some point I'm probably going to get this, but I'm very healthy right now. So there were no reasons for health concerns.

QUESTION: When exactly did you get sick in 2021? Can you share the progression of the illness and at what time did you realize you might be in trouble?

SALIER: I came home from work October 1 and sat down on the couch, which wasn't typical of me to feel that kind of tired. I was visiting with my wife and told her I just felt kind of off. After dinner I headed off to bed, and I didn't leave the bedroom for another ten days, except to go and get COVID tested the next day. COVID just completely wiped me out.

There would be little stints after I went back to bed when I would fold clothes or something, but after ten or fifteen minutes of that I just wanted to lie back down again. During the first four or five days, I kept thinking I would eventually kick this, and I would be okay even though the body aches were very extreme.

But then I started to swing the other way. I would think I took a step forward and then I would take several steps back. My wife took me down to a clinic in Osage, Iowa. First we had applied through Mayo for monoclonal treatments, and we never even got an acknowledgement. So we went down to the Osage clinic and I lay down in the back of our Expedition on the drive. The physician looked at me and said she had one bag of monoclonal left, but said I could not have it because she was triaging it for people at death's door and she didn't think I was at that point.

I inquired about ivermectin and she said she didn't prescribe that. I came back home to Minnesota and I was really starting to turn for the worse. It was getting to the point where I would fall asleep praying because I knew I was losing and I needed a miracle. I could feel myself going. The body aches were extreme. There were times I had to wad up into a ball to try to make it bearable. We tried Tylenol. We tried aspirin. They would alleviate things enough that I could try to lie on my back and get some rest.

I had a consistent fever between 102 and 103. We were monitoring my blood oxygen levels and they were dropping down into the low nineties. I was starting to have a lot of cognitive trouble. I would know what people were saying to me but I was having a really hard time communicating back. My kids would come to the door and ask if I was going to be okay. I was starting to get desperate. I didn't have a primary care physician because we were fairly new to the community, and the physician I used to have in Osage had been fired for some kind of COVID conflict.

QUESTION: What was the next step for seeking out help?

SALIER: My wife had been paying a lot of attention to options. She got sick with COVID about a third of the way through my illness, but wasn't as bad as me. She pounded me with the vitamin D and she would make me get out of bed every couple of hours, and make me walk around and take as many deep breaths as I could handle. We were trying to ward off pneumonia or anything like that settling into my lungs, but we didn't know where to turn next and were getting scared.

Thankfully, God intervened. Next thing you know, a mutual friend of Steve Deace and I happened to call me on an unrelated thing, and quickly figured out through my inability to communicate that I was in big trouble. He got a hold of Steve, who was able to get Dr. Mollie James headed my way.

That absolutely saved my life as far as I'm concerned, and you will never convince me otherwise.

QUESTION: Whether as a soldier or a farmer, you are used to powering through things. How often had you encountered something that had debilitated you to this degree?

SALIER: I think there was one time in twenty-five years of farming that a buddy of mine came and did chores for a day and a half because I was too sick. Otherwise, sick or whatever, there was work to be done so out I went. I always called myself a one-man fighting hole. It was me and all the work that needed to be done, and there were all those little faces at the dinner table depending on you.

QUESTION: There are two layers of inhibition to getting treatment. There is finding a doctor because there is a tiny percentage who will deal with you, and there is finding a pharmacy that won't practice medicine and deny prescriptions. Let's start with what did Dr. Mollie James prescribe?

SALIER: We first talked with Mollie eight days into me being sick. For my wife, who was also sick, she prescribed ivermectin and hydroxychloroquine and thought that would be able to stop the stage she was in. However, Mollie said I was already into the cytokine storm. Mollie kept asking my wife if she could sit me up when I was talking on the phone, because I was so exhausted and would flop back over.

I remember her telling my wife that within forty-eight hours I would be in the hospital because I was going critical, but she also didn't want to panic us because she knew how to stop this. She said hydroxychloroquine would not help me because I was beyond the stage for it to be effective. Instead, I got ivermectin, steroids, vitamin D, a nebulizer, fluvoxamine, Pepcid, and a number of other things. She said ivermectin would be crucial because it has effectiveness at both the viral stage and the cytokine stage, but we couldn't get a pharmacist to fill it. We were denied both the hydroxy and the ivermectin by the pharmacies.

QUESTION: This is the deadly crossroads that hundreds of thousands, if not millions, of Americans found themselves in. Particularly during the latter half of 2021 during the more dangerous delta variant. There was a forty-eight-hour window when you had moderate to severe COVID and needed to ward it off, before it became critical and difficult to treat. Ivermectin was the crown jewel of treatment. Why did they deny it?

SALIER: This part I remember vividly, because I remember my wife walking into the bedroom while on the phone crying and saying, "You can't just not fill a prescription because you don't want to." Then she hung up and said that Walmart refused to do it. I had just been told by Mollie that I had forty-eight hours before I would have to go to the hospital, and from there I would have a fifty-fifty shot of coming out of there alive.

Needless to say, we were scared. There is a difference between having a riot unfold in front of your position when you are with a group of highly trained Marines in Somalia, and something coursing through inside of you that there is nothing you can do about. The first one you can face down, stand up to, and will yourself to do your job. With the other one, you are helpless. That is scarier than anything I had ever experienced.

We got a hold of Dr. James on a Saturday. She got a hold of the exact same Walmart pharmacist and verified the need for the prescription. He even told her no. His position was that ivermectin was not FDA-approved for COVID and therefore he felt it was dangerous. He also hung up on our doctor. So Mollie asked if there was another pharmacy. We sent in the prescription to Hy-Vee and the pharmacist told my wife he couldn't fill the hydroxy or ivermectin. He said if he entered it into the computer for COVID, the computer kicked it out. So the corporate structure of Hy-Vee decided they weren't going to allow it.

My wife came back home and we were truly panicking. It was Saturday evening and the clock was ticking. Where do you go and what do you do? So in the end I used my farming experience. I've ridden a lot of horses and used ivermectin on those horses. My wife had some she had grabbed from the local farm store. We held hands and prayed. We asked Mollie and she said that as long as it is pure ivermectin it is the same product, albeit with a different potency. Then Dr. James looked at the product label to ensure there were no other ingredients in there, because sometimes they can mix in a different dewormer that would indeed be toxic.

After we hung up, my wife and I looked at each other and said we needed to gamble. Either we take vet medicine, or we gamble that not only am I going to pull something out of a hat, but that she isn't also going to end up in the same situation I'm in. So we held hands and prayed and got apple sauce, and shot the amount of ivermectin we needed into it and put it down the hatch.

Eight hours later, I knew I was winning. I could feel it. I wasn't going to die. And my wife had the same effect within six hours. Keep in mind I had other drugs too, but my wife got only ivermectin. The hydroxy never came. She took only horse paste and it turned her around in six hours.

I had been pretty sure I was not coming out the other side of this. And when you do, it is pretty emotional. I got out of bed the next day and walked outside after being in my room for days and days and my children cheered. I wrapped a blanket around me and watched the sun set over our creek with my wife, and it was the most beautiful thing. It is in no small part due to the tenaciousness of my wife in being relentless for me while being sick, Steve Deace for quickly getting me hooked into Dr. Mollie James, and Mollie fighting the fight all the way through with us.

QUESTION: Did you take subsequent doses of the horse paste?

SALIER: Yes, it was like a five- or maybe a seven-day run. Something like that. I know we went through two tubes of it between the two of us. We got better for less than twenty bucks.

QUESTION: When were you able to return to work?

SALIER: I went back around day nineteen, I think. The strength was the last thing to return. I have a pretty physical job. Dr. James did try and continue to pursue getting my ivermectin prescription filled. She found a place in Florida that would send it out as fast as they could, but they were being inundated. I did get the shipments about ten days after taking the horse paste. I think it was about $200 for a full course for both my wife and me.

QUESTION: So the pharmacies were practicing medicine by withholding an FDA-approved drug when there is not a single day that goes by for them where something isn't pre-scribed for something off-label. Did the pharmacist tell you what you should be taking for COVID instead and what could make you better?

SALIER: No. Here's where I come down on all of this. The doctor can prescribe it. The pharmacist can fill it. But the final check on all of this is me. Nobody can force me to take it. It can arrive at my home and I can sit it on my counter and say no. It is my call when it comes to my health. Not some phar-macist's but mine.

When you strip me of that, you not only strip me of human decency and pride, but you strip away the very free-doms and liberties that I have stood for my entire life. Please explain to me how when we buried the guys coming out of Iwo Jima or D-Day or the War of 1812, if this is where we end up? Why did they die if we are just going to throw away our individual liberties like that? That has me more enraged than almost anything else, because they stripped me of my ability to make my decision. We are a free country and I am a free man. I will determine for myself my own destiny, and I, not you, will strive for the best for myself and my family.

QUESTION: The fall 2021 period in the Midwest was a tough time with delta variant. You had a good outcome by the grace of God with Dr. James, and despite the medical profession and the government colluding against you. What other people do you know who didn't have access to what you did because you were a farmer?

SALIER: My wife's step-grandmother was flat-out locked up in a nursing home and died alone from COVID. There are two other families who I was able to connect with Dr. James, and she saved them both. There was another farm family who told me later that they didn't even bother with a doctor, and just went ahead and took the horse paste ivermectin. None of us that did have had any side effects.

QUESTION: You have filed a federal lawsuit against both Walmart and Hy-Vee for their immoral and inexcusable denial of care, which nearly cost your life. Where do things stand on that front?

SALIER: Both Walmart and Hy-Vee moved for dismissal on various grounds. My attorney showed them all the grounds on which Minnesota allows them to deny a prescription in a forty-six-page response, and that none of them applied to my situation. We are still waiting to see where things go from there. I've never been a litigious person. I've never sued anyone. This is way outside my comfort zone, I'm not litigious at all, but this type of destruction of our culture and liberties via blind trust in so-called "medical experts" has to come to a stop.

CHAPTER 9

Pierre Kory: The ICU Doctor Who Saw Firsthand Ivermectin Works

I t was the testimony heard 'round the world.

Most people were convinced for months that there was no way to treat COVID outside of some future miracle vaccine or therapeutic. Although there were individual doctors successfully treating COVID patients from day one, most people and doctors never heard of the concept of COVID treatment. That is until Dr. Pierre Kory, a Wisconsin-based ICU doctor with a New York accent, testified about ivermectin before the U.S. Senate Committee on Homeland Security on December 8, 2020.[90]

While the politics of COVID became increasingly partisan over time, on that December day, anyone watching Dr. Kory's testimony before Chairman Ron Johnson saw an ICU doctor who is also a pulmonologist in deep distress about the number of people dying with their lungs destroyed—and how it didn't have to be that way. Until that point, the entire debate over COVID centered around how much should we lock down, who is at risk of dying, and when are the amazing vaccines going to be approved? Kory had a message for people that if we only treated people early with the right corticosteroids and ivermectin, most deaths would have been avoided, especially for the original strain of the virus circulating before the vaccine arguably created stronger variants.

Much to his shock, Kory found out that for the first time in history, YouTube had taken down a piece of congressional testimony—his impassioned plea for the government to promote treatments.[91] Mind you, Kory didn't mention a word about lockdown or masks, and didn't diminish the threat of COVID—if anything, he painted a grim picture of the pulmonary pathology he was experiencing on the frontlines from day one. He simply wanted to save lives.

Together with Dr. Paul Marik and several other ICU doctors and pulmonologists, Kory founded the Front Line COVID-19 Critical Care Alliance Prevention & Treatment Protocols for COVID-19 (FLCCC), which focused solely on providing the public and practitioners with early-treatment, late-treatment, and long-term recovery protocols for COVID. Doing the job the NIH refused to do—and eventually opposed—Kory constantly updated and informed the public on the latest clinical and academic information on best practices for treating COVID. Thousands of physicians around the world used his protocols to save countless patients.

One of the FLCCC partners, Dr. Joseph Varon, was able to use the protocol for all his patients at United Memorial Medical Center in Houston, Texas. Because Varon is the chief of critical care services, he was able to apply proper treatment protocols across an entire hospital—perhaps the only one in the entire country. He attests to witnessing a drop within inpatient COVID mortality—both among critically ill and those on regular wards—to just 4.4 percent of COVID patients as of August 2020, as compared with the 22 percent mortality rate across the country.[92]

Imagine what would have happened if, from day one, the NIH did what Kory was doing instead of censoring and marginalizing those who sought to treat early? What is the benign, innocent reason why NIH didn't? In order to understand the depth of the human rights violations from the denial of treatment, we call upon Dr. Pierre Kory to share his story on behalf of the FLCCC doctors, so that never again will doctors be censored for using safe drugs to treat patients in need.

· · · · · · ·

QUESTION: Let's start at the beginning. You were working in the ICU and different places treating COVID patients. You are a pulmonologist, which is really the specialty involved in treating the lungs, the bread and butter of this virus. How did you discover ivermectin, and can you describe the mechanisms of how it helps against the virus?

KORY: When we saw this coming after hearing about Wuhan, then Lombardy and Seattle, I was the chief of the critical care service at the University of Wisconsin. Once the threat was real and the New York outbreak exploded, we just started to prepare different options, and ivermectin was never in our protocols at the beginning. We only adopted it for early treatment in the fall of 2020.

What we started out with was trying to treat the virus in the ICU when doctors were overrun, and we were running out of ventilators because we couldn't get these patients off them. The disease was so bizarre because most people who get critically ill and need to see an ICU specialist generally adopt a trajectory. It will start to improve slowly, and you can get them off ventilators in days or sometimes a week, or they will continue to decline and then die. I've had ICUs where 20 percent of my patients die, but here they were not getting better and they were not getting worse. They were filling up ICUs and we were running out of ventilators.

Our first protocol was called MATH Plus. That was centered around corticosteroids along with a number of other medicines we thought were effective. In a lesser-known hearing than the one in December, I testified in the U.S. Senate back in May 2020 for the use of corticosteroids, and did it at a time when every national and international health care agency had on their protocols "do not use corticosteroids."[93] I got really criticized for that call and people thought I was going to cause harm. There were some disagreements at work with a lot of my leaders, and then seven weeks later, Oxford University completed its large, randomized controlled trial[94] and corticosteroids became the standard of care overnight (albeit as we learned later not the right steroid). So ivermectin was not my first rodeo to find a drug that worked that is not understood by the rest of the medical system.

QUESTION: Looking at your COVID treatment protocols, how come almost all of them are over-the-counter early treatments?

KORY: When you look at our protocol, every component has a significant evidence base. Ivermectin has an overwhelming evidence base. They are combination therapy protocols because this disease is really complex. These are safe, cheap, over-the-counter medicines I treated people with across the country.

Now I have a global network of colleagues in many other countries. I've yet to meet a doctor who has adopted ivermectin in their practice who said it didn't help any of their patients. Not one. Ivermectin was really helpful in all phases of illness but it was most impactful in prevention. For people who have not gotten COVID, if you take ivermectin weekly, it prevents the contraction of COVID. I've been on ivermectin all this time. I take it every week and I haven't gotten COVID even though I am constantly around COVID. Large cohorts of health care workers in India and Argentina were prophylaxing with ivermectin for many months and very few get COVID. Its highlight is protective use. It's also effective, however, as an early treatment when taken with first symptoms. My dream is for the world to put ivermectin in its cupboard. The earlier you take it, the more effective it is. Generally, within twenty-four to thirty-six hours after first symptoms, people were feeling much better.

QUESTION: What's the history of ivermectin?

KORY: Ivermectin is a well-known antiparasitic drug that really transformed the health status of huge portions of the globe. Its discoverers won the Nobel Prize in 2015.[95] It's so safe it is often given without a prescription in public health distribution programs. A decade ago, researchers started testing ivermectin against viruses—Zika, West Nile, HIV, and influenza—in the lab and it was effective.[96] Then we saw in early April of 2020 it was effective against COVID-19 in a test tube, so people started using it clinically.[97]

It has profound antiviral properties. We aren't entirely clear why, but I think its main mechanism is that it binds tightly to the COVID-19 spike protein and prevents entry into the cell, which is why it is a good preventative. It also interrupts replication and has numerous anti-inflammatory properties for the unfortunate minority of people who go into the pulmonary phase and need to go to the hospital. We have also found it to be phenomenally effective for long-haul COVID and even in postvaccine injury.

The behavior of the government and medical establishment on ivermectin is so bizarre and quite sinister. We know what the world would look like if we used ivermectin as prophylaxis. There are numerous examples of very forward-thinking health care ministries. The best example is in Mexico City, when they were getting crushed in the second wave so much that they were literally running out of hospitals and oxygen. They did a test-and-treat protocol across all of their outpatient centers. They expanded their mobile testing units and people who tested positive with rapid tests got an early treatment kit with ivermectin, aspirin, and paracetamol.

What they showed is that the hospitals started to empty within two weeks, deaths started to plummet, and they had 25 percent occupancy in hospitals by March 2021. There was a 76 percent reduction in the need for hospitalization when they treated early. They also replicated the protocol in a number of states in India in their huge wave, and they broke free from the WHO protocols and saw massive reductions in deaths, case counts, and hospitalizations.

QUESTION: How come doctors with decades of experience didn't know this about ivermectin and early treatment?

KORY: It's a product of a health system that favors for-profit medicines and excludes those that aren't. Ivermectin is off-patent and is ridiculously cheap and widely available. It won't make anyone money. And to get a seat at the table, you need a team of $800-an-hour lawyers to sit down with the FDA. Everybody demands these randomized-controlled trials, which is really silly because there are other ways to determine if something is safe and effective. Plus, we were in the middle of a deadly pandemic, and needed to act fast with so much on the line.

Repurposed drugs often get actively opposed, and that's when things really get ominous and what has changed me as a physician and a citizen in this society. When I put up the preprint of all my evidence on ivermectin, I literally thought it would be a world-changing paper, but it was basically ignored.[98] Ivermectin has to disappear in order to make room for the other drugs that are coming in the pipeline. The vaccine push looked at it as a foe, which is really sad because we clearly needed more than vaccines.

We are reaching levels of absurdity around our behaviors. The system is literally putting itself between doctor and patient with what it is telling doctors to do and use. Remdesivir doesn't work and isn't even recommended by the WHO. You are using an antiviral in the hospital and we know the only time they work is in the first few days of an illness. And it is $3,000 a day and you have to be admitted to the hospital to use it. There were also legions of people who died from insufficient corticosteroid therapy. The dexamethasone is a very low dose for someone crashing onto ventilators with inflamed lungs but that's what the trials used. Nobody wants to think themselves through things like this disease anymore. It is sad and frightening.

QUESTION: There was a lawsuit filed in Washington in June of 2022 over the denial of treatment for COVID. I'm sure one of the great frustrations you've had is the lack of an honest and open hearing of the data. You could get that in a court of law, where discovery is a two-way street. Is there an opportunity with these kinds of lawsuits to finally get some data out of this that the public has not been shown?

KORY: I've said for a long time it is time for the lawyers. It is time for the judges. It is time for the courts. We've done everything we could to get good, pragmatic, sound, and data-driven evidence-based advice out there—and we get attacked for it with narratives from agencies that are clearly being controlled by pharmaceutical companies. They do not want a generic repurposed drug, and the actions they've taken to try to suppress the evidence of efficacy of ivermectin has been vast and rapacious for over a year now. They are selectively presenting and misrepresenting the actual data.

QUESTION: As a physician who has treated people for COVID since the early days of the pandemic, can you share the clinical outcomes you've seen firsthand?

KORY: I wrote the definitive review paper more than a year ago. After we saw some trials popping up around the world about ivermectin, I started using it in my practice. My first patient had been sick for two weeks and took ivermectin on a Sunday night. On Monday she had no fever, her heart rate was back to eighty, and she felt like the cloud has lifted. That experience continued in other patients for many, many months and was shared by doctors around the world. It's not every single patient but it is the vast majority. Obviously, there are combinations of medicines but at the beginning, ivermectin was a very robust medicine based just on my personal experience. But the medical system considers that the lowest form of experience, even though it's only what has driven advancements in medicine for hundreds of years.

However, in modern medicine, that is discounted as anecdotal—especially if it can't make anyone any real money. Yet, it is real, the patients I successfully treated are real, and the data is there.

I've never heard of a doctor who has used it who says it doesn't work. The only people who say it doesn't work are those who *don't use it.*

QUESTION: **During the initial wave of the pandemic, how many patients would you estimate you treated with ivermectin?**

KORY: I began using it in the fall of 2020. Trials started popping up all over the world that were all really positive. Since then, I've used it for about 400 people, and I've had three COVID hospitalizations and one death. And that death was an eighty-seven-year-old with a number of comorbidities. The only other person who went to the hospital was someone who didn't get to me until after ten days of symptoms.

QUESTION: **One of the things that hasn't been pointed out about doctors like you is that you guys aren't picking** and choosing from among the most promising of patients to stack the deck with your data. That's why I think your anecdotal data carries more weight. You guys were often getting patients who were on their last legs and out of hope because they could get nowhere with their other physicians and they were coming to you out of desperation, yet your data was still that promising. Is that a fair characterization?

KORY: It is, because we treat anyone who is ill that reaches out to us. When I started using hydroxychloroquine, I thought it was equally as effective as ivermectin and in some cases even stronger. The war on hydroxy was fought in 2020, though, and I became an expert on ivermectin, and what I saw being propagated from the top of every agency and blaring through major media was a PR campaign against ivermectin. I had to watch doctors being told not to use it across the world and become convinced it was a horse dewormer and nonsense medicine. It was all propaganda.

QUESTION: In 2022 there was a much-hyped "study" condemning the effectiveness of ivermectin. You did a three-part series on your Substack taking it apart.[99] Can you give us a summary?

KORY: That trial is what I would call a textbook example of how the pharmaceutical industry manipulates science. They know how to design and conduct studies to fail, so if they want to show the efficacy of a drug, they know how to design that for their products. There are books written about the manipulation of studies that the pharmaceutical companies themselves sponsor. In this case, there were literally forty different actions they took to try to show that ivermectin doesn't work.

One of the most egregious was they allowed the control group easy access to ivermectin. It is really hard to show a medicine is better than itself. It didn't show any benefit from ivermectin *because they were all on ivermectin.* That was the most brazen of tactics they did. We believe they actually showed a massive benefit from ivermectin, and they had to manipulate the data to bury it. I say "believe" because we can't empirically prove that because they won't share the data. In fact, we can't empirically prove anything, including their own claims, because they won't share the hard data.

They made public statements that the hard data would be available to all upon request at the end of the trial, but all of the investigators have gone dark. They are hiding, because they know this is fraudulent. But with the help of the media and *JAMA,* which is where the study was published, the headlines were screaming almost with glee that ivermectin didn't work.

This is not unique to ivermectin. They've done it many times over the years for any threat to their bottom line that comes from a generic repurposed drug. It's been a decades-long war and this has had a mass impact on humanity for many other ailments.

What they did in a global pandemic against one of the safest, most widely available, and inexpensive medicines that had the qualities to be a global cure is nothing short of an assassination. They had to destroy ivermectin because it would have dried up their markets and the hospitals would've emptied.

Ivermectin is the single most threatening medicine to the bottom line of the pharmaceutical industry in the history of medicine.

CHAPTER 10

Nicole Sirotek: When Health Care Couldn't Care Less about You

When one thinks of a hospital nurse, one conjures up an image of compassion and care. It has been said that "nurses dispense comfort, compassion, and caring without even a prescription."[100] They are the bridge between the doctor and the patient and spend most of the time with the patient during trying times. Yet, so many of them were swept into the spirit of the age as care turned to malfeasance and compassion turned to cruelty.

One nurse who remained the paragon of care, comfort, and compassion is Nicole Sirotek. She worked as a critical care and emergency transport nurse in Elko, Nevada, but travelled across the country to work in Queens, New York, during the outbreak in March 2020. On May 4 of that year, she posted a viral video visibly traumatized by what she described as "gross negligence and complete medical mismanagement" causing patients to die in droves.

"Stay out of New York City for your health care," she warned. "They don't care what is happening to these people." Well, unfortunately, as the pandemic spread to other states, nobody could avoid the hospital mal-care as this mode of treatment became the uniform standard of "care" throughout the nation. Although Sirotek claims she was feeling suicidal, she eventually bounced back and created American Frontline Nurses, an organization dedicated to helping patients navigate the hospitals, challenge the doctors on bad treatment options, and guide them to better care at home.

Like Dr. Mollie James, Sirotek saw the worst of the worst inside the hospitals throughout the pandemic. What she witnessed was a sea change in hospital treatment that is reverberating far beyond COVID. To understand where the level of care, compassion, and comfort is holding in America's hospitals so that we can better understand how to hold the current system accountable, we call Nurse Sirotek to the witness stand:

· · · · · ·

QUESTION: You were one of the original whistleblowers in New York after going there to volunteer during the initial phase of COVID. What, if anything, has changed for you as a health care provider since that initial dramatic experience?

SIROTEK: As the pandemic has changed, the narrative has changed. It's not so much COVID now because the virus is starting to live symbiotically with its host. But we've allowed two years of deplorable hospital care, so that has sadly become the standard across the United States. We are seeing lack of care, negligent care, inappropriate care, and medical discrimination on levels we've never seen before in the United States. I've worked hospice before and I've worked plenty of terminal cases. Pain management is always an important part of that kind of care, but what is happening now is that they are pushing it entirely too early. They are literally trying to sedate and medicate you to the point that you are just not an active participant in your life. And there's a push to get you on a DNR status as soon as possible, just because the outcomes statistically are not good.

But once you sign that order, many hospitals and providers will look at that as an order for the absence of care rather than a different type of care. So, once you sign, they won't give you antibiotics or steroids or anything other than sedation and pain meds, essentially leaving you to die. This is going on across the country. People are just trusting their providers and not understanding their rights and their options.

QUESTION: You just used a term—"medical discrimination." Can you quantify that for us? What did you mean by that and how pervasive is this problem?

SIROTEK: A lot of what we are dealing with is medical discrimination. We had a gentleman whose heart was damaged from the two Pfizer vaccines and he needed a heart transplant. They would not put him on the transplant list until he got the booster. I said the booster will literally kill him. He has next to nothing in cardiac function, which is why he needs the transplant. Our team of nurses gets about five cases of medical discrimination a week from across the country, where people in organ failure are denied transplants on account of these shots.

Another huge issue we are dealing with is those who are in suicide crisis. We get twenty to thirty of those calls a week. Ages range from as young as tweens all the way to folks in their sixties who are in mental health crisis because of everything that has gone on the past few years. They've lost their home. They've been isolated. They can't function in society anymore. They have drug and alcohol relapses. Some want to take their own life, and we are trying to get them into facilities to get the help that they need, but they are being turned away because they are not vaccinated.

We had one teenage girl who was the victim of a gang rape. The parents had family members who died from the vaccine, and they didn't want their daughter to take it. This meant we had to fly her three states away from her family to a mental health facility to get the services she needed for suicide crisis. That's another example of what I mean by calling it medical discrimination.

Another example is a Canadian family who had a family member get the vaccine in order to take a vacation to Mexico. He ended up developing a bunch of blood clots. Once they stabilized him, we had to fly him back to Canada, but they would not allow the flight to land because the flight team and the pilot were not vaccinated. Ultimately, they had to land in the United States, refuel, and then take ground transport into Canada in an ambulance.

QUESTION: All for a shot that even its manufacturers admit has waning efficacy, thus requiring frequent boosting, and therefore greatly elevating the risk profile with every injection. Let's go back to the person you mentioned whose heart was damaged by the jab. Can you give us further details about him?

SIROTEK: He was a healthy man in his forties who lived an ordinary life. He wanted to "protect Grandma" and "do the right thing to stop the spread." He trusted the system and the system betrayed him.

He got two shots. He had some symptoms the first time, but it was the second one that did him in. He ended up with myocarditis. He has what is called an ejection fraction, which causes heart failure because the cardiac muscle is not designed to grow like a regular skeletal muscle. Once your heart enlarges and then shrinks, it becomes sloppy and you have poor cardiac outcomes, such as low levels of oxygen-rich blood pumping out to your body.

He's in heart failure. He has microclot issues that keep going to his lungs. He has poor quality of life. He's on oxygen and all these meds. He just wants to be put on the transplant list, and he can't obtain access because he's not boosted. And again, he's not boosted because the initial set of shots is what did him in.

QUESTION: Is this "medical discrimination" as you call it just happening in certain parts of the country more prone to accept and thus promote the preferred narrative, or is it happening pretty much everywhere?

SIROTEK: The worst of it is occurring in Democrat-run states like California and New York but we are seeing it somewhat in Republican-run states such as Texas and Florida as well.

For example, we had a person in Florida who was in a car accident. He had fractures in his lower back and he went into the ER, but because he would not allow a swab for a COVID test, they denied him care. They discharged him and he went to two other hospitals before he finally received care. Technically he would test positive because he just had COVID a couple weeks ago, and sometimes it takes time to completely pass through, plus the PCR tests are completely faulty to begin with.

QUESTION: Therefore, you're saying even in the red states we don't have a COVID off-ramp within the medical system. Even if we have it at the governmental level, it is imbued in the medical system. Do you believe the medical system is getting worse and not better?

SIROTEK: We've dealt with medical kidnapping cases, when they won't allow you to leave to go somewhere else for the care you need, which they won't provide. If you don't go along with their protocols, they will literally not allow you to leave the hospital, or if you have a child, they will weaponize child protective services and the police against you. They will try to tell them that you are an unfit parent.

This stuff wasn't happening five or ten years ago. Never have I seen anything like this. Typically, with a transplant list they would require vaccines, but you could almost always obtain medical or religious exemptions for them if needed. We've never had this level of discrimination before when it comes to lifesaving care.

With regard to the medical kidnapping problem, in the past, you had a right to a secondary consult and to take alternate treatment. I spoke with the father of a thirteen-year-old boy whom the hospital would not give food and water to because he had COVID and they said it was just in case they had to intubate him. Mind you, he was on just one liter of supplemental oxygen. What killed him was four days without food and water. The father said he trusted them. One of the last things his boy said was that he was hungry. The family has post-traumatic stress disorder from dealing with hospital systems. How many more people are we going to send to these mini concentration camps before we unite and say we want actual health care, not sick care and not death care?

QUESTION: Is it fair to say our technology and techniques have obviously gotten better, but the care itself has gone backward?

SIROTEK: They always teach us in our policy analysis courses, and it doesn't matter if you're a doctor or a nurse, that the United States spends 10 percent of its gross domestic product on new health care tech and pharmacy. However, if you go to a country with a universal health care system—and trust me they have their own problems that are no better than our country's, just different—they are repurposing all kinds of drugs to maximize them for different diagnoses.

In South America, we have little old ladies on Viagra for pulmonary hypertension. They use ivermectin for herpes. All these other countries who we think are below the United States in standard of care are excelling at the care part of health care. There are designer medical systems popping up in Mexico right now, where you can get the care that you want for a fraction of the cost, but also with American doctors and American-quality facilities.

We have everything that you could want in the United States, but you have to waste so much time with the bureaucracy and the medical-industrial complex that you risk dying before you get the state-of-the-art treatment. The fact that the United States in lagging behind this methodology of repurposing drugs is embarrassing.

A lot of drugs that the hospitals won't use or tell you about are incredibly cheap, so the pharmaceutical companies don't profit from them. This is why they keep sinking money into cancer but never actually cure cancer. The treatments are barbaric. Chemotherapy is barbaric. But if you can create a new drug that has only a slightly better effectiveness than the old drug, you can now patent it and make more money. It is like a racket.

FDR had the New Deal when he put all this money into social work programs trying to stimulate the economy, which we are still paying for eighty years later. Is this the "new" New Deal, where you guys just keep cranking money into pharmaceutical companies to keep the world going around by keeping us sick?

QUESTION: How do we change this paradigm?

SIROTEK: We aren't going to fix the old model of health care, so don't try to Band-Aid it. We are abandoning it and walking away from it. We are moving away from the HMO/PPO pharmaceutical run racket, and we are going to a more or less cash-based system that is focused predominantly on primary care and early intervention.

I think we are moving to freedom-minded medicine because you vote with your dollars. The only way to make change is to hit them where it hurts and that is in their pocketbook. If we take our consumerism away from these medical industrial complexes, and start going toward patriotic nurses and doctors and clinics and concierge medicine and telehealth and things like that, we are going to see freedom-minded hospitals where the consumer is put at the forefront. Would you continue to frequent a restaurant that gave poor customer service and a poor product? No. And your health is the number-one thing you need to take care of.

CHAPTER 11

Ralph Lorigo: Why Live with Ivermectin When You Can Die on a Ventilator?

R alph Lorigo has witnessed what few other lawyers have. He went up against hospital lawyers who fought to deny patients the right for family members to administer ivermectin—a Nobel Prize–winning, FDA-approved drug— even after they conceded that the patient was as good as dead. Then, in certain cases, after Lorigo won in court to administer the ivermectin, the patient inexplicably turned around and is alive to this day.

Yet, those same hospital doctors and lawyers would remain unmoved, would deny the same treatment to subsequent patients, and even fight all the way to appellate courts to block it for dying Americans with no other recourse. What is the benign, innocent explanation for this?

After being admitted to the New York State Bar in 1974, the Buffalo-based attorney achieved a stellar career, earning much success in real estate and other lucrative areas of law. A member of the legal establishment in good standing, he was even nominated once for a judgeship. He didn't need to take on the entire legal and medical system with very labor intensive and extremely emergent hospital malfeasance cases. But he was flooded with calls from desperate families across the country, who turned to him to help fight for the right to try against COVID one of the safest and most successful drugs ever developed.

At this stage of his career, he could've easily passed on taking on such a leviathan. However, he chose to rise to the occasion.

What he discovered through the course of individual litigation and stories from victims needlessly losing loved ones to untimely deaths is a story that has not been fully told. Yet, it will reverberate long after COVID, as it demonstrates a lingering degree of cruelty, malfeasance, and scientific corruption in America's hospitals that we once thought was limited to countries like China.

We call attorney Ralph C. Lorigo to the stand to enlighten the public about the gravity of the hospital war on ivermectin specifically, and what has become of American hospitals in general:

• • • • • •

QUESTION: You've been practicing law for almost five decades. Of all the areas of law you've covered, it's doubtful you ever expected to delve into the denial of treatment during a pandemic. How did you end up becoming the "right-to-try-ivermectin lawyer" in America?

LORIGO: In my practice, I started working for another lawyer and then as a sole practitioner working all the different legal fields a suburban lawyer would work. My parents were real estate brokers, so I had a lot of real estate clients at the beginning, but I taught myself criminal law, family law, litigation, all different aspects. As I progressed, I hired lawyers to the point I had six staff attorneys working for me and I had a very good practice. I'm now a commercial litigator in business law.

I was in the middle of a deposition and I got a text from a good client of mine that his eighty-year-old mother-in-law was rushed to the hospital with COVID and given a 20 percent chance of living. Her son had come up from Georgia and did his research and convinced the ICU doctor to give her ivermectin. On the second day after she was admitted into the ICU, she took just one dose and experienced such a dramatic improvement that she was off the ventilator and out of the ICU.

She started to decline, though, and the COVID floor doctors refused to give her more ivermectin. My client thought maybe I could find a way to convince the hospital, so I had the son and daughter come to my office and I listened to the situation. After hearing their story, I decided we were going to sue the hospital for declaratory judgement. We were going to bring an order to show cause on an immediate basis, and ask a court to order the hospital to give her the ivermectin.

We were doing this ex parte, which means we don't have to inform the hospital in advance. The litigation papers were prepared and signed the next morning, and by noon that day I got a call from the judge. I knew him very well and he asked me what this was all about. I explained the situation. The judge signed the order to provide ivermectin and then it had to be served on the hospital.

Within a half hour of it being served, I got a call from a lawyer who told me he represents the hospital, and that the court order is ineffective and should have never happened. I asked him what he was concerned about—after all, I had relieved the hospital of all liability. He replied, "Judges can't prescribe medicine." We hung up and the court contacts me and the judge wants to have a conference later that day.

I contacted the son and got a hold of the family doctor, and he is aware of what has happened. I asked him to write me a letter prescription for the ivermectin, which he does. He was an older family practitioner, but he knew she got one dose of ivermectin and that she did better.

We had the conference with the judge and the judge agreed the hospital had to enforce the prescription over the hospital's denial. I won and the hospital administered the ivermectin that night. Six days later, my client was better and left the hospital. This ended up in the local news, and it was most-read story in Buffalo for five days in a row. From there, I started getting calls from lots of other people.

QUESTION: Can you highlight any of those cases that stood out in the subsequent months and how the hospitals fought for the right to kill?

LORIGO: I got a call from a woman whose sixty-seven-year-old mother was in the ICU on a ventilator for several days. You couldn't even go into the hospital and visit her. On New Year's Eve, the family stood outside in the parking lot praying at the window. We prepared a lawsuit and it came before the judge. He contacted me, signed the order, and we served it on the hospital.

The hospital's attorney got involved, but the order stayed in effect and the hospital claimed it didn't have ivermectin. The daughter went to the drug store and bought it for eighty-three cents a pill. She brought it to the hospital, and again a woman whose family was told to say their last goodbyes left the hospital and is still living today.

Another case that stood out happened on Good Friday in 2020. I knew that judge for decades, so I called him and explained the situation. He told me to email him the papers and scheduled a conference call with the hospital attorney—and this was the same hospital as before, again. She went through her little litany and said the hospital didn't want to give the ivermectin because it's not FDA-approved for COVID treatment. But the judge said there was a court order like this before and the hospital administered it.

So the judge ordered the hospital to administer the ivermectin to an eighty-one-year-old man who had dementia issues. But they wouldn't let the wife into the hospital and he had been in there for weeks on a ventilator. His wife was very concerned that without interaction with somebody, he wouldn't survive. So, I went back to the court to allow her to visit him. The judge asked us to go to his chambers and told the hospital's attorney to let the wife in for a reasonable period of time. She agreed and we got an order for one hour in the morning and one hour in the evening every day. That man took the ivermectin and he survived, too.

However, not all cases had happy endings. Time is not on the side of patients on ventilators who have a slim chance of survival. The hospitals often fought us every step of the way, knowing that even if we eventually won, the patient would be dead before we could administer a long enough course of ivermectin.

A case that will forever stand out in my mind was a woman in her fifties who had been on a ventilator for about thirty days. The husband who went to see her every day convinced the infectious disease doctor to prescribe her ivermectin. The pharmacy called the administration and the administration said no.

The husband and I talked to the doctor, and the doctor said he would be cooperative, but in the end he wasn't and finally stopped talking to us. However, her husband had access to the patient portal and got the prescription printed out. I won the case and the hospital was obligated to provide the ivermectin.

This lady was in bad shape, but was getting better after five days of ivermectin because the ventilator was doing less work. Yet once the five-day prescription ran out, her health declined again. We had to get a second court order based on a new prescription after the head doctor at the hospital wrote a scathing affidavit against ivermectin.

That's how I got to know Dr. Pierre Kory, who used to be at this hospital. When he heard about this case, he penned an affidavit for us with all the studies that showed ivermectin is safe and works. Kory is triple board-certified and is just stellar. He helped us win that second court order.

So, the hospital gave her another five days of ivermectin, but then they stopped. We pulled the patient portal and the doctor had written to give it for thirty days. We went back to court, and in front of the judge, they called the doctor to the stand and he said he wrote the prescription for five days despite what he put in the portal.

The hospital leaned on that doctor to write the prescription for five days after he had originally written something different in the patient portal. I made the doctor read the patient portal in court and he didn't know what to say. He said there had to be a mistake with the dates. He was stammering.

I told the judge my client had been on a ventilator for fifty-three days, and I wanted to put my client's husband on the stand to counter what the doctor said, but the judge said she had to adjourn. That was on a Thursday and the judge said they would reconvene the next Tuesday. My client died on the Sunday in between.

QUESTION: Did anyone representing the hospital in any of these cases—whether it be doctors, lawyers or administrators—ever say what their alternative treatments were?

LORIGO: No, and I even ended up suing one hospital system six different times! Back in those days, ivermectin was a five-day protocol. The hospital gave the ivermectin but they never asked for a hearing. Here's the way it works legally. I bring a lawsuit for declaratory judgement. Lawsuits take a long time to get heard, but I'm bringing an order to show cause and asking for a mandatory injunction. When you ask for an order to show cause, it is usually called a temporary restraining order. You are usually asking to stop something. I'm asking for a mandatory injunction so I'm asking to perform something so the degree I have to get to is higher.

I generally have to prove four things. I have to prove the likelihood of success on the merits in the lawsuit. I have to prove irreparable, imminent injury. I have to prove the balancing of the inequities in my favor. And I have to prove that there is a public purpose for granting the injunction. In the lawsuits, the hospital attorneys constantly deny all four of those things while offering no alternatives.

QUESTION: Would you cite for them in your dealings with the hospitals that ivermectin was an FDA-approved drug in general, and even won the Nobel Prize in 2015 for saving so many lives?

LORIGO: Yes, but they would always respond with "there aren't enough studies." They were reading out of the Big Pharma playbook that the FDA and CDC put out. During the first few months of COVID, they were trying to put forth a vaccine that hadn't gotten anywhere yet, and all they knew was that they had a protocol to put them on a ventilator and give them steroids and antibiotics. Many of those people died like that in those first several months.

QUESTION: Did you ever bring up to the judges that the hospitals weren't willing to experiment with something we know is safe, but they were willing to use an expensive standard of care like remdesivir that we know was pulled from an Ebola trial because it caused liver toxicity and kidney failure?

LORIGO: It came up all the time. Here's what I was armed with as we progressed through this. After the first three cases, I got connected to the Front Line COVID-19 Critical Care Alliance (FLCCC) and started talking to them on a regular basis. They looked at repurposing drugs like hydroxychloroquine, but ivermectin was found to be better in so many ways.

As this progressed, I was doing all this research and looking at all the pros and cons; I went to the World Health Organization website and looked up the adverse effects of remdesivir and ivermectin. In less than two years, remdesivir had 7,890 adverse effects, 560 deaths, 945 cardiac events, and 743 renal failures. In thirty years, ivermectin had zero deaths and 5,400 total adverse reactions.

I had all that in an affidavit that went to the judge in every one of my lawsuits. Remdesivir is an extremely toxic drug. It had very few tests before it was approved on an emergency basis. It costs more than $3,000 a shot. And the government gives a 20 percent bonus to hospitals to use remdesivir. We presented all of that.

QUESTION: The morgues were full of people by that point and the doctors and administrators would still fight you tooth and nail to the point of appealing decisions, even after losing at the district court level, when they knew people had no hope of survival if they were left on a ventilator?

LORIGO: Yes, and after early on when I was winning case after case, and most were being saved, the hospitals started to fight me even harder.

I remember one time the hospital appealed the case of a sixty-seven-year-old woman who had gotten COVID visiting her daughter and ended up on a ventilator for about twenty days. The daughter was even told to come and say her goodbyes.

The daughter got a hold of me and I brought the ex parte order to show cause. I convinced the judge of our case via video conference, and he ordered the administering of ivermectin, but the hospital refused to administer it. The daughter was in the hospital with her mother, and the hospital told her they would not obey the court order. The daughter put me on the phone, and I told the doctor it was not a question of their decision at this point. The doctor gave me the name of the hospital lawyer and I asked the in-house lawyer if the hospital was going to direct a doctor not to obey a court order.

She didn't answer and when I asked a second time, she simply hung up on me. I brought a motion for contempt on a Friday, served it on the hospital on Saturday, and Sunday night, the hospital emailed their motion to set aside the court order. Then on Monday, they sent another one to stay the court order. The judge was on my side and we won. The judge told them they had to let our doctor treat her with the ivermectin. She's also still alive today, but even after she left the hospital, the lawyers were still appealing the merits of the precedent of the case, if you can believe it!

QUESTION: Almost as if to say, "How dare she survive?"

LORIGO: I've had numerous clients tell me doctors have said they think they should consider pulling the plug, and when the clients tell them they want to try ivermectin for their loved ones, the doctors tell them no because that could hurt them. That's the twisted logic they've actually used. That it could hurt them more as they're already dying.

The protocol is set by the administration and not by the individual doctors. In many of the cases, the administrators have testified that the doctors don't have a choice, even if they are willing to give ivermectin. Now, the big question is why.

QUESTION: Do you have numbers for how many ivermectin cases you litigated, how many you won, and how many of those cases survived?

LORIGO: I won the great majority of the cases at the beginning, but it got so hectic that at one point in September 2020 I got fifty cases. We were going like crazy and I hired another lawyer just to do ivermectin cases. Everything else, I had to set aside. I lowered my hourly rate substantially in order to do ivermectin cases, but at that point I was working ten hours a day, seven days a week. I was having hearings twice a day in December of 2021. I would estimate I won 70–75 percent of the initial hearings, but then when we had actual testimony, I started to lose cases because using local ICU doctors against my telemed doctor didn't work.

QUESTION: How much did the FDA's war against ivermectin, which started in late August 2021, play a role in swaying judges?

LORIGO: It was in every answering paper, that article with the picture of a woman and a horse claiming it was just a horse dewormer. But the reality is that the article came from the veterinary division of the FDA and what it really says is don't self-medicate with animal medication. It was couched in a whole different language and all the mainstream media picked it up. The FDA tweeted that you aren't a horse and you aren't a cow, but there was a sentence in the article that initially said if you are prescribed ivermectin for an FDA-approved use, get it from a pharmacy and use it as directed. But then they changed it by taking out "for an approved use."

The attorney general for the state of Nebraska made a big deal out of that one sentence because he said it was an acknowledgement that you don't have to use ivermectin for an FDA-approved use and it can be used off-label. The U.S. Supreme Court has held that off-label use is legitimate, legal, and often medically necessary and the FDA has agreed with that—but not for ivermectin.

I concluded they had to discredit ivermectin to justify the emergency use authorization they wanted for the experimental vaccines. You can't have an effective and available treatment in order to get an EUA from the FDA.

QUESTION: To hear you describe the layers of bureaucratic hell that they are willing to impose just to get what they want is ghoulish, but did you ever encounter any argument you thought was a valid point?

LORIGO: No. There are so many doctors who stopped prescribing it because of intimidation. I've had doctors say they believe in ivermectin and give it to their families, but that they couldn't help me out any more in court. I'm going to be seventy-five years old, and this is something I would never have believed could happen in my life. Hundreds of thousands of people have died without the need for it. It is so heart-wrenching. In so many of those situations, those people died alone.

CHAPTER 12

Jenna Campau and Brian Festa: You Will Take a Shot You Don't Need or You Won't Get the Healthcare You Do

One of the most barbaric and demonic aspects of this entire biomedical state that has been created since the advent of COVID is the denial of treatment, including organ transplants, to those who don't get the shot for medical or religious reasons. It is a degree of discrimination and apartheid none of us could have imagined, especially at a time when courts are forcing hospitals to perform chemical castration or "transgender" surgery under the guise of antidiscrimination law.[101]

What began in a few radical hospitals in some blue states has now become the general rule. No matter how much information comes forward that the shots do not work, especially for those who are immune-suppressed or suffering organ failure. No matter the mounting evidence of damage to the organs caused by the shots. No matter your prior immunity status, what risk factors you have, or how dangerous the shots are to you—you will be getting the shots, and sometimes even boosters. Legitimate religious and medical exemptions are being categorically denied.

This policy is as illogical as it is immoral and inhumane. The safety and efficacy of these shots were never studied in people with organ failure. The same doctors and hospitals that refused to allow established safe medication like ivermectin to be used for COVID patients with no options because the efficacy against COVID wasn't studied in accordance with their standards had no problem forcing the shots on those in organ failure with no studies on efficacy or *safety*.

In reality, it was known from day one that the shots failed to stimulate immunity with this subset of the population. Researchers at Toronto's University Health Network (UHN) Transplant Centre studied the T-cell responses in organ transplant patients who had prior infection without the shots versus those who had the shots without prior infection.[102]

In April 2021, Mayo Clinic researchers published their findings in the *American Journal of Transplantation* that solid organ transplant patients enjoy limited antibody responses from the shots.

"We report seven SOTs with undetectable or low titer antispike antibodies who developed COVID-19 infection after receiving one or two doses of the SARS-CoV-2 mRNA vaccine," wrote the authors in a letter to the journal. "The clinical presentation and course of these patients were comparable to those of SOTs who had COVID-19 infection and have not been vaccinated."[103]

A Johns Hopkins study published as a letter in JAMA in March 2022 found that only 17 percent of a sample of 436 organ transplant patients had detectable antibodies from the Moderna shots.[104] "Our study shows that [immunity] is unlikely for most transplant patients, and one could guess that our findings could also apply to other immunosuppressed patients, such as those with autoimmune conditions," Johns Hopkins University surgeon Dorry Segev wrote in Medpage Today.[105]

In fact, not only do the shots not work for the recipients, but if anything, using organs from donors with the shots might be exceedingly dangerous. A U.K. study found thirteen solid-organ donors who likely died from vaccine-induced thrombosis and thrombocytopenia stemming from the AstraZeneca shots during two of the early months of vaccination in 2021. So what happened when ten of their organs were given to recipients? "There were seven major thrombotic or hemorrhagic postoperative complications in six recipients resulting in the loss of three transplants." One of the patients died within a day of cardiac arrest.[106]

Thus, if anything, there should be a rule *banning* the shots for organ donors and recipients. Yet, Jenna and Daniel Campau suffered the denial of a kidney to their seventeen-year-old daughter Alisa, who was in renal failure.

The Grand Rapids, Michigan, couple adopted their daughter from Ukraine to bring her to freedom here in the United States, but then faced the worst form of discrimination, one that that could end her life. Spectrum Health/Helen DeVos Children's Hospital denied Alisa acceptance to the organ list because of the Campaus' religious beliefs opposing the COVID shot.

Worse, in what has become one of the most odious habits of the biomedical tyrants, her nephrologist filed a Form 3200 medical neglect report with Michigan Children's Protective

RISE OF THE FOURTH REICH

Services. Hospitals and medical practitioners have been engaging in medical kidnapping throughout the pandemic to deny bodily autonomy as well as parental rights to anyone who doesn't participate in their great human experiments.

With the help of the nonprofit We The Patriots USA, Jenna and Daniel are bringing a lawsuit against Spectrum Health/Helen DeVos Children's Hospital as a result of the religious discrimination against their daughter, Alisa. Brian Festa, an attorney and cofounder of We The Patriots USA, has been helping numerous other clients facing similar life-threatening forms of barbaric discrimination.

Thankfully, as this book was going to print, We the Patriots USA had achieved the legal victory needed to obtain the health care Alisa Campau deserves. But because the Campau case represents thousands of other similar forms of discrimination that continue to occur in the medical system, we call Jenna Campau to the stand, along with Brian Festa, whose organization funded her lawsuits and other similar ones, to inform the public and lawmakers on the extent of this illogical, illegal, inhumane, and life-threatening form of discrimination.

◾ ◾ ◾ ◾ ◾ ◾

QUESTION: Brian, let's start with you. Why is your organization supporting legal action here?

FESTA: Jenna's daughter Alisa is being denied a lifesaving treatment for end-stage renal disease. She's being denied treatment due to her refusal to take not only the COVID shot, but also the flu shot and other vaccines, because she has sincere religious beliefs and medical concerns about the shots. That's what is so dangerous about this from a legal perspective. The precedent that is being set is that this isn't just about the fog of war during the height of a pandemic anymore, or when we are in emergency lockdowns. Now, it is going to be anytime you need what they call "lifesaving treatment"—whether it actually is or not—they can deny it on the basis of refusing the COVID shot or any shot.

Prior to 2020 or 2021, when did you hear about anyone being denied an organ transplant for not getting the flu shot? You didn't. Now it has become the new standard. Even if this isn't affecting you personally at this moment, you should be very concerned about this case because if this is allowed to stand, then this will be the new standard of care in every hospital in the United States. Imagine being told you can't have lifesaving cancer or heart surgery simply because you didn't get your annual flu shot, or your fourth COVID booster. It's insane.

QUESTION: Jenna, could you describe being united with your daughter in the United States, and then how you found out she had renal failure?

CAMPAU: We met our daughter back in 2012 when we were on a family trip in Ukraine. We had already adopted our son from the same institution, but it wasn't until 2019 when she became officially available for adoption, so we started that process and brought her home in June of 2021.

We already knew that she had some serious kidney issues, but we knew we didn't have a full picture. By August, her health had declined quite a bit and she ended up going on a regular dialysis schedule. It was confirmed she was in stage four if not stage five renal disease. She has only one kidney and it is very obviously not working properly, so she is in dire need of a transplant.

QUESTION: Can you talk about the timeline of getting on the transplant list, the treatment in the hospital, and how it changed once they found out you didn't want to give her the shot?

CAMPAU: They started the process of getting her on the transplant list by the end of 2021, and we were trusting that they knew what they were doing. Then, within a couple of months after she was on dialysis, we were informed that if we were questioning or resisting vaccines that they would consider it noncompliance and they would involve the authorities if they saw fit. We asked them for a written copy of what their required protocol is so that we wouldn't be surprised by anything else. At first, we thought there might be some wiggle room and they might be willing to negotiate. But it has become very clear that is not the case at all and they filed a report on us.

QUESTION: Wait, so not only did they deny you a place on the transplant list, but they reported you to child protective services?

CAMPAU: Yes. We did not know until January 2022 that there is something called an evaluation process, where there isn't an official beginning to all the technical layers of the process to get on the transplant list until they see a certain level of compliance. At this point, it's all about compliance with vaccines, and that they are insisting on a combination of vaccines including for COVID, and a number of others that we all along have felt we can't go along with.

QUESTION: Did you show them any data about waning efficacy for the COVID vaccine, or the escalating risk profile? Were the people you are working with even phased by that information?

CAMPAU: We brought this up when we could sit down with all the people on our daughter's team and discuss these things together. But when I look at the after-visit notes, it says we never brought up any of these things. And in a phone call I had with the Patient Relations and Ethics Committee several months ago, it was suggested I draft an email and lay out bullet points and include links for whatever I felt was appropriate to explain our objections, which I did, and again it was as if it had never been said.

QUESTION: Did you try to go to a different hospital?

CAMPAU: We started to investigate other transplant programs across the country, and I got on internet forums with other families experiencing similar discrimination. We went to a facility in Indiana because I had talked to them on the phone, and was assured that they did not require the COVID vaccine in particular. When we got there, we started consulting with this doctor and about twenty minutes into our conversation, she said that she was in touch with our facility, and let them know to tell us that they had changed their policy and now required the COVID vaccine as well. It's been so strange to watch all this happen so quickly behind the scenes.

My oldest daughter is thirty now, and when I questioned something or declined something with my pediatrician when she was a baby, that was the end of the conversation, and we didn't have any pressure put on us. I naively thought that was still the case. When I asked the hospital social worker if the vaccine was such a sacred cow to her that she would risk a girl we had just brought all the way over from Ukraine being removed from our home, she said it would be up to child protective services. So that's been just hanging over our heads and now a report has been filed. Their goal is to use CPS to force whatever the medical cartel wants to require. Any religious or safety objections just don't matter in their paradigm.

QUESTION: So Brian, where does the law stand on this hospital/child protective services power play, or does it vary state to state?

FESTA: It's better in so-called red states in general, but the state still has way too much power over parental rights and parental autonomy and it's really dangerous and scary. Medical kidnapping is exactly what is happening right now. If it can happen to baby Cyrus in a state like Idaho, it can happen anywhere. These doctors need to find themselves in court, and so does the state if they act against parents. There is no credible scientific evidence to support the need for a COVID or a flu shot if you are going to get a transplant. In fact, the science is quite the opposite.[1] They will have to answer to that in court, and we are very confident they won't be able to.

---

[1]   Festa is not a physician and none of his statements herein
    should be construed to constitute medical advice.

I have not seen a case like this go all the way to trial yet. In some cases, on the private level outside of court, the hospitals have backed down to keep it out of court. Because this isn't just about the science but the religious discrimination angle as well, they will have to answer for that too. Title II of the Civil Right Acts makes it illegal to discriminate against someone in a place of public accommodation on the basis of one's religious beliefs. And hospitals that offer goods or services to the public are places of public accommodation. Any doctor who refuses treatment based on the patient's religious beliefs is violating that law.

The Department of Health and Human Services also has an Office of Civil Rights within it, which was created under the Trump administration, to address this kind of discrimination. There are a number of counts against these hospitals and doctors from various legal angles, so we are prepared to go all the way if that's the direction they choose, but we would rather resolve this quickly because somebody's life is at stake. If we do have to go to court, though, it will set a precedent for thousands if not millions who could be denied critical medical care just for holding fast to their religious convictions.

QUESTION: Brian, what drove you to take on these kinds of cases?

FESTA: This is personal for me. My son was very seriously injured by a flu shot when he was just a baby. He has multiple lifelong autoimmune conditions and deficiencies. He needs to get very expensive treatments every week for it and his immunologist has confirmed it is because of the flu shot. So, it's personal that they are requiring someone who is already in a compromised immunological state to get a flu shot. It defies logic.

QUESTION: Jenna, your daughter is almost an adult and has a mind of her own. How does she feel about all this?

CAMPAU: The idea of having free choice and a voice for herself coming here from Ukraine is something she is just now figuring out as she is getting command of the English language. At first, we didn't want to tell her a lot because we didn't want to scare her. But even before we got her home from Kiev, she said she absolutely never wanted the COVID shot. When they came to her orphanage to administer the shot, they only gave it to the boys and to the female staff who were beyond child-bearing age. So that seemed pretty telling to her.

But if not getting the shot keeps her from being placed on the transplant list before her eighteenth birthday, it's the difference between nine to twelve months and four to six years, in terms of when the actual transplant would likely take place. That is time we likely don't have…all for an outdated, ineffective, and dangerous shot.

CHAPTER 13

Robert Malone: The Man
Who Knew Too Much

The American people were told they were receiving a vaccine that was more or less in line with the safe technology they have come to expect the past several generations. However, what they actually produced, supposedly at warp speed, was anything but ordinary.

It was people like Dr. Robert Malone who should have been brought into the development process, assuming the medical establishment really desired a safe pursuit of mRNA technology for vaccines. As one of the founders of the technology, Malone could have easily flagged so many concerns from day one, and could have guided the regulators on what to look for when analyzing the safety of gene therapies. Unfortunately, no such input from real experts like Malone was ever solicited. What is the benign, innocent explanation for this?

How is it possible they spent more than a decade unsuccessfully coming up with a safe and effective vaccine for SARS-COV-1, but they were able to make it so for

SARS-COV-2—which we were told was a "novel corona-virus"—in barely six months? There are only two possible answers to this question, and they are not reconcilable.

Either these vaccines rank among the greatest scientific achievements in all of human history, or we have recklessly injected over twelve billion doses (as of July 10, 2022) of a potion with an escalating risk profile into our species.

So which is it? Few human beings alive are as qualified, let alone willing, to answer that vital question for us than Dr. Malone. In order to help us understand this mRNA technology that was used, and whether it was implemented with the proper oversight, we call Dr. Robert Malone to the stand.

• • • • • •

QUESTION: Please begin with a summation of your extensive experience and credentials in the field of virology and, specifically, with your pioneering of mRNA vaccine technology. What is it that drew you to it?

MALONE: I'm a Maryland licensed physician and scientist trained at UC-Davis, University of Maryland, University of California, San Diego Salk Institute, Northwestern University Feinberg School of Medicine, and at Harvard Medical School for a postgraduate fellowship in clinical research, particularly international clinical research. I've had additional training specifically in medical ethics and clinical research ethics. Much of this is mandated training required if you want us to manage clinical trials or serve as a principal investigator.

I began my career as an undergraduate working in a retro-viral virology lab, focused on breast cancer at UC-Davis. And while I was there, one of my two mentors, Murray Gardner, serendipitously was deeply involved together with Preston Marx and eventually Luc Montagnier in understanding the retroviral basis of acquired immunodeficiency syndrome (AIDS), particularly using a nonhuman primate model. Coming off of this background of two intensive years in which I basically functioned as a graduate student at UC-Davis, I received an MD PhD scholarship at Northwestern, but elected to take my graduate work at UC-San Diego because I was very passionate about the application of retroviral biology to the indication of gene therapy. I went there because there were two leading retroviral-vector gene-therapy specialists: Ted Friedman, and Inder Verma.

I qualified for the program at UC-San Diego by scoring in the top fraction of 1 percent in my graduate record exam on biology. So I was readily accepted there and progressed rapidly through the curriculum and was in a series of graduate rotations in basic virology and recombinant DNA. I'd also done some work in retrovirals in RNA viral biology when I was at Northwestern as a first-year medical student.

I was accepted into Dr. Inder Verma's lab at the Salk Institute, which was a main part of the molecular biology and biology labs at the Salk at a time when there were very few graduate students. Inder was one of the leading retrovirologists in the world, having characterized reverse transcriptase for Dr. David Baltimore, who received the Nobel Prize for his work with reverse transcriptase. Inder was a full professor before the time he was thirty. When I joined the lab, he was in his early thirties.

Under his direction, I focused on questions relating to the packaging of retroviruses for purposes of retroviral gene therapy. And in order to do that, I sought to develop a system that would allow me to use modern recombinant DNA technology to ask precise questions about the structure and function of the packaging RNA sequence in retroviruses. To do this, I needed to develop methods or discover identified methods for producing large quantities of purified RNA and delivering them into cells that would complement those RNAs, resulting in the production of infectious retroviral vectors. The series of discoveries that I had in the laboratory in the late eighties, when I was working on these problems, led to both the awareness that gene therapy technologies of any form could be used for vaccination purposes, and specifically, that mRNA could be manufactured in bulk and purified and worked with.

With the discoveries I made about the structure of RNA and the necessary sequences and elements to make that RNA function, I was able to achieve reasonable levels of RNA delivery and expression in a wide variety of cultured cell lines. And then in embryos, particularly frog embryos, a series of patent disclosures was filed, which resulted in fights between different investigators at UC-San Diego and the Salk.

As I was caught in the middle of this, I had a nervous breakdown and chose to resign with my master's in lieu of PhD, having already completed my oral qualifying exams. I went to work for a small biotech company called Vical and brought my technology protocols and reagents there. And within a couple of months, we had the discoveries that are now called naked DNA delivery, and had filed the patents that eventually led to nine issued patents covering the platform technology for delivering DNA and RNA into tissues and animals and its use for vaccine purposes. That all goes back to 1989.

I then completed my medical degree and finished an internship at UC-Davis. And then because I was successful in writing grants and contracts during my internship year—I had been awarded approximately a million in grants and contracts—I elected to become a faculty member rather than complete my pathology residency. At that point, I set up a laboratory and grew it to about six faculty members in the field of polynucleotide delivery and gene therapy. I had a number of other patents and fundamental discoveries relating to the use of positively charged fats to deliver polynucleotides into cells and tissues. This is the cationic lipid technology. And from that, there are still multiple marketed cationic lipid compounds sold into the research market.

I was then recruited from UC-Davis and my laboratory was moved to the University of Maryland-Baltimore across the country. In the subsequent few years, I started a company, which was part of the objective of the university of Maryland in hiring me, and then had to close that company because the objections of the dean of the school of medicine. I had been hired basically by the overall director of the provost of the campus at large, but the dean of the school of medicine objected to using facilities at the school to start up a company even though it was funded by the state.

So we closed that, but about that time had a series of inventions and discoveries relating to using pulse electrical fields to deliver polynucleotides for vaccination purposes. And that eventually gave rise to another startup company called Vical that also operates in San Diego now, and is developing DNA vaccines for coronaviruses. At that point, I left the University of Maryland and joined Uniformed Services University of the Health Sciences in Bethesda, the military medical school, and worked on a breast cancer program. I set up a research facility in Western Pennsylvania with a breast cancer tissue banking operation.

Subsequently, I accepted a position as an assistant clinical director of DynPort Vaccine Company right after the anthrax attacks in late 2001. DynPort at the time had just received the prime system contract for all biodefense related products advanced development for the Department of Defense. So at that point, I worked on all of the major biodefense vaccines—plague, tularemia, anthrax, smallpox, Venezuelan equine encephalitis virus, and a number of other products, including antibody products.

And then I pivoted my career to focus on regulatory affairs and clinical trials, such as clinical development. And I've been doing that ever since at a number of facilities, including Solvay Pharmaceuticals for its influenza vaccine contract with HHS's Biomedical Advanced Research and Development Authority (BARDA), and various contract research organizations that were vaccine focused.

I've worked at a phase 1 clinical research facility in Baltimore, and basically developed a broad understanding and capability, particularly focused in the area of biodefense medical countermeasures—both drugs and vaccines.

I had many large contracts from my clients. I won or managed billions of dollars in grants and contracts, including for government clients. I've done projects, for instance, a cooperative research and development agreement with the Defense Threat Reduction Agency (DTRA) that identified a number of repurposed drugs active against Zika and working closely

STEVE DEACE AND DANIEL HOROWITZ

with DTRA. At their request, I basically parachuted into the company called Newly Genetics and spearheaded the Ebola vaccine project that was sold off with my assistance to Merck vaccines, and eventually became the Ebola vaccine that we know today that's licensed.

So, in summary, I have a career that spans discovery research and fundamental technology all the way through advanced development and licensure of a variety of medical products. And it spans molecular biology, virology, immunology, pathology—all the way through medical clinical research and regulatory affairs, epidemiology, and all the associated disciplines.

QUESTION: It is vitally important for you to have restated all of this for the record as we now get into the specifics of COVID. What was your trigger as a dedicated scientist in this field? When did you first sense something smells rotten in the state of Denmark, if you will? When did you sense this is not passing the smell test and something is not right?

MALONE: It was gradual for me. But that process began with a phone call I got from infectious disease doctor Michael Callahan. He was in Wuhan in the fourth quarter of 2019, and called me on January 4, 2020. Since that time, I had been focused on drug repurposing for the novel coronavirus and worked a number of different contracts and helped build over $150 million of grants and contracts through this epidemic largely with Department of Defense, but also with BARDA.

Those associations gave me an awareness of the government actively blocking various early treatment options. Ivermectin was one example. In that case, I had worked with a couple of senior scientists in the U.S. and in Spain to launch a special volume of Frontiers in Pharmacology, focused on drug repurposing for treating the novel coronavirus and had actively solicited a review on ivermectin from the now-famous Dr. Pierre Kory.

And then I saw that article arbitrarily and capriciously blocked from publication because of somebody interceding with the overall senior director of the Frontiers publication series. Someone that was not disclosed who it was at the time. The article had been through rigorous peer review, the fees had been paid for, the abstract had been published, and I'd never seen anything like that in my experience.

Then my own papers and those of many colleagues were pulled and reviewed in an arbitrary fashion, to the point I and other editors decided to resign and close down that journal. That was one of the first major triggers of an awareness that something wasn't right here. Then there was a series of other events involving conversations with a physician in Canada, who shared what was going on in Canada with mandates and efforts to vaccinate children with an experimental product.

Next, there was my ongoing dialogue with three senior members of the FDA and the office of the commissioner in which we are all perplexed by the government's position about hydroxychloroquine and ivermectin. The discussion with those individuals also focused on the potential risks of the vaccine. I was aware of the risks of spike protein being biologically active because of the work I was doing in drug repurposing, and I mentioned this to them. They communicated it to the review branch, and what came back was that the review branch of the FDA had no concerns about the biologic activity of spike protein, which I found really unusual.

Then there was the push to mandate these emergency use authorized products, which flew in the face of fundamental medical ethics and informed consent. As well as he requirement that patients be allowed to elect and to choose to take an unlicensed product with informed consent. Thus, I saw the mandates as a breach of medical ethics.

Then, I received the Japanese common technical document, which virologist Dr. Byram Bridle had identified and reviewed, and was shocked to find how sloppy and incomplete the nonclinical package was within that document. And that kind of set the whole thing in motion, as I had spoken out about the medical ethics breaches and the fundamental regulatory breaches of international standards that I observed with the Pfizer product based on the Japanese common technical document.

This all led to me being included in a famous podcast with Bret Weinstein and Steve Kirsch in June 2021, in which I discussed what I knew about the risks of the vaccine and the spike protein, and then that kind of cascaded as information became available. I found myself in a leadership position, with information about the risks of vaccine and the various governmental efforts to mandate the vaccine coming at me daily. This is the cascade of events that led to me becoming increasingly aware that what was being done was a breach of normal clinical research standards, nonclinical research standards, and medical ethics.

QUESTION: How in the world did it ever get off the ground with professional vaccinologists when this technology was discussed for this novel coronavirus vaccine? It's become abundantly clear that at its most basic level, this thing codes your body to produce a pathogenic spike and the lipid nanoparticles distribute this all over your body so that you're producing this thrombotic spike pretty much everywhere. This elicits inflammatory autoantibodies in a response and that's not controlled to one area, but potentially in every organ. And then the lipid nanoparticles seem to be very inflammatory themselves. Even a layman who does the research can see this at this point, so how could anyone in the vaccine-producing business from day one have thought this was okay, and in what sort of appropriate framework did you conceive the idea of mRNA use for other vaccines?

MALONE: The initial conception of the technology was that one of the fundamental flaws in the gene therapy paradigm is that it's not very efficient, as all of the existing technologies were inefficient, so that the gene that was inserted with the virus—or whatever your technology—was widely distributed into a small number of cells all over the body typically. And that this introduction of DNA, because it was all DNA or viral DNA based, would result in a certain number of events involving recombination into the genome. Those events were intrinsically risky in terms of cancer cells or other types of insertional neurogenesis problems.

And furthermore, with the existing vaccine—the existing gene therapy technologies at the time, which continue to be used at present—they were all designed for high-level, long-term expression of the recombinant protein. As such, the problem is that if something goes wrong—if the protein is toxic, for some reason—there's no way to correct it and recover it. There's no way to recover. The patient is stuck with that problem. You can't go in and surgically remove it because there's these random scattered cells all over the body that have this gene therapy.

And so with the advent of my conception that you could use RNA as a drug, the fundamental basis of that was not just the technology of being able to demonstrate that you could introduce it and you could manufacture it at large quantities and what the structure needed to be in order to make it work, but the idea was that with RNA, because it normally has a half-life of a few hours at most, if there was something that was going wrong with the genetic therapy, the RNA would naturally degrade rapidly and it would no longer be in the body. It would be cleared and patients would heal themselves.

Also, the application that I promoted at the time as the entry-level application was the one that I was aware of that required very, very low levels of protein. And that was generating an immune response, ergo, a vaccine, because the immune system is a natural amplifier of a biologic effect from a very small amount of protein. So that was the genesis. It started off with RNA as a drug because it had these intrinsic safety advantages, and then the application of vaccines as the entry-level medical indication for use of the technology.

Now, moving toward the present, in the latter nineties, about a decade after I did all this work, I was contacted by a scholar at the University of Pennsylvania named Kati Karikó, who was impressed with what I'd done and wanted to get involved in RNA delivery and this vaccine indication. And so I spoke to her about the problems with the tech, which were that it was highly inflammatory in particular, as well as inefficient, but introduced her to some senior scientists in the RNA world that were working on stabilizing RNA. I then invited her to a conference that was held in Annapolis that

I was organizing. Kati was working with a gentleman named Dr. Drew Weissman.

Weissman is part of Tony Fauci's close circle of people that Tony has personally trained. And Kati and Drew recognized in the literature that there was evidence that if RNA included a modified uridine-base called pseudouridine, that it would be more stable, and in particular, less inflammatory for an RNA.

So they took the work that I had done—the technology with the RNA synthesis and the structure of the vector—and instead of using a cocktail of a A, U, G, and C to manufacture that RNA as separate bases that would be polymerized, they used a cocktail of A pseudouridine instead of standard uridine G and C to manufacture the product. They found that when they did that, and they injected it into animals, they didn't have a strong inflammatory response in the same way as before. And it produced very high levels of protein.

On this basis, they had a patent issue and then began touring the world, promoting the idea of RNA vaccination using their modification. That's the basis for their claims that they invented mRNA vaccines and should be award the Nobel Prize, and were awarded the Alaska Award and many other global awards for their modification to what I'd done. The thing about what they did by adding the pseudouridine is they overcame the problem of the hyperinflammation that had bedeviled the cationic lipid-based (positively charged fats) RNA delivery systems.

But what they didn't realize, apparently, is that one person's reduction in inflammation is another person's immunosuppression. So, we now know that pseudouridine is actually very carefully regulated in the cell. It's not used in a distributed way all through an RNA. It absolutely is used to regulate inflammation and inflammatory responses in cells and it is used to extend the half-life of the RNAs that a cell might provide if it chooses to modify some of those uridines to form pseudouridines.

Basically, what they did was take a very crude approach, put in pseudouridine all the way through the mRNA molecule, which is absolutely not what natural RNA has, and then used that for the injections. They still subscribed to the theory, as did Pfizer and Moderna, that these RNAs in the vaccine would last only for a short period of time in the patient. And they also subscribed to the theory that they would stay in the deltoid after injection, but the data showed that they didn't stay there. In fact, the mRNA goes all over the body and produces remarkably high levels of protein.

What wasn't appreciated until very recently, because no one did the studies (even though they should have, and the FDA should have required them), is both the biodistribution and the pharmacokinetics of the therapeutic. This reveals to us the duration of the drug product in the body and how long it is active. What we now know is these hypermodified RNAs that aren't really natural RNAs—manufactured by way of the University of Pennsylvania patent—are both apparently immunosuppressive and absolutely result in very, very long-term stability of the RNA, so that the RNA is able to be recovered from lymph node biopsies in humans for at least sixty days, if not much longer. This is absolutely not the way that a natural RNA works.

Thus, what they ended up developing and ultimately using in all of us was a molecule that in some ways is more like DNA, but also has some of the characteristics of RNA, which

RISE OF THE FOURTH REICH

can be used to produce protein, and it still has this extremely long half-life and this immunosuppressive property.

To that end, what was placed in all our bodies is fundamentally different from what I had proposed and its behavior in humans is fundamentally different, and it absolutely should have been rigorously tested to demonstrate safety and its pharmacokinetics and its biodistribution. But that was not done, it was not asked for, and was not required by the FDA. That was a major dereliction of duty on the part of the FDA. They absolutely did not do what they were supposed to do, and that came in two forms. They didn't do the fundamentals and they didn't apply the fundamental standards of good laboratory practices for what they did do.

And then the FDA, for some strange reason, applied the checklist for a standard vaccine technology when they should have applied the checklist for a gene therapy technology. I was one of the first to point out that this was actually a gene therapy technology, and I was resoundingly fact-checked and demeaned about having said so. However, in the SEC filings for both Moderna and Pfizer, they specifically acknowledged that these were gene therapies.

The reason why I believe there was such pushback to the term is because had they acknowledged that they were gene therapies, which they were, it would have revealed that the FDA was asleep at the switch and not applying the checklist of a novel gene therapy technology. That would've included the genotoxicity reproductive toxicology analyses that the FDA did not require Pfizer or Moderna to do.

So there was very widespread dereliction of duty down to the level where a lot of the tests that are reported weren't actually done with the actual biologic material with the vaccine itself, but with other RNAs, such as luciferin RNA and other surrogates. Had I submitted a package like this for one of my clients, as a regulatory specialist, I would've expected the FDA to immediately reject it and tell me to go back and do the work that I had failed to do.

The next question is why. You had collusion and cooperation and advocacy for this technology between the Vaccine Research Center under Tony Fauci's oversight and University of Pennsylvania with Drew Weissman, Tony Fauci postdoc researcher, and BioNTech. Then there's Moderna, which was developing and eventually deployed a vaccine that was engineered by the Vaccine Research Center at NIH. There had never been an mRNA vaccine widely deployed in the world ever, but there was a clear belief from Dr. Fauci that this technology represented the future.

There were also the nongovernmental actors. At that point, it had a major investment and support from Bill Gates and his foundation, who believed this was a fundamental advance in technology. It had clear, explicit backing from the leaders of the World Economic Forum who believed, among other things, that it represented a step forward toward their agenda of transhumanism. They speak about this in their own documents. And the logic was that if the RNA vaccine technology could be deployed, it would create a situation in which those that were supporting this tech would've overcome the ethical objections that they knew existed to genetically modified organisms, including humans. If there was a crisis like this that they were able to use this type of gene therapy technology for, it would have the advantage of then overcoming ethical barriers to willingness of the population to accept other genetic modifications.

There had never been anything like this deployed before. There were a number of highly influential individuals, including Tony Fauci and Bill Gates, who very actively promoted the technology. The Vaccine Research Center, which had experienced failure after failure after failure, historically, to develop a vaccine that was licensed—including West Nile, Ebola, a universal influenza vaccine, and most notoriously HIV, which was the very reason why the Vaccine Research Center had originally been created. All of these had been major failures, despite billions in funding from Congress. And they had gone through a series of technologies, including DNA vaccination and adenoviral vector vaccination, and believed that they finally had a winner technology that they were going to very actively promote, which was the RNA vaccines.

It's also important to remember that the RNA vaccine technology was basically brought off the shelf and actively advanced because of a funding program from the Defense Advanced Research Projects Agency (DARPA) that was implemented a few years ago. DARPA had actually seeded most of the mRNA drug and vaccine technology startups through this historic program. But up until the time of this event, those startups had largely failed.

Moderna was a failing company because of all the toxicity and other problems and failure to show effectiveness for their various syndications with the mRNA technology. But in this case, for some reason, it was pushed despite other options being available. More traditional vaccines, such as Novavax, as well as early drug treatments were available. All these things were largely suppressed to push just this one technology that was kind of a poster child, a golden child, of all the major players—DARPA, the Gates Foundation, the World Economic Forum, and Tony Fauci.

QUESTION: So you provided the background as to why they pursued this technology, in addition to what it is. Moving forward, obviously the Moderna CEO announced they have fifteen more messenger RNA vaccines in the pipeline. In the past, we could assume a bad vaccine design would go by the wayside either because it wasn't profitable or it wasn't feasible to develop, but is there a concern that we're now on a new paradigm where they're able to get some sort of approval for something that should never be approved—despite concerns of inflammation and other health risks?

MALONE: The FDA is completely compromised now. The world can no longer rely on them as an objective rigorous assessor of safety and effectiveness. Some of the fatalities here are the credibility of the FDA, the credibility of the CDC, the credibility of the NIAID, the credibility of the hospital systems, and the credibility of physicians. Substantial damage has been done through this policy of rushing out products before they're ready and kind of taking a "damn the torpedoes" approach, combined with all the censorship and propaganda and defamation.

What I mean is the things that have been done that are breaches of the law and fundamental bioethics go on and on and on. They've basically destroyed my industry, which is why I've been such a vociferous objector as I saw this happening.

QUESTION: Knowing what you know today, would you say that it is not worth pursuing mRNA for vaccines in the future, even for pathogens that don't contain a pathogenic spike or something with similar toxicity?

MALONE: I think that the use of pseudouridine was ill-conceived, rushed, and should have been much more rigorously tested, but the idea of mRNA as a transient way to produce a protein on short notice? There's a lot of fundamental good things about that. And remember that mRNA can work without the cationic lipid, though it's not required. There are companies like CureVac in Germany that don't use the pseudouridine, and Moderna wasn't going to use it but they were arm-twisted into doing it. But originally, it was only BioNTech that was gonna use the pseudouridine. CureVac is backed by an interesting character named Elon Musk, and is busy developing a rapid-manufacturing, small-scale platform for mRNA vaccine products.

The idea behind this is still viable, and I published it in a paper a few years ago, which is basically about rapid response vaccines. There's undoubtedly a need for this ability to quickly develop a vaccine candidate product on a very abbreviated timeline for a novel engineered or an unexpected inner species crossover virus. That's not to say that it should be deployed globally without adequate testing, but having the ability to rapidly manufacture something that can be used in a *limited* way as an experimental use authorized product still has enormous need and merit.

But it's one thing to build that for, say, Special Forces, who might be willing to accept it with appropriate informed consent. It's a totally different thing to jam it by mandate into millions of arms, or billions in this case.

QUESTION: After everything we know about all the inflammatory reactions and the autoimmune diseases we're seeing, what are your biggest concerns about the long-term medical adverse effects to the general population?

MALONE: The data is increasingly suggesting that particularly with people receiving three doses, there seems to be a dose-dependent immunosuppression, which is associated with reactivation of latent DNA viruses, particularly Epstein-Barr Virus. That's really what's responsible for a significant fraction of the malaise, achy joints, things like that, that people experience as a post-vaccination syndrome. And this immunosuppression also does appear to be associated with an increased risk of cancers, and in particular, more aggressive cancers than might otherwise be normally observed.

Therefore, the long-term risk here that we have is particularly with the folks that have received three or more doses. They have substantial longer-term immunocompromise with the consequences of viral reactivation immunosuppression. This is when people talk about the AIDS or acquired immunodeficiency syndrome associated with the vaccines. They're not talking about HIV as much as they're talking about this T-cell deficit that's associated with is.

There's also, of course, the myocarditis problems. If you do the rigorous assays in a prospective fashion, what's observed is that the *majority* of patients who receive these vaccines develop at least a subclinical myocarditis, and this is why the high-performance athletes are so wary of these products— because they're being actively monitored for their physiologic functions. Because they're being so carefully monitored in their performance criteria, oxygen lung capacity, and the like, they're able to see 5 or 10 percent decreases in their function. In a high-performance athlete, that's the difference between winning and coming in with the rest of the pack. So that's why there's so much hesitancy there.

And if you apply that kind of prospective analysis, what's discovered is that the vast majority of people who are vaccinated have some degree of cardiac damage from these mRNA products.

QUESTION: So do you believe that the long-term risks from the mRNA vaccines are worse than those from the adenovirus vector vaccines, and is it because of the pseudouridine?

MALONE: Yes, it's a combination of things. So the pseudouridine is a new addition to the story, but we clearly have toxicity from the lipid nanoplex itself. And we know that because Moderna did studies on an influenza vaccine—so no spike protein was involved—and at a one hundred microgram dose. Eighty percent of the patients enrolled had adverse events and about 40 percent of them had grade-three adverse events. That's absolutely not an acceptable level of toxicity, but that's intrinsic to the nanoplex.

It's a combination of the pseudouridine incorporating into the RNA and the toxicity of the lipids and the toxicity of the complexes as a whole, which is separate from the toxicity of the spike.

So, we've really got three categories of toxicities. We got the payload toxicity—that's your spike issues. We got the cationic lipid and associated nanoplex toxicity. And we have the toxicity of the pseudouridine incorporating molecule, which is not really a natural RNA; it's something else altogether.

QUESTION: Can you look in your crystal ball six to twelve months from now? What are some things that you forecast based on current trend lines and the data that you have access to? What do you believe will either be more prevalent than we know now or will be things we will be talking about as they relate to the COVID vaccines, COVID treatments, anything involving COVID? What do you forecast six to twelve months from now will be the primary discussion? *(We asked Dr. Malone this question in the spring of 2022.)*

MALONE: Well, on the treatment front, the Merck and Pfizer drugs are really fairly toxic and not particularly effective. That will come to out publicly. The deadly nature of remdesivir will become more and more clear. The safety and effectiveness of the early treatment strategies that Drs. Tony Urso, Ryan Cole, and Peter McCullough and everybody have been promoting will become clearer. So it will become clearer that there were unnecessary deaths due to suppression of early treatment.

As for the vaccines, because the Pfizer data package will continue to roll out and continue to be nitpicked, you'll learn more and more about the various malfeasance that's occurred. There will be increasing awareness of the reproductive risks and the coagulopathy, stroke, blood clotting, autoimmune disease, and this kind of chronic malaise of the post-vaccinated. Those risks will be known to a greater extent. I think that there'll be increased awareness of the damage to immune systems and the dangerous consequences of that.

I'm increasingly focused on what has been done under the guise of COVID by the World Economic Forum and its acolytes, and the logic of transhumanism and human modification. I think that if I have my way about it, that's gonna become much more a part of the national dialogue. And there'll be a growing awareness of the intentional infiltration of the Western democracies by the World Economic Forum, specifically its young leaders trainee program.

The narrative, I think, is gonna turn more along the lines of COVID being a gross overreaction. And seeing that increasingly now, as people are talking about the overly pessimistic projections of morbidity and mortality that drove global policy and national policy information is going to become more and more common knowledge—that the stress scenarios were grossly overstated, and that threat scenario was weaponized for a variety of purposes that had nothing to do with public health.

CHAPTER 14

Brook Jackson: Malfeasance or Malevolence?

Let us begin with questions that likely have no comforting answers.

How is it that three-quarters of the COVID deaths globally occurred precisely after the vaccines were released in December 2020? How is it that numerous countries throughout 2021 and 2022 reported more cases per 100,000 among the vaccinated than the unvaccinated? How is it that there is zero correlation between high vaccination rates and lower COVID case or death rates, and some studies show varying degrees of reverse correlation?

How is it that already in February 2021, Pfizer (according to court-released documents) knew about nine pages' worth of injuries and maladies covering nearly every part of the body?

How is it the Vaccine Adverse Effect Reporting System (VAERS), which is known to woefully underreport the scope of vaccine injury, reported 1.33 million adverse events, roughly 166,000 hospitalizations, and over 29,000 deaths, as of July

2022? How can something go from being heralded as perfectly "safe and effective" by every government and medical entity on earth, but then turn out to be response for more self-reported adverse events than any vaccine in human history?

To illustrate the dichotomy between the promise of the vaccine, and the sobering reality, consider that the *New York Times* predicted on December 13, 2020, that at 95 percent efficacy, there would be just 131,200 COVID cases in the U.S. Without the vaccines, they predicted there would be roughly 2.4 million cases.[107]

In reality, there were over sixty-eight million more cases from January 1, 2021, through early July 2022. Just from December 2021 until July 2022—after a majority of adults were vaccinated and most seniors had been booster—there were almost forty million cases!

Clearly, this was not some innocent mistake. The gap between their promise based on the trials and the reality is simply too wide to bridge. Undoubtedly, Pfizer had to know their trial data was fraudulent. However, we need not speculate as to that point.

Enter Certified Clinical Research Professional Brook Jackson, who was hired as a regional director for two of the Texas clinical trial sites for Pfizer's contractor, Ventavia Research Group, during the phase 3 trial. She will testify to damning evidence of fraud at every stage of the trial protocol and implementation.

The soft-spoken Texas mom, who has worked as a clinical trial auditor for many years, was hired by Ventavia in the critical month of September 2020 to oversee site management of the trial centers in Fort Worth and Keller, Texas—two of Pfizer's 160 clinical trial sites. She was fired before the end of the month after reporting documented evidence of fraud, fabricated data, and violation of clinical trial protocols at every level of the operation. According to Jackson, the entire trial had been unblinded, thereby sabotaging the crown jewel of the science behind randomized controlled trials.

Because of the impending federal court case over her termination, Jackson was unable to apprise the public of what she knew for a full twelve months after she was terminated. She first divulged her allegations, including the bombshell fact that the trial participants in her sites had been unblinded, to the *British Medical Journal*. The rough details of her allegations were published in an article in *BMJ* on November 2, 2021.[108]

As of this writing, Jackson's allegations are the subject of a federal complaint in the U.S. District of Eastern Texas against Ventavia, Pfizer, and Pfizer subcontractor Icon PLC for wrongful termination and violating the False Claims Act.[109] However, her claims and accompanying evidence point to more than just fraud, but a willful disregard for human life by knowingly injecting the entire world with a dangerous concoction. We therefore call Brook Jackson to the witness stand to hold Pfizer accountable for mass injury and death caused by their shots:

· · · · · · ·

QUESTION: Let's start with the inputs that can make all the difference in determining the outcome of a trial. Can you design a trial plan/program to get you the desired outcome you want? When we saw the original Pfizer data that says 91 percent reduction in COVID with only a small number of people experiencing adverse reactions, you are alleging straight-up in your federal complaint that there was fabrication and falsification of blood draw information, vital signs, signatures and other essential clinical trial data. You aren't just saying that they violated protocols like safety and privacy, but are you straight up saying it was fabrication?

JACKSON: For this trial specifically, what my former company did very well was market their study. They were very good at advertising open spots in the study. We were in the middle of a medical district with a lot of physician offices. Texas is a very diverse state so the demographic was diverse. The outlook on clinical research was typically favorable. So it was the perfect opportunity for Ventavia to quickly enroll many participants in Pfizer's study, which is what they needed. But there was such a rush to allow Pfizer to get to market first that they enrolled participants who were not eligible based on prior medical history.

We were not reporting adverse events or, oftentimes, there was a delay in following up on them. One suspected vaccine injury took eleven days before there was any follow-up and those are required to be reported to the sponsor within twenty-four hours, so they were ten days late. This kind of stuff happened daily. My reporting it to my managers started on day two of me being there on September 9, 2020.

When I first walked into the clinic, we started talking about the things that needed to change. I was hopeful. My recommendation was to immediately stop enrolling into the study so we could quantify what errors had been found, so we could alert Pfizer of the things they needed to know about, specifically the unblinding of the approximately 1,200 patients that had been enrolled to date. They were at three locations in Texas. All the patients enrolled in those sites had been unblinded.

It's truly hard to overstate the importance of this finding. I want to point out that several months into the trial, the patients were purposefully unblinded by Pfizer, a fact known to the FDA and the public, but the unblinding I am talking about happened *prior to that*. I'm not a scientist and I am not a doctor, but when patients are blinded in a trial, there is a reason for that. It's to prevent bias from being injected into the study, and that was especially important for this vaccine study because of how the trial was designed. They decided to pause enrollment and we would go through these charts more carefully and involve the sponsor because of the unblinding; in addition, the storage of the vaccine wasn't being monitored, and it was out of range for months based on the protocol's specified temperature range. *We should have immediately quarantined that vaccine.*

There were also other important breaches of elementary clinical trial protocol. The new CEO of Ventavia is still in the study and her children are as well. At the time of the enrollment pause, they were bringing friends and family in to quality control the data. I was shocked. I couldn't believe it. It is actually in Pfizer's own protocol as part of the exclusionary criteria that no family members or friends are supposed to be enrolled in the study. You can go to Ventavia's website, where the new CEO Marty Anderson is introducing herself, and she tells you that she is a clinical trial participant herself.

It's concerning that they had no regard for following the protocol, which is the gold standard for the type of study they are running, especially for a product that would be universally distributed or even mandated like never before. I found more than twenty-five patients that I audited did not meet inclusion criteria. Some of the participants were on medications that would exclude them; others had medical histories that would exclude them. The first question that popped into my mind with the CEO and her children was whether they got to pick which arm of the study they participated in. Did they get to choose getting the vaccine?

QUESTION: How do you follow up on who did and who did not get COVID during the study, and who experienced adverse events?

JACKSON: Ventavia was severely understaffed when I was over at these clinical trial sites, especially the one in Fort Worth. We had five exam rooms and sometimes only four or five coordinators. When you are seeing more than forty patients a day, it is impossible to make sure you are conducting the visit with patient safety and protocols in mind.

That's why I'm 100 percent confident things were missed and adverse events were not reported. They were not able to follow up with patients. That's where the fabrication of data comes in. If there was a data point that was missing on the charts we were auditing, they would just fill it in blindly! I watched a clinical research coordinator fabricate a blood pressure reading because it was not collected at the time of the visit.

QUESTION: You've already discussed the nature of some of the disqualified people participating in the trial, but what about the quality of the people administering it? For example, who actually stuck the needles in the arms and what can you

tell us about the shots themselves? You lay out in your federal complaint that you witnessed the unblinding of participants, using unqualified people to inject, needles that were the wrong size, different concoctions not pursuant to protocols, members of Ventavia leadership being enrolled in the trial, signatures being forged, and data being backfilled and forged with the COVID vaccine. Can you provide some specific examples of those allegations?

JACKSON: There was such a push by Pfizer and Ventavia to enroll, enroll, enroll. The faster the better. I don't think Ventavia cared about the reasons behind the rush. They were worried about the money and being first to market. Ventavia was mainly paid on a per-patient basis, so every patient they enrolled was money in their pocket.

They were putting unqualified people in important roles, such as preparing the shots, administering the vaccine, and storing the contents. During my first day when I was getting to know my staff, it really stuck out to me that the receptionist at Ventavia was also responsible for being the unblinded vaccinator. To prevent unblinding or unmasking, she was the only one to know what the participants were getting. There should have been a backup.

But she was a receptionist, and in between those duties, she would be responsible for preparing and injecting these study participants. When I went to look at her qualifications and her background, she had zero medical experience. She had donated some time to a children's hospital or something like that. Other than that, she had worked at a restaurant before coming to Ventavia.

The unblinded vaccinator at a different location had been a medical assistant but had zero protocol training. She had already injected I can't tell you how many participants. Thus, not only were some of the vaccinators unblinded due to their other duties, but they were also unqualified from a medical standpoint.

This is not just about spilled milk from the past. This is about making sure this never happens again. Somebody has got to stop Ventavia from enrolling patients into any more trials. Their bread and butter are vaccines. They are a preferred site of many pharma companies, Pfizer specifically. The last time I checked, Ventavia was enrolling in forty clinical trials and these studies are a mess.

Just how sloppy is their oversight? On one monitoring visit, which is conducted by either the pharma company itself or the contract research organization (Icon), the first thing that stuck out to me when I read the report was death. It was a death the monitor found during the visit to go over the data that the site had not reported to the institutional review board. *A death is something you report immediately.*

In recruitment, you can look at a certain disease processes and you can include certain patients in a trial and exclude others, but I've never seen a direct target of high-risk patients and of patients that fall into a high-risk category of catching a disease, such as health care workers and first responders. They were targeting this group of people. Even knowing Ventavia was so far behind in their data entry and they were receiving mislabeled samples in the laboratory—red flags that Pfizer and Icon were both aware of because I was included on those emails—they still incentivized Ventavia to enroll more by offering them a bonus. And they offered them an increase in the number they could enroll weekly, as long as they could guarantee they were from that high-risk category.

The bottom line is that all of the data you see publicly is all scrubbed and is not from the original trial site paper trail. That is what makes the Pfizer data bogus from head to toe from the day they released it. You are never going to see the site-level data unless those of us on the inside show you. What the public will see, what the FDA has been sued for, is the cleaned-up version of what is at the site level. So even if you succeed in FOIAing those documents, they will not reveal the errors I saw firsthand.

To give you an idea, when Ventavia is seeing a patient, every data point is captured on paper. So, we have source documents with date of birth, age, height, weight, sex, comorbidities, medical history, and medications. It follows the trial from start to finish and everything is captured on paper.

From that source, all that information is transcribed over into an electronic platform that Pfizer uses. So that opens the possibility for there to be errors into that transcription. Then they have somebody from Icon come to the site and compare the paper source against what was entered into the electronic system. There's an audit trail. I've looked at the electronic data that has been released by the FDA *and that is the cleaned version of what Pfizer wants you to see.*

Everything I am telling you, I have internal documents, text messages, phone calls, and audio recordings to back it up. Everything.

QUESTION: You also allege a failure to secure informed consent. What exactly does that mean?

JACKSON: In order to participate in the study, you have to sign an informed consent form. It's pretty long, about twenty pages, if I'm remembering correctly. That is something a coordinator is supposed to make sure the patient is fully informed about. The sites were so busy and so understaffed that it became the job of the marketing team, kind of like a call center, to explain the ins and outs of the study visit so that when they came, they were ready to go. When patients got to the site, they were brought to an exam room, given the informed consent, and shown the place to sign.

QUESTION: Can you describe the events that led up to your dismissal?

JACKSON: On the first day I was there, I had to step in on an informed consent that was being given. They were doing a quick overview and I intervened and went over it in detail with the patient, which took about two hours. You are talking about a novel virus and a novel vaccine and a mobile app to capture any adverse events. It takes at least some time to understand that, but they were so interested in getting patients in and out that hundreds of patients were improperly consented. There were even missing signatures and missing dates.

My management team just told me to put all of it on a list because they were so overwhelmed with what I was bringing them. Then the next time I opened up a chart I had flagged because the patient's signature was missing, the signature would now magically be there, even though it was obvious the patient would not have had enough time to return. *The staff must've just forged it.*

They chose the route of lies and cover-ups rather than cleaning up the trial because it was all about quotas and time. I have a text message from one of the managing members at Ventavia that says not to inform Pfizer we were pausing the study, and instead to tell them we are actually in a perfect place.

When I first started, I was excited about the pause because I thought they were taking me seriously, and we were going to make things better. But when I saw that message, I was gutted. They were just going to clean things up so they didn't get in trouble. They actively forged data. I was deflated. I knew what Ventavia was doing and I didn't want to be complicit in their scheme to cover up fraud.

I was eventually called in to discuss the pictures I had taken about various things I had documented, and I took them only to show my managers what I had found. I felt like I was being interrogated. My manager was attacking my integrity and asking me what my intentions were in taking the pictures. I'm crying in the audio because I was so upset.

After that meeting, I went home and talked to my husband and we made the decision I was going to talk with the FDA. In that complaint I listed *fourteen* different concerns I had about patient safety. That is what this is all about for me. These patients are people. They matter, they are in danger, and this clinical site is operating beyond its legal, moral, and scientific scope. A few hours after I filed the complaint, I got a call from Ventavia and I was fired after less than three weeks of work. I filed a False Claims Act lawsuit against Ventavia, Icon, and Pfizer and the case immediately went under seal, which means I was ordered not to discuss the study.

QUESTION: For seventeen years, you've been working on vaccine trials. Before the COVID vaccines, you worked with Ventavia previously. Did you ever feel uncomfortable with anything you saw about safety, protocols, cutting corners that would affect the confidence in the safety or efficacy of the therapeutic you were working on before this trial?

JACKSON: Absolutely not. My experience is going on twenty years with site management level and clinical research organization experience in all phases of medical device, pharmaceutical, and biologics trials to include vaccines and infectious diseases. I've never been a part of any phase or size of clinical trial where I saw as much misconduct as I saw with Pfizer's phase 3 vaccine trial for COVID-19. I have global experience in clinical research, and I have worked in other pharmaceutical studies where Pfizer was the sponsor. I had never seen any misconduct like I did with the COVID study.

Ventavia Research Group continues to be invited by all the Big Pharma companies. They are pretty big players. There has to be some accountability for what they have done. I also want government accountability. I alerted the FDA about Ventavia's misconduct, and when I spoke to the inspector at the FDA for over an hour, she said the same thing but there was no action. And it's not just Ventavia that needs to be held accountable. Pfizer is responsible for the overall conduct of the study no matter what. When I realized that after the initial sixty days they had to investigate, they weren't going to do anything but kick the can down the road, that also makes them complicit in this fraudulent scheme to cover things up.

On the FDA's own website, they say they rely on the pharmaceutical company's data in order to determine whether or not to approve a medicine or a vaccine. There is no safety net for the public. If Pfizer and their contractors play loose with the data, the people will never know—until they experience the harms with real-life human tragedies, as we've witnessed since 2021.

QUESTION: How did this experience, and what you went through, alter your view of the way COVID was treated and perhaps the vaccine approval/testing process as a whole?

JACKSON: I was one of those people who woke up really late. I'm not a political person. I have a small family and we do lots of soccer and volleyball, and I kind of stayed away from all of that. We are not antivaxxers. We typically get our flu shots every year. But my mind has been changed and my life has been turned upside down because of this virus, the vaccine, and what I happened to stumble into in terms of all the fraud and misconduct that I've seen from the clinical trials to the federal government.

Now I find something that shocks the hell out of me every day.

CHAPTER 15

Stephanie de Garay—Erasing the Vaccine Injured from Humanity to Serve the Sacred Cow

How is it that as of February 2022, there were already over 1,000 peer-reviewed studies discussing vaccine injury, yet there was never any desire to investigate, much less pull the faulty vaccines?[110] Clearly, this was the intention during the clinical trial itself—to see no evil and hear no evil about any injuries.

While Brook Jackson's testimony offers a glimpse into how the Pfizer clinical trials were fabricated, Stephanie de Garay's testimony about her daughter's severe, life-altering injury during the trial reveals the human cost of that fraud. It also provides a harbinger of what was to come as the entire global population became not a human trial but an animal trial.

Stephanie de Garay and her husband were eager to get back to normal life after the lockdowns and, like so many other Americans, were convinced that accelerating a vaccine trial was the only way to "earn" back our freedom and way of life. Thus, they signed up for Pfizer's clinical trials along with their three children. Ultimately, the parents weren't accepted in the 2020 adult trials, but their three kids participated in Pfizer's twelve-to-fifteen-year-old and sixteen-to-seventeen-year-old trials.

It is a choice that the de Garays wish they could take back.

Their twelve-year-old daughter, Maddie, suffered life-altering paralysis, neurological damage, and multiple systemic inflammatory and debilitating syndromes within hours of receiving the second dose of Pfizer in January of 2021.

One would have expected that if a healthy twelve-year-old suddenly became disabled from the shot within hours, Pfizer, the FDA, and Cincinnati Children's Hospital, which was the trial site investigator for Maddie, would have immediately diagnosed and treated her injury with compassion. One would have expected all the players involved to study every pathophysiological angle of the vaccine injury, properly document it, warn all the other trial participants, and help fund research into diagnosis and treatment of those injuries.

But then one would learn the hard way to no longer expect those things, because compassion is in short supply here in the Fourth Reich.

Instead, in the new biomedical supremacist world where we find ourselves, to this day Pfizer and the FDA refuse to recognize the severity of Maddie's injuries. Cincinnati Children's Hospital refuses to diagnose this as an injury resulting from the shot they administered. Maddie's debilitating injury was never properly recorded in the clinical trial data. There was no effort to study the origins of her injury and find the culprit within the concoction of the shots. The de Garays were left on their own for legal and medical help as expendables, and an inconvenient testament to what was to become the most sacred product in the history of mankind. Maddie's story is a microcosm of millions of ignored injuries.

See, you were made for the sacred cow; the sacred cow wasn't made for you.

After all, if a twelve-year-old girl who becomes nearly paralyzed from the waist down and needs a feeding tube as a result of the shot in the *actual clinical trial* never resulted in acknowledgement—much less treatment, studies, and policy changes from Pfizer—how much more should all those injured outside the trials expect to be recognized? To our government, pharma, and most hospitals and doctors, those who suffer in silence simply don't exist. The vaccines are completely safe because anyone injured wasn't really injured. It either never happened, is just in their own mind, or is a coincidence. In Maddie's case, they used all three excuses.

It wasn't until the de Garays found a private doctor who wasn't beholden to insurance companies that Maddie was diagnosed with chronic inflammatory demyelinating poly-neuropathy (CIDP) resulting from the vaccine. CIDP is a rare, horrific disorder of the peripheral nerves that targets the body's nervous system and results in gradual sensory loss and weakness associated with loss of reflexes. Indeed, it was one of the hundreds of maladies listed in Pfizer's confidential docu-ment ordered released by a federal judge, which demonstrates they knew about CIDP as an associated injury no later than February 2020.[111]

So that this can never happen again to another child, we call Stephanie de Garay to the witness stand to tell the world the horror of her child's vaccine injury and the response to it.

● ● ● ● ● ●

QUESTION: Can you tell us when you got involved in the Pfizer children's trial and describe your thoughts in deciding to go ahead and volunteer as a participant?

DE GARAY: We found out about the trial from a friend who was in the Pfizer trial for adults at Cincinnati Children's Hospital, and my husband and I actually signed up first in July of 2020. We received all the paperwork they had through email, and then all the communication suddenly stopped, so we just assumed there were a lot of people that were in the trial and we weren't needed. Fast-forward several months later and that same friend had a son enrolled in the teenage trial. My middle son, Lucas, found out about it and expressed a desire to join.

So, in terms of the motivation, there was a small monetary compensation for it; I think it's like a thousand bucks or a little more over a period of two years. But for a kid who couldn't work and also wanted to have a life, this was a great opportunity to take off the mask and get back to normal life.

My friend, because she was in the trial, was unblinded and we knew she had received the actual vaccine and had no reaction to it. I also knew several adults and kids who were in the trial, so I was not worried when Lucas asked to do it. Our other two kids, Gabe, the older brother, and Maddie, the younger sister, found out and wanted to participate in the trial too.

Keep in mind, these kids and everybody had been in lockdown, thus the fear had been placed into them and we'd been told all along that these vaccines were going to make it all go away. This was our ticket to freedom. Both my husband and I were frontline workers—I work in a school and my husband works in health care—so we were planning on getting it early anyway. Now they had the opportunity to get it early and we figured they were going to be safe. Our mindset at the time was we believed everything we were told.

QUESTION: At what point did you realize you were in for trouble—that this is not what you were told and what you were expecting?

DE GARAY: The kids got their first dose on December 30, 2020, and there was no issue at all with any of them. Then Gabe got COVID, so he didn't get his second dose, per the trial protocol. That's the way the trial worked, like if you got COVID and it was verified, then you don't get the subsequent dose. Gabe was actually sick for a very long time. To this day, I don't know if it was just from the COVID, the vaccine aggravating the COVID, or vaccine injury. My guess is he got COVID from the vaccine, and indeed he was later confirmed as having gotten the actual vaccine, not the placebo. Lucas ended up getting the placebo, so obviously he had no issues.

As for Maddie, after the first dose, she had the typical symptoms where she had fever or her arm swelled up, and she was tired, but that was everything we expected. Lucas and Maddie both got their second doses on January 20, and Maddie had said, "Man, it hurt way worse than the first one." Neither of us were really that concerned at the time. They got the shots late in the afternoon after school, but then in the middle of the night, she came into our room and said, "I don't feel right. Something is wrong; can I sleep with you?"

Maddie was almost a teenager, so she never came in our room to sleep in our bed anymore. Yet, she crawled in between me and my husband, which was even more odd, so clearly something was wrong. In the morning, we told her she didn't need to go to school, knowing that we had been warned ahead of time that she could feel similar symptoms to COVID for a day or two following the vaccine. She hates missing school, so she asked to go at the regular time and told me she'd see the nurse if she was feeling ill. Somehow, she made it through the day and walked through the door of our home…barely.

My husband works from home, and Maddie barely made it to his office, which was right inside the door. When he saw her, he noticed her fingers were white on the tips, looking ice cold. We saw that her toes looked the same and she had edema-like swelling all over her body. You couldn't even touch her back because she had these zapping pains going up and down her spine. Her entire body hurt really bad, she had a horrendous headache, and probably her worst symptom was excruciating pain in her lower abdomen, near her appendix.

My husband immediately called the hotline for trial participants, and they said that they were going to call right back. So, he called me at work and informed me Maddie was suffering some sort of reaction to the vaccine. I can hear her in the background yelling, "Mom, my heart feels like it is being ripped out through my neck."

That's when I got scared and left school to immediately go home. By then, the trial line had called and they said to take her to take her to Cincinnati Children's, which is where the trial was being held, because the doctor that was the principal investigator, Robert Frenck, would be able to have access to our charts and they'd be able to compensate us for any bills that we had. So, we drove about thirty minutes away, all the while monitoring her vital signs.

When we got to the ER, they checked for appendicitis and they did basic blood work and a urinalysis. When they checked for appendicitis, it didn't show anything, so they gave her an IV Tylenol, and Zofran for nausea. She did have blood in her urine, which is not normal, but they sent her home because she felt better.

Shortly after she got home, all the symptoms rocketed up again and just continued to get worse. So, between then and April, she went to the ER ten times, and then she was hospitalized three times. The first time for three days at the end of January, the second time for a week in March, and then for a month and a half beginning in April when they also had her in inpatient rehabilitation. It progressed over time and her condition deteriorated; she ended up eventually having to have an NG tube to eat. She got to the point where she could not swallow at all and could not walk at all. She's still in that state today over a year later.

QUESTION: Could you describe more specifically the symptoms she has suffered with the past year, what the diagnosis ultimately was, and what the consequences for her quality of life are?

DE GARAY: Maddie can't feel her body from her waist down, and because of that she can't tell when she has to pee until her bladder is overly full. It gets to 1,000 mL in her bladder when she goes to the bathroom once a day. For a typical person, going to the bathroom with 200 mL is a lot, so her bladder is really stretched right now. Additionally, she has gastroparesis in the stomach muscles, which prevents her from emptying her stomach. She has vision problems too. We've been to several eye doctors and specialists, and they cannot figure out what they can even give her, so everything she sees is blurry or double.

Most critically, she can't swallow food. Maddie can still swallow her saliva on a typical day, but if she gets a sore throat, she can't even do that. She's been on an NG tube since April 2021, so she gets all her nutrition through the feeding tube, but she mainly survives on formula because we can't get enough fluid in her given that the pump can't go very fast. She also has a PICC line and gets an IV for additional hydration every day.

In terms of mobility, she can't feel from her waist down and is wheelchair-bound. She can move her legs if she's lying in bed but can't move them against gravity. You can put a pin into her, and she won't feel it at all, and her reflexes are messed up as well. Picture if your legs ever felt completely numb with pins and needles—that's how she *always* feels.

QUESTION: Is there neurological damage as well?

DE GARAY: On March 12, 2021, just one day before the data cutoff for Pfizer's twelve-to-fifteen-year-old trial, Maddie had an MRI of her spine. There were some minor abnormalities that they explained away—everything that was abnormal they explained away. When she woke up from the MRI, she was unable to walk to the bathroom; they had to put in a catheter. When they finally had her stand up, she dropped straight to the ground. Before that day, she would be hunched over and take tiny steps so she could walk (barely), but now after that, she could not walk at all.

At the time, the way they explained it was that it was probably due to the anesthesia, so we believed them. But now, after talking to lots of people and after her similar experience after the second MRI later in June, we know it was an allergic reaction to the gadolinium-based contrast from the MRI. Did she pick up that allergy from the shot? Who knows.

Maddie was in inpatient rehabilitation from the middle of February until June. When she left inpatient rehab, she was able to walk in an abnormal manner, so her legs would shake and her leg would drag. She was able to walk like that with a walker, but if she let go of the walker, everything would spin like being on a boat. During the MRI of her brain in June, they used a different anesthesia. But once again, she woke up and could not pee, and when this one was done, she lost control over the movement in her neck.

Eventually, she was able to move her neck by the time we left, but she could not support it at all. So once again, she left there unable to walk again or hold her neck, so we left the hospital like just like that—in worse shape than before.

Later on, with additional testing, we discovered she had a reaction both times to the gadolinium-based contrast from the MRI. To this day, we don't know if that was a pre-existing allergy (she never had an MRI before) or something generated by the inflammatory response to the vaccine. We also found out she is allergic to heavy metals as well. So, a lot of times people develop allergies—and this is something I never previously knew—from vaccines or viruses.

QUESTION: Can you describe Maddie's quality of life at this point? Physically, she's confined to a wheelchair, but what about in terms of functionality, learning, thinking, processing information, speech? Is she still in a lot of pain?

DE GARAY: She is in a wheelchair. She can't take showers by herself. I have to help her to the bathroom and put on her pants. She has lost her independence, most of it, but she can get around in her wheelchair if she's on a hardwood floor. In terms of her brain, she gets exhausted very easily. She was going to school for an hour and a half to two hours a day, and then we were doing a modified workload at home where I would work with her. She will mix up words and not even realize that she's doing it—that's getting worse actually—and she'll just call things by the wrong name. I know what she's talking about and now we just joke about it, because that's life.

Maddie suffers from constant pain in her back and her neck. She still has problems like supporting her neck. She is similar now to a baby that you hold up its head by supporting its back, but sometimes it'll bobble to one side or another.

QUESTION: Let's take this back to early January 2020 before the Pfizer shots. Maddie is a typical twelve-year-old girl—can you describe her physical condition at that point?

DE GARAY: She was in awesome physical shape. She's one of those kids that would try a sport and would excel. Throughout her life she played soccer, volleyball, and gymnastics. She did dance, she did TikToks, and taught herself to walk around on her hands. I have a bunch of pictures of her (right before she got the second dose) walking around on her hands. She even did rock climbing. She was very strong, nonstop, and anything she would try she would just be able to do it and just picked stuff up.

QUESTION: So, there were no physical conditions or learning disabilities before that?

DE GARAY: She was diagnosed with ADHD like countless other kids these days. So she did take Vyvanse, but only when she was in school. And she had been diagnosed with dermatographia, which is when if you scratch yourself, your skin raises and you get hives. That's it.

QUESTION: Let's go back to the trial phase of Operation Warp Speed, when there was so much hope for the vaccine. Many of us would have thought at the time that if you would have taken a twelve-year-old girl in a clinical trial, for a vaccine for which the ingredients and technology certainly was novel, and within a day she gets severe systemic and multipronged reactions to it that degenerate and lead to a de facto paralysis and lack of functionality indefinitely, that you would have had a team from Pfizer and the FDA examining every aspect of the of this. Is that what happened?

DE GARAY: Not at all. I have never spoken to Pfizer—ever. The first time I talked to the FDA was many months later, early in 2022, and it was only once, and nothing was done. I filed an adverse event report in VAERS. The first communication I got from them was this year as a year follow-up. They never followed up on the initial report. They approved the vaccine in May 2021, and she didn't have the MRI of her brain until June of 2021. They did no tests like an electromyography

(EMG) and she can't feel from the waist down. They did the most basic tests they could possibly do where they knew nothing would show up, and they diagnosed her with functional neurologic disorder a day before they submitted the EUA on April 9, 2021.

April 8 is when Cincinnati Children's Hospital put into her charts "functional neurologic disorder" as the diagnosis, which is basically saying that this is in her head and it's all psychological. The principal investigator, who's supposed to be the advocate for the participants in the trial if anything was to happen, works for Cincinnati Children's Hospital and he can get into her records. Between January and April, there are notes in her chart showing he talked to all the specialists prior to her appointment. She had to see a psychiatrist because they put her on antidepressants, which we've since taken her off.

She's done cognitive behavioral therapy and physical therapy because if you have functional neurologic disorder that's what is supposed to resolve it. It did not work. She never got better, but they still diagnosed her with functional neurologic disorder. The psychiatrist collaborated with the principal investigator, Robert Frenck, who diagnosed her with functional neurologic disorder and anxiety.

He had two virtual visits with Maddie, so not in person, never met her before, and he's the one who diagnosed her with the functional neurologic disorder. The allergist talked to the principal investigator and did zero tests. There's so much that has happened to her that I can't even tell you all of it. She had rashes all over her body, she had blisters in her mouth in the beginning, and she had lumps on her head and the allergist did zero tests.

Nothing.

Anything that wasn't basic care, we had to ask for. They just did normal blood work and they did do an endoscopy. All these tests showed abnormalities but there always was an explanation for everything. There was blood in her urine basically every time they did urinalysis, and they tried to blame it on her period, which also came ten days after she got the vaccine and it was like she had given birth. I'm not joking. It was horrible for her very first one.

QUESTION: You're telling us your daughter was a child participant in the actual clinical trial for the most used experimental vaccine in human history, and yet after she suffered a series of systemic reactions there was little to no desire to follow up, or even properly diagnose, from all the investigators supposedly all over it? And you're saying the only conversation you had with the FDA was because you filed the VAERS report?

DE GARAY: It wasn't even because I filed a VAERS report. It was because somebody else who was injured got a call set up with them and pulled me into it to give me time with the FDA. One thing to note, because this is important, is that while I was in the hospital with Maddie, her story went viral. That was by accident. At that point, I thought Maddie was the only one injured by the shot, so I was going to keep this personal. I was trying to be respectful in the beginning until they figured it out. I had posted something on Facebook asking for prayers and my uncle asked me if I could make it public so that his church could pray, so I said okay and it went viral overnight. That's how her story unintentionally got out. From there, God was in control.

Because of that, we found out about another individual who was in the AstraZeneca trial and was injured. Somebody saw Maddie's story and told the other injured person about it and connected her with me through Facebook. At the time, she was being seen and studied by the NIH, along with some other people (all adults) who had also been injured. The paper just came out in 2022 from that study. That doctor could not treat Maddie because she was a child, but he did talk to her neurologist, which is why they did all this additional testing after the vaccine was approved.

He told the neurologist to assume that this is real and that he recommended intravenous immunoglobulin. The neurologist, for a short time, told us that the more he saw us, the more he knew this was not functional neurologic disorder. And then all of a sudden, we got a message from him in my chart—he didn't call us or anything—saying it's functional neurologic disorder and we recommend that you do cognitive behavioral therapy, which if you remember, we had already done. This was also during the time the study's doctor stopped talking to the participants and responding to them. So, somebody was told to shut up.

We never signed a waiver. There was an informed consent that basically said you could have a sore throat, swollen arm, fever, or maybe some aches and pains for about two days. Or that there is a possibility of an anaphylactic reaction or other reactions, but they will compensate for any of the medical bills related to the trial as they determine.

QUESTION: So where does that stand? Obviously, you have endless medical bills. How much has Pfizer paid you?

DE GARAY: Pfizer paid me nothing. Cincinnati Children's paid for the hospital bills that we incurred at their hospital only, and that was after we got a lawyer involved. They did not do it initially. That's not for all the medicine that she was prescribed that didn't help her and made her worse. That wasn't for all the lost wages that I incurred because I was a contract worker at the time. That wasn't for a lot of expenses. We ended up moving her care out of Cincinnati Children's to another local, smaller children's hospital, just as a holding place.

In April, 2021, she did qualify for long-term care for a year because she was in the hospital for over a month. It would pay for the copays that we couldn't cover starting in April 2021 through April 2022. Anything before that is the stuff that we had to fight with Cincinnati Children's, which was the big bulk of it. They wouldn't even give us a wheelchair in the beginning, so we ended up getting one on our own. It wasn't until November 2021 that they finally gave her a custom wheelchair. We had to have ramps installed in our house and none of that was covered. We had to put in hardwood floors so she could roll around. We had to make her shower accessible. All these things that you don't think about, they all add up.

But once you tell them that she was in the vaccine trial, that's a red flag because nobody wants to run any tests because they know something's going to show up. She was in the trial. At this point, people know that there've been reactions, and her reactions line up with all these medical papers that have come out. So, they don't want to be the ones that say she has this or that because that's career sabotage. They will be fired.

QUESTION: Can you tell us a little bit about the VAERS reporting, what that experience was like, and what it demonstrates in terms of the likely underreporting factor globally?

DE GARAY: I'll talk about VAERS and I also want to explain what they're monitoring and how they monitor during the trial. They don't use VAERS for the trial. If anything happens, the principal investigator reports the incident to the sponsor, which would be Pfizer in our case, and Pfizer reports it to the FDA. There's no VAERS report.

So, I filled out the VAERS report because they wouldn't tell me what symptoms were reported for Maddie to the FDA, and I wanted people to see what happened to her and I wanted it documented. It took me three days to be able to file that VAERS report because of the amount of information and because it would keep timing out. I would have to start all over again because it wouldn't save the existing information. It was a nightmare.

With the trials, all they're doing is they monitor you for a week or two. They use an app and they're soliciting information on all those limited side effects they tell you about. Did you have abdominal pain? Was it mild, moderate, or severe? And did it require hospitalization or an ER visit? Was there diarrhea? Arm swelling? A fever? Muscle aches?

But there is nowhere to put that you have electrical shocks up and down your spine, that your fingers and toes are white, that you have a rash all over your body, that you have blisters in your throat, and that you feel like your heart is being ripped out for your neck—none of that. There's nowhere to put that on the app. There's nowhere to document it. The instructions are you call the trial line—you don't email, you call—and it's only monitored for a short period of time.

QUESTION: To this day, have you seen an official report of her adverse event?

DE GARAY: No. I've asked. When I did talk to the FDA, I said I wanted to know what was reported for Maddie's side effects and they were supposed to get back to me, but never told me. We have asked the principal investigator repeatedly. We even have a recorded phone call with one of the people who worked at the trial, because they had called about something else and my husband interrogated them. Still have not gotten an answer.

You can manipulate the data. They know the tests that can confirm autoimmune issues, so if you don't do those tests then you won't confirm it. Then it's like it didn't happen.

QUESTION: You mentioned Maddie's story went viral. Did it get picked up by any mainstream media outlets?

DE GARAY: The closest to the mainstream media was Tucker Carlson on Fox News, and also *Fox and Friends* did an interview with me. However, the *Fox and Friends* interview has disappeared. It's like it never happened. It aired live. You can't find it. It's nowhere. Just like Maddie's long-term injury.

CHAPTER 16

Jessica Rose: The Data Is the Thing by Which We'll Catch the Conscience of the King

The final principle of the Nuremberg Code quite reasonably and morally established a guideline that has been violated repeatedly by the Fourth Reich:

> *During the course of the experiment, the scientist in charge must be prepared to terminate the experiment at any stage, if he has probable cause to believe, in the exercise of the good faith, superior skill and careful judgement required by him that a continuation of the experiment is likely to result in injury, disability, or death to the experimental subject.*

Imagine being one of those scientists leading the experiments for Pfizer, Moderna, and the relevant government agencies. At what point would they have known that the greatest experiment ever conducted upon mankind was going to result in widespread death and injury? That is the question for our next witness, a Canadian viral immunologist and biologist, who is prepared to show categorically that the date was January 2020. That's right. Every day this experiment was continued past the very beginning was a violation of the Nuremberg Code.

We have a pharmacovigilance tool called VAERS, which is operated by the CDC. This is not a mere survey of vaccine injury. It is the one and only safety net for the American people, and even much of the rest of the world against damage done by vaccine products approved by the FDA. This was the system created by the CDC in 1990 in exchange for exempting the manufacturers of all liability for injury and death caused by their products. Thus, especially when the government knew it was introducing a novel and risky product at breakneck speed en masse for the public to be used immediately, VAERS was the most important system they should have monitored with the vigilance of a hawk from day one.

An unprecedented increase in thousands of maladies, including record numbers of deaths, should have spawned an immediate cancelling of the authorization for these shots. Especially given how hard it is to fill out a VAERS entry, the stigma against doctors identifying the shots as the culprit, and the known underreporting factor.

What Dr. Jessica Rose is prepared to show is that either they never watched the system, or they did and weren't fazed by the genocide-levels of safety signals, making it unclear which one is worse. Dr. Rose has become the foremost expert in the VAERS data for the COVID shots, having monitored an endless stream of trends since the first month of the release of the shots. As an applied mathematician, immunologist, computational and molecular biologist, and biochemist, Dr.

Rose is eminently qualified to compute, analyze, and interpret the level of concern from VAERS reporting and warned the world about the sickening safety signals from day one.

Because there is no way that similar scientists working both for the vaccine makers and the government, as well as other high-profile promoters of the shots in the medical industry, could not have seen these same glaring and blaring safety signals, we call Dr. Jessica Rose to the stand to show the world the extent of the injury data, when it began, and when it should have been known.

· · · · · · ·

QUESTION: Your expertise in multidisciplinary fields is uniquely suited to analyze data concerning vaccine injury trends, and also interpret what is undergirding those injuries. Can you give us your mathematics and scientific background?

ROSE: I acquired this weird fascination with viruses when I was five. This runs deeper than getting degrees. I am really fascinated with pathogenic viruses, so in order to explore that, I took the academic route and started with an applied mathematics degree, which means you are taught using mathematical modelling techniques to do viral kinetic analysis, dynamic analysis, and epidemiological analysis.

We were taught how to learn about viral dynamics within a host, and also transmission, using math. I had such a good time that when I was finished, I wanted to apply that skill practically. I started an immunology degree, which is the hardest thing I've ever done. It was fantastic and I had an excellent advisor, who was also a bit of a black sheep like me. He was an HIV pathogenecist, so I got to do what I really wanted to do—study HIV—which is one of the most interesting viruses to me.

That was a joint project, half math and half immunology, and I actually got to play in the level-three lab. It was really fun. Then I attended a conference in Ohio with all the overlords of HIV, immunology, and mathematics and I met my soon-to-be PhD advisor. He took an interest in what I presented, and was astounded that anybody was doing the same thing he was doing in his lab because there are only a handful of us who approached HIV pathogenesis from the applied mathematics point of view.

So, as it turned out, I ended up going to Israel to do my PhD in computational biology, which was meant to also be on the subject of HIV but it ended up being about cytomegalovirus (CMV) and hepatitis B. This was my first go-round with big data. They needed somebody to find some patterns using mathematical modelling techniques within this very large data set that was testing an oral analog of ganciclovir, which is an anti-CMV drug. I completed that and I switched to bacteria to do a postdoc looking for Rickettsia, which is a pathogenic bacterium, and analyzing the strains using molecular techniques. Then I moved on to another postdoc in biochemistry, where I was looking at memory proteins, which was also extremely interesting. So, as you can see, I've had my feet in many ponds.

For me, there has always been this focus around viruses and I love math. I'm good at pattern recognition, so I'm good at analyzing data. When they declared the pandemic, I was meant to give all of that up to go to Australia to become a professional longboarder, and that didn't happen because you couldn't travel. Instead, I decided to teach myself to use a statistical programming language and the data set that I used to enable that was the VAERS data out of the United States.

The reason I decided to do that was because very early on in 2020, I started to notice things weren't lining up with regard to the fear surrounding the coronavirus and the reality. I thought they would be injecting people pretty soon and I was anticipating that VAERS was going to become pretty interesting—and it did.

It's a huge data set now. It has millions of reports in it, which has never happened with any other vaccine before.

QUESTION: Many would assume the CDC, FDA, or even Pfizer/Moderna would have been monitoring the VAERS system aggressively, given that we're injecting a novel vaccine technology against a novel coronavirus—and we've never developed a successful vaccine against a coronavirus before. But if they were, they certainly did a good job keeping that on the down low. So, it's been left to analysts such as yourself to inform the public on what the data says. At what point did someone with your expertise in pattern recognition discover that this ain't your grandfather's vaccine?

ROSE: Right away in January of 2021, and you don't need expertise for that assessment to have been correctly made. What you would have needed is basic information on how VAERS functions as a pharmacovigilance tool. So, if you detect a safety signal—a safety signal for death, for example, has been historically fifty people—in the context of a biological product like a flu vaccine, then you pull the product. Fifty has traditionally been the cutoff.

In January, we are talking about the month after the roll-out in the U.S. and Israel began on December 17, *and we already had more than fifty deaths in VAERS*—and that is even before we address the underreporting factor within a complex, self-reporting system. Thus, we already had a safety signal from only death, but it is even worse than that. We also already had safety signals from hundreds of adverse event types. We are currently up to over 14,000 *different* adverse event types reported (as of July 2022). We had neurological signals. We had cardiovascular signals. We had pathological signals. We had immunological signals. We had death. We had hospitalization. We had disabilities. You name it. We had already had all the signals in January 2021, before most of the public had even been injected yet.

QUESTION: Are you saying, from a pattern recognition standpoint, the traditional modus operandi of pulling a product after discovering fifty deaths in VAERS was predicated on the fact that if there are fifty such entries, which are pretty exhausting to type in because they can take a long time, the assumption is that is just a fraction of what is really out there, correct?

ROSE: Precisely, yes.

QUESTION: You said there were already 14,000 different adverse event categories. We now know from court-released documents that Pfizer, and likely the FDA, knew no later than February of 2021 that there were nine pages of maladies, or what looks to be more than 1,000 categories of adverse events they observed. To the best of your knowledge, does it appear that most if not all of them are represented in VAERS?

ROSE: Oh yes. And more.

QUESTION: Right away, people assume there are always going to be a certain percent of adverse reactions to any therapeutics—even generally safe ones. Over 400 Americans per year die from using acetaminophen, as just one example.[112] So, the key is the denominator. In the case of acetaminophen, hundreds of deaths are a scant percentage of the $1 billion spent per year on Tylenol.

Similarly, the COVID vaccines have a really big denominator, since at the time of this interview, over five hundred million doses had been administered to Americans. Given that vast denominator, it's probably not enough to say it has the most adverse effects, to be fair, because it's also the most injected. Therefore, what do the percentages, or the numerator, say about the safety of these products? Are they really that less safe than what we've become accustomed to with normal vaccines?

ROSE: I wrote an article on Substack about this very thing.[113] I compared the number of adverse events, as per the number of people who were injected, with the three COVID products in the United States versus the flu products. Just the flu, which is one of the more accessed therapeutics annually. I didn't factor in any of the other vaccines. It was just to see what the ratio was.

There is about a two-and-a-half-times difference in the denominators, but that ratio did not transfer to the number of adverse event types, or to the number of adverse events themselves—not even remotely. There was no comparison. The number of injections being the same did not translate to the number of adverse events.

Therefore, it is not because the number of injections being higher for COVID that we are seeing this exorbitant increase in the number of reports. There's no comparison. We are talking about a difference between 39,000 average number of adverse event reports for all vaccines combined for the last thirty years, versus 1.2 million in 2021 for just three products! There's no comparison.

But the patterns were recognizable in January 2021. I wrote a paper on this at the time. All the predictions I made back then—and worse—have sadly come to pass.

QUESTION: As it stands at the time of this interview in July 2022, there are more than 29,000 deaths, more than 165,000 hospitalizations, and almost 200,000 doctors office visits reported in VAERS from the COVID vaccines. Why do you believe this system is woefully underreported? Those numbers alone would have gotten any biological product pulled by an exponential factor. Why do you believe they are underreported, and not overreported because anybody could be filling this out and making something up?

ROSE: We never need to talk about the underreporting factor because the numbers are so horrific already, but it's just human nature that underreporting exists. There are only going to be a certain percentage of people who suffer an adverse event who are going to report it, and there are a variety of reasons for that. However, in this case, there are so many adverse events occurring.

This is how I would paint the picture: you are an ICU doc. You just completed a fourteen-hour shift. You know, because you are an experienced physician, that when ten people who came into the ICU that night with cardiac events were between twenty and thirty years old, and just had their second COVID injection, you know that those are likely caused by the injections themselves. One single VAERS report takes at least thirty minutes to file online. After such a long, grueling shift, are you really going to stick around just to make stuff up? Especially since if you don't complete each sequential page on time, you get booted off the system and have to start all over again. That's a lot of information to fill out, which makes it difficult to fake.

Not only that, but there is this atmosphere in hospitals right now where you are not even really allowed to suggest that the injections are causing any adverse events. You are mocked. You are gaslit. You are belittled. If anything, the doctors are being disincentivized to fill out the reports. And patients are going to their general practitioners, they know that something is horribly wrong with them and they know that it's because of the injections, because they were completely healthy before and the doctor mocks them. I've heard of doctors telling patients to leave because they merely suggested it was the injections that caused their issue, so why would that doctor file a VAERS report?

The good part about it being a volunteer system is that the individual patient can still file the report, and the person who is suffering might actually be the best person to do it because they have all the details. *I've calculated that the underreporting factor for injuries may be as high as thirty-one, based on the Pfizer phase 3 clinical trial data and their rate of adverse events.* I think that it probably varies between adverse event types. For death, specifically, my data analyst instincts tell me a factor of ten is a decent estimate.

QUESTION: Thirty thousand deaths would be just as much a violation of the Nuremberg Code as 300,000. Isn't it true that CDC was supposed to have an office that was constantly monitoring this, and putting out tables based on the weekly VAERS updates?

ROSE: Yes, but that was not done. We know that because a recent FOIA request proved it. They claimed that is how they would be assessing the damages and they have not been doing it.

QUESTION: What is the benign, innocent explanation for that?

ROSE: There isn't one. Moreover, there can't be one.

QUESTION: Isn't it true that VAERS mostly captures injuries that occur pretty shortly after the time of the injection, and that the realm of possible injuries that festered, were latent, or didn't go kinetic until much later, are extremely underreported? So when you look at VAERS in 2022, when the vaccine intake was much slower than in 2021, because most people who wanted the shot or were forced to get it were already injected, it seems like the rate of myocarditis reporting seemed to increase. Hence, is latent myocarditis something that could be a ticking time bomb over time?

ROSE: Yes. I dare say that is a component, and I dare say that this data appearing later is the backlog filling. I think it is a combination of things.

QUESTION: Obviously this VAERS reporting demonstrated a threshold to pull the product from market really from the time the distribution began, as you've demonstrated. At about a year and a half later, what are the most concerning safety signals being hinted to, or screaming bright red from VAERS, using applied mathematics as well as understanding the mechanism of action of this shot?

ROSE: It is a weird time to ask me this because I am on this trajectory leading me very close to the underlying destructive cause. The immunological adverse events have been piling up from the very beginning. That makes sense to me because the systemic nature of the damage points to some kind of immune dysfunction.

That doesn't really perfectly explain to me why we are seeing bleeding and clotting at the same time, for example. It doesn't explain the fibrin agents embalmers are finding. What does explain that are amyloid plagues. I've been doing research of immunological problems such as autoimmune disorders and amyloidosis.

Something that is also extremely concerning, that is related to this, are prion diseases like Creutzfeldt-Jakob. This is very rare. The background is about one in one million Americans per year will be diagnosed with Creutzfeldt-Jakob. We are now well above that according to VAERS, and that is with a very low underreporting factor. What's more concerning is that this number is going up every week.

That is a bad sign.

Just to be clear, one report of Creutzfeldt-Jakob in the context of a biological product is concerning to me, because it is not something you want to mess around with. If you get diagnosed with it, you have about a year to live and there is nothing you can do about it. You want to talk about fearing something? Viruses are not what you should fear—this is. It makes the proteins misfold in your brain and basically your brain goes to mush. There are already forty-six reports of prion diseases in VAERS right now!

Needless to say, that is scary.

Amyloidosis is another concern. In terms of clinical destructiveness and life alteration, there are 51,438 reports of disability within the context of these products. I know people who have been put in wheelchairs who were previously healthy.

QUESTION: What about the more immunological responses like autoimmune disease? We are seeing a lot of shingles. Do you suspect that autoimmune and/or immune suppression are going to be among the longer-term effects of these shots?

ROSE: Yes, I think that as people keep injecting themselves, they become progressively more immunocompromised. If you have a reduction in CD8-positive T-cells after injections, it's not good because those are the T-cells that kill virally infected cells. HIV is the same kind of problem except you have a reduction of CD4-positive T-cells, which are the generals of the immune system. Both of these T-cells are vital to this sector of the immune system, and if you have a deficiency in either one, it is not good news.

In the case of latent viral infections like herpes zoster, which manifests as shingles, this is also a byproduct, in my opinion, of immune factors being disrupted or dysregulated. These immune components are supposed to be maintaining these viruses that you have in your body in sort of a dormant state, but they aren't doing that as well anymore after the injection of these products.

We don't really know why but we know it is happening. You can't deny it. You can see it with your eyes clinically. The amount of people who are reporting herpes zoster manifesting as shingles is off the charts, and it is not just herpes. There is Epstein-Barr virus, cytomegalovirus, Hepatitis, and there's also cancer. The data pattern shows the mechanism of protection against the emergence or reemergence of these problems is being compromised somehow by these injections.

QUESTION: The body's mechanism of fighting cancer is kind of similar to fighting viruses. When you have a depletion of some of these killer cells, is there a long-term concern you are going to make people more vulnerable to various types of cancers? Is there any pharmacovigilance data in VAERS or elsewhere that would seem to indicate that there might be a "Houston, we have a problem" moment when it comes to cancer?

ROSE: Yes, and there are multiple facets to this one.

The first is the most important one and that's what the oncologists I know are saying as well as ones who are actually still being diligent doctors. There are patients, who have been in remission for years, coming out of remission shortly after their shots. They are seeing rare cancers. They are seeing more cancers. Cancers coming in younger people. VAERS confirms this.

The number of cancer reports is very high, but what is more alarming is that the number of reports of rare cancer is also really high. There are cancers that generally appear in young people occurring only in old people and vice versa. We are talking about breast cancers in males. Breast cancer is the number-one cancer being reported, but there also are leukemias out the ying-yang.

We are seeing bad signs and it doesn't look good. It very much aligns with this immune dysregulation or compromisation theory. If the protective mechanisms to keep cancers at bay are lost, then we will see a resurgence of cancers.

QUESTION: The 800-pound gorilla in the room is the reproduction of human civilization. Published early on in the FDA summary basis for regulatory action on Comirnaty, they noted missing information on use in pregnancy and lactation. It was obviously very clear early on that the effects of the vaccine on sperm, or concerning pregnancy, the fetus, or a nursing child are not known. As we currently stand mid-2022, what is the sum total of the evidence we are seeing that are red flags—or downright injuries—as it relates to the reproductive system of both men and women?

ROSE: As far as I know, the studies they did pertaining to fertility were absolutely lamentable or not done or not complete. They did no genotoxicity studies. They did no carcinogenicity studies. As far as I know, they didn't look very hard at what would happen with fertility.

Having said that, we were told explicitly that once injected, these products would stay in the injection site or the local draining lymph node. We know now, according to Pfizer's own data that was court ordered to be released, that the lipid nanoparticles were heavily distributed to the ovaries and the testicles and they concentrate there. The purpose of the lipid nanoparticles is the delivery vehicle of the payload, which is the messenger RNA that is the coding material for the spike protein.

So, what is the effect of lipid nanoparticles slipping their way into cells in the ovaries? We have no idea. And what is the effect of massive of amounts of spike protein being produced at those local sites? We have no idea. Those studies were not done. Not only that, but the information that this bioaccumulates in the ovaries and the testicles was withheld. That's shameful considering that there is a paper that remains published to this day in the *New England Journal of Medicine* that is promoting the safety of these products for pregnant women.[114]

The fertility data is not good, and you can look at this from two points of view. You can look at it from the point of view of women who are getting pregnant and losing their fetuses, having miscarriages or spontaneous abortions. You can also look at this from the point of view of stillbirths. Both of these are happening at higher rates than we've ever seen before in the context of biologicals from both VAERS and on-the-ground reporting. I have two well-known doctors in Canada who were told by the doulas and the nurses in two specific hospitals that the rate of stillbirths was really, really high. And when one of them spoke about that publicly, she was taken away to a psychiatric hospital, and the other one was beaten in court.

This is not a joke. It actually happened.

The precautionary principle dictates to us that if there is even a sign of danger, we don't need causation, especially when we are talking about the fertility of women and men. We need to stop. We need to talk very loudly about this. We don't need to censor people. And we need to find out if this is happening because we don't know yet. We have a lot of signs that women's fertility is being affected. Women's menstrual cycles have been completely dysregulated from the very beginning.

I remember in Israel they started rolling the vaccine out really soon, most people got it, and the women started talking about having dysfunction in their menstrual cycles. I'm not sure if it's the vaccine, and nobody knows yet. That's exactly the point, and why we need to find out. Because if the damage is cumulative, or if this extends through the generations, we might be in really big trouble. What I'm saying, from a scientific point of view, is we must thoroughly investigate if this could really reduce the population.

QUESTION: In other words, ubiquitous menstrual cycle dysregulation alone doesn't prove with the preponderance of the scientific method that the vaccine will sterilize people. But it certainly does signal some smoke; perhaps you ought to pull the products until you can conclusively confirm they're safe?

ROSE: There are two things that everybody needs to know. One, there wasn't enough data collected with regard to pregnancy safety. There is not enough data, period. There is nobody on this planet who can definitely say what is going to happen to a pregnant woman if she gets injected with this. Nobody. If anything, the data points to it not being good for women in their first and second trimesters to get them, because it greatly increases the odds they will lose their baby.

Two, if there is even an iota of a concern about fertility, we have to stop and figure that out first before proceeding, let alone promoting and forcing people to take this.

QUESTION: Roughly three-quarters of the COVID-related deaths in the world took place *after* the vaccine products were released. And in many countries, especially in the Pacific Rim that seemed to do very well that first year, almost all their deaths occurred after the shots were released. The more they injected, the more they infected. Most people never heard of the concept of a leaky vaccine, suboptimal antibodies, non-sterilizing vaccines, antibody-dependent disease enhancement, or original antigenic sin. All these concepts are new to your average person. But is it not a fact that to anyone working as a vaccinologist, or similar disciplinaries in the manufacturing companies and the regulatory organizations; this is as simple as the ABCs. How could they have not understood the risk of creating viral escape and making things worse? Isn't that part of Vaccinology 101, that you have to make sure when you are going with a non-sterilizing vaccine that it doesn't make it worse?

ROSE: Yes, and the thing is we've been trying as a species to create a vaccine against coronaviruses for decades. We've never been successful because they are highly adaptive. If you knew about this, you would say that there would never be a coronavirus vaccine that would work for very long.

I know most people don't understand that, but the very smart people doing the work behind the scenes absolutely know this stuff. And the policymakers also knew they were pushing the original version onto people who were probably immune, and it is not going to work against the new so-called variants. And now they are chasing variants.

They passed a new policy now that basically means no clinical trials are required for variations of these products, and by the way, that includes self-amplifying mRNA products, which are being trialed right now.

QUESTION: Can you describe what self-amplifying mRNA products are?

ROSE: Basically, it means that instead of needing the host cell machinery to propagate itself, it carries its own luggage in order to do that for itself. So, the claim is that this is awesome because you will need only a small dose of it in the beginning, but we don't know anything about the byproduct of what doing this is going to be. I'm not going to speculate because it is not my field, but it terrifies the hell out of me. I've written a Substack about this as well.[115]

The thing that scares me the most is that this was always in the plan. There is a version of the Pfizer product that everyone is getting that is the self-amplifying version. It is in the trials now. I guarantee that not one of the people participating in those trials has any idea that they are being injected with something that is different from what has been described before, as is this messenger RNA that uses host cell machinery to translate into the spike protein.

QUESTION: Obviously, from the get-go, to even pursue children as candidates for an experimental shot violated the Nuremberg Code in the sense that the benefit could never outweigh the risk—because the risk for them has always been close to zero. But the fact that they pursued children way after it was clear the vaccine didn't work, and then even babies the following year when we saw negative efficacy and the pathogen for which they were immunizing against was long gone, does this pose any long-term danger to their innate immune systems? What sort of long-term effects do you see to children's immune systems because of these shots?

ROSE: The injection circumvents the innate system and the innate system is powerful in children. It is proven to be highly effective. Children don't suffer from COVID-19 in a bad way. To go after them is preposterous for that reason alone. It makes no sense to even make it an option to inject children with this. It is a beautiful blessing that children have not been affected by this.

As far as what the shots are going to do to children long term, I do not have anything good to say about that. They are touting that the benefit of these shots is the reduction in severity of symptoms and that is starting to prove to be not so true as well. But the risk could be death. If I'm weighing the risks and the benefits there, I think I am going to choose not to inject myself.

I don't really want to say anything about the babies yet because I don't want to be too morbid. Let's just say I'm keeping a close eye on VAERS. There are already more than 2,000 reports in VAERS for zero- to five-year-olds, and that was *before* they said they could roll out the EUA product.

QUESTION: **Wait, these shots were not authorized until June 15, 2022, for the cohort of six-month-olds to five-year-olds, and you are telling us there are already 2,000 reports predating that? Could these perhaps be due to children from the clinical trials?**

ROSE: Some of them, yes. But there are simply too many of them to all be from the clinical trial. There were only a few thousand children in the clinical trials, so unless all of them ended up in VAERS, which I suppose is possible, it is not only the children who were in the clinical trials.

A doctor from Canada had injected over 500 children aged zero to five before the vaccines were approved for that age group because he felt it was his duty to protect them.[116] Of course, we have no follow-up on those babies. We don't know if they suffered any adverse events. I'd imagine that those reports, even if they were submitted to the Canadian system, may not have made it in because those reports in Canada are vetted by people who have a vested interest to make sure that the products don't look bad. But at least we know for sure there were babies being injected off-trial.

QUESTION: **Did this doctor lose his license?**

ROSE: Are you kidding me?

QUESTION: **By the time this interview will be read by the audience/jury, it will at least be early 2023. Can you think of something pertaining to these vaccines that we'll be discussing in six to twelve months that isn't quite on our radar yet, looking at the data patterns you're seeing?**

STEVE DEACE AND DANIEL HOROWITZ

ROSE: Babies and small children dying, and I'm so sorry to say it. But the data trends point to forthcoming cardiac problems and deaths in those cohorts. The rates are low right now, because there aren't enough data points yet. But we shouldn't be seeing these signals at all, and we are already well above the fifty deaths in children aged zero through eighteen. Nothing makes sense. There are no rules.

CHAPTER 17

Kristen Meghan Kelly:
E-MASK-ulation of the Human Body,
Civil Rights, and Common Sense

If a government can force a human being to cover his route of inhalation in order to access public accommodations and criminalize breathing without a mask—what exactly can a government *not* do to you? Which fundamental right remains that you still retain for yourself?

It's not just that our government officials beginning with Fauci knew from day one that masks don't work against respiratory viruses.[117] It's that they knew they were harmful, knew they were never meant for children under any circumstance, and knew that there were better controls of hazardous environments than cheap Chinese cloth that wouldn't denude humanity of its dignity and bodily autonomy. Yet, they nonetheless chose the most inhumane and illogical breach of human sovereignty by controlling the most vital parts of all human beings down to the age of two. They then engaged in the most egregious form of discrimination, shaming, and even apartheid against those who did not and even could not comply.

They kept these policies in place for years on end—and in many cases, to this day—despite irrefutable evidence and lived experience demonstrating that they absolutely did not work. The policy was so Orwellian that one French researcher, after studying case rates in thirty-five countries with six hundred and two million people, concluded in a peer-reviewed paper that masks "may have harmful unintended consequences."[118]

There is an entire industry of industrial hygienists and hazardous exposure experts inside and outside of government who were aware of the danger and lack of efficacy of masks. It's just that they chose to go along with this atrocity. However, one such expert chose to speak out and serve as an expert witness in court cases and at legislative hearings to bring the truth about source controls, personal protective equipment, and how the protocols for dealing with them were breached with a degree of ferocity that is only matched by its degree of unscientific insanity.

Retired Air Force veteran Kristen Meghan Kelly, a mother of two in Michigan, is a senior industrial hygienist who has worked in the field of hazardous exposure protection for two decades. She is not only a subject matter expert who can attest to the abuses of basic legal standards, medical and safety protocols, and human rights violations inherent in the mask mandates, but as a sexual assault survivor is also a victim of the mask regime herself. Like so many who suffered trauma, she was unable to cover her mouth without triggering a panic attack resulting in cardiac arrhythmia and vertigo. Before the claimed public health emergency, she was previously exempted by an occupational health physician from respirator use due to two medical issues. She represents so many of those forgotten human beings with disabilities who were denied access to public accommodation and even medical care for not being able to wear this ill-advised and ineffective medical device.

Because Mrs. Kelly has experienced every aspect of this issue from so many angles and has represented so many victims of this regime, we call her to the stand to share with the world the magnitude of the atrocity of what is probably the most intimate violation of bodily autonomy in modern history.

• • • • • • •

QUESTION: Typically, in your line of work there is an assessment of the nature of the hazard you are up against, the options available to combat it, the evidence of what works, the safety concerns, and then how to confront it safely. Throughout COVID, how have the various layers of government and the medical field upheld or disregarded those principles?

KELLY: Industrial hygienists are exposure scientists and what gets conflated in the minds of the public is that we are just OSHA liaisons, and we just deal with administrative issues of compliance. That is a very small aspect of this profession. In reality, we are really engineers and scientists, and we must anticipate, recognize, evaluate, and control a wide array of hazards. More specifically, we work with public health professionals and health care workers. Industrial hygienists aid in identifying the hazard through evaluations. We utilize a multidisciplinary approach and review to understand what these hazards do to the human body and we track the trends of symptoms through public health professionals. That means we are informed regarding the hazard at hand and we even pass that information on to doctors with whom we are consulting.

In navigating a hazardous exposure threat, we use this multidisciplinary approach. We look at different conditions because when it comes to controlling a health hazard there is never a situation where it is one size fits all as far as the controls needed. We follow a practice called the "hierarchy of safety and controls" and we start at the very top and work our way down the inverse pyramid. When we are implementing these controls, they must have something called a risk-reduction rate. We know when we are dealing with an aerosolized virus, engineering controls go through dilution, destruction, and filtration technologies to provide—at a minimum—a 90 percent risk reduction rate.

When we talk about the bottom-of-the-barrel selection of controls, which is personal protective equipment like N95 respirators, we wouldn't promote those respirators as the best respiratory protection due to their limitations regarding aerosol exposures, difficulty to quantitatively fit test, and their assigned fit and protection factors. We would use a powered air-purifying respirator (PAPR). Although respirators are control methods, they are among the least desirable. After a certain amount of time, people are inattentive and do not wear them properly, and they lose their efficacy and ability to control the hazard.

This conveys why we do not rely on or promote masks; they do not seal, creating gaps that result in a less than 1 percent risk reduction. Masks have no governing health and safety criteria and are not rated against an aerosol, and we know this in view of the fact that proper control measures have their own rating and limitations assigned through the National Institute of Occupational Safety and Health (NIOSH). Under their guidance, masks are not considered PPE, nor are they regarded as source control for an aerosolized virus, reiterating that they cannot form a facial seal.

When implementing a control, we first ask ourselves: does it work? Masks do not prohibit aerosols from being inhaled or exhaled, but engineering controls do! We can declare masks stop some large droplets of fluid; nevertheless, is not the primary route of transmission in this case concerning an airborne aerosolized virus. We commit to addressing the greatest hazard, and that is the spread of infectious aerosols, which are inhaled into the deep lung and which masks are unable to stop.

From there we ask: does the solution—in this instance, the mask—do they bring about harm and create a greater hazard? As expected, masks can create a greater hazard as they are documented as causing the wearer to inhale less O2 and additional CO2, they are not designed to be worn for prolonged periods, and they are not designed to be worn by children or individuals with a wide array of medical issues.[119]

Consequently, this entire policy was all in shambles from the day it was promulgated. We didn't utilize a multidisciplinary approach or review. We didn't follow the hierarchy of controls. And we had not conferred with the actual subject matter experts, industrial hygienists such as me, who deal with controlling hazards at the source, daily. In these situations, consulting with nongovernmental experts is key, as there is less likely a conflict of interest and intimidation of released information. Instead, our government went straight to the public health professionals and the doctors. Everyone has a role, but when you skip one, the rest all falter.

Thus, the deviation of our government from personal protection, source control protocol, and safety is as dramatic as a heart surgeon one day opening a patient from the back rather than the front.

QUESTION: What would have happened, pre-COVID, if a group of businesses told their employees or customers you can't come here, you can't work here, and you can't be serviced here unless you wear this PPE—no exceptions, no fit test, and no health test?

KELLY: Masks and respirators are classified as medical devices because they have the ability to impact the body and proper gaseous exchanges. Respirators are regulated through NIOSH. We know these medical devices require medical clearances, and there is a long list of exceptions as to why individuals may not medically be able to tolerate these devices, such as autism, PTSD, asthma, hypoxia issues, vertigo, cardiac issues, and the like. Thus, in a normal setting outside of a pandemic, if an employer mandated such medical devices, OSHA would have fined them into the ground. 29 CFR 1910.134 requires businesses to have a written respiratory protection program in place. This encompasses a health risk assessment and exposure data documenting how it came to be that respiratory protection was needed and proof the hierarchy of safety and controls was considered. Although masks are not considered respirators, OSHA does have guidance on the elective use of masks in the workplace.

Elective use is a fundamental issue to remember; this is because OSHA wouldn't anticipate requiring masks in the workplace, as it is viewed as elective use for situations like nuisance dust and individual allergies to nonhazardous substances. There is no standard on using masks for a virus as it was and is not the answer in risk mitigation. We know the requirements for implementing the use of even an N95 respirator; it's egregious to assume masks should be mandated without regard for capabilities to control the hazard and their health impacts. Additionally, 29 CFR 1910.132 places the responsibility on an employer to ensure specific PPE is rated for the hazard at hand. Rightfully so, one may argue these restrictions and requirements apply only in occupational settings. Accordingly, mandating covering noses and mouths with breathing barriers is not an issue that is capable of being anticipated in the world of health and safety.

Where a standard exists, there is a hazard, but where there is a hazard, there is not always a standard!

I know as an industrial hygienist if I required employee masking against an aerosolized virus, I could have my employment terminated or lose professional credentials and certifications. The possibility of criminal charges exists if I select an improper control method that leads to injury, illness, or death. When you knowingly recommend improper control methods causing greater harm, there are consequences. Some may relate masks as part of the public health code "no shirt, no shoes, no service." Except none of their choices for protection are classified as PPE or medical devices.

Masks impact breathing and the proper gaseous exchanges needed for body systems to properly function. I sit here as an exposure scientist with twenty years under my belt and wonder how we let this happen. It was so criminal. Where are my colleagues? Where is OSHA?

STEVE DEACE AND DANIEL HOROWITZ

QUESTION: OSHA not only failed to follow its own policies and protocols but was actually one of the agencies tasked with promulgating and enforcing the mask policies in the government and recommending them in the private sector. What is the most egregious part of this deviation from their established science and protocols?

KELLY: We must always follow the hierarchy of controls, pursuant to OSHA's guidance, yet this precedent was abandoned. Industrial hygienists implement controls, and there *must* be follow-up investigations—regularly. For example, I put hospital workers in respirators and ensure they have increased air exchanges and positive pressure in their operating rooms and negative pressure rooms for isolation areas. These evaluations are scheduled on a quarterly, semiannual, or annual basis. I have to return to interview staff and ask how things are going. I conduct air measurements and monitoring. In certain situations, I may conduct a form of presence and absence sampling by conducting swipe samples of several surfaces.

In other words, I have to verify the confidence in the controls implemented—something our government refused to do. There have been times I discovered improperly selected and failed controls. I had identified employees working around respirable carcinogenic metals dust and were wearing half-face respiratory protection when full-face was needed. Workers were complaining of sores in their mouths and irritation of the eyes. Yellow and green chromate dust was present in their eyes.

Yet, in the case of the federal government, they put out all these categorical, sweeping, and unprecedented mandates and rules and never went back and verified the confidence in these controls. That right there is why I ponder where OSHA is, for the reason this requirement is a huge part of program management within OSHA. We must provide documentation. If I'm consulting as an industrial hygienist to a hospital and I do not have a report showing that I went back to verify confidence in any controls that I put in place, there is a major cause for concern in my ability to support the right for employees to have a safe and healthful work environment. Where is the accountability for OSHA?

QUESTION: Indeed, two years into the pandemic—still with no updated assessment of the government's masking policy—a German study found almost all the children who wore masks experienced dangerously high levels of carbon dioxide, beyond acceptable levels.[120] Would those working at NIOSH or OSHA have known this was always an inherent risk?

KELLY: Absolutely. Let's use health care, for example, that's where you still see the most mandates existing. If I were to suggest that in a health care setting all the other controls are not lowering the hazard enough to an acceptable limit, and I, therefore, needed you to wear a respirator, there is no data to back up that assertion. I also know that masks do not fall under OSHA's respiratory protection standard, and that is because they were never designed for prolonged use as a control method for this hazard. When selecting a respirator, you first determine the level of exposure through air sampling. Under OSHA's 29 CFR 1910.134, when we cannot identify or reasonably calculate an employee's exposure the employer shall classify the atmosphere to be immediately dangerous to life or health (IDLH). There is no occupational exposure limit for a virus. This would mean full-face pressure-demand supplied air with auxiliary self-contained air supply. Visualize that for a moment.

These devices impede your gaseous exchanges. When we cover our nose and mouth, the body's natural response is to increase our respiration rate. If I determine an employee must wear a respirator, training on its limitations and approval from an occupational health doctor is required. I've managed respiratory protection programs for more than 75,000 people and completed program requirements on an individual basis.

When you listen to the federal or state government, or even private corporations, issue a blanket mandate for a medical device that can cause great harm to different individuals, that is a deplorable breach of settled protocol. I also believe it was criminal for doctors to go on the mainstream media and say there are hardly any medical issues that would preclude someone from covering their face. That is simply not true and ignores the science existing in the realm of occupational safety and health.

Where were the occupational health doctors speaking up when governments were imposing a one-size-fits-all control on our entire country when we're not permitted to do that ourselves in any other context? Why were they silent?

During the initial rollout of these tyrannical and negligible mandates, there were patrons fainting in parking lots while loading their goods, as well as construction workers laboring by themselves in hundred-degree heat with breathing barriers on and sweating. Once those masks become soiled, they further prohibit your proper respiration. Having an improper level of hemoglobin, impacted by improper gaseous exchanges, can cause a domino effect impacting body systems.

Extended mask and respirator use, as a blanket solution, mirrors the unethical and illegal act of mandating the use of oral prescription medication to patronize a business—without knowing about your allergies or previous adverse issues with that medication. Prescriptions require consideration by your physician to review your medical history as improper use can lead to death. Turning to masks and respirators, 3M and Honeywell tell us improper use of these devices can lead to death. These are the facts we chose to ignore due to selectively picking data for different agendas, and we omitted the actual science that has existed in this profession for over forty years.

Under OSHA's respiratory protection program, elective mask use activates the requirements under 29 CFR 1910.134 Appendix D. I would provide those individuals with training regarding the limitations of use because such suboptimal breathing barriers can provide a false sense of security. You don't just hand out respirators like gloves. A recent trip to a Walgreens unveiled Honeywell N95 respirators on a small table, removed from the boxes, exposing this PPE to cross-contamination. If this were identified in an occupational setting, two years ago, the employer would be subject to a citation for handing out personal protective equipment that requires medical clearance, training, and a fit test. Now we are handing out soiled respirators with no training to the average layperson. This is all wrong!

QUESTION: Does this explain why we were never told to mask up during our entire lives during flu season?

KELLY: Yes. All the professionals with a modicum of ethics prior to 2020 knew that not only would masks be completely useless, but also that masking could never be implemented as a blanket approach because there are so many preexisting genetic and human health issues that can impact the ability to cover your nose and mouth for eight hours a day. We've abandoned all the science and protocols.

OSHA standards aren't law, but they are enforceable by law. Take note of the information on the boxes of N95 respirators. The manufacturers' warnings convey they are not for consumers or children. Specific respirators are determined by an industrial hygienist or another subject matter expert like an Occupational and Environmental Safety and Health Professional. That health clearance is required. You must be fit tested on a specific size and model, and trained on proper use, cleaning, storage, and disposal. You must be trained to recognize the adverse issues of use. We cast aside all of that! I will parrot these key requirements like Zuckerberg's propaganda of wearing a mask to protect Grandma!

We are causing great harm to the people of this country and to our children, who never, under any circumstances, were included in historical studies of how masks and respirators impact the human body.

QUESTION: Children had to wear masks all day every school day in almost every corner of the country. Are you saying that before COVID, recommending to put a mask on a child, much less mandating it, was a nonstarter?

KELLY: It's been known for decades that we do not mask children or place pregnant women in respirators for prolonged periods without consulting with a credentialed individual in fetal protection, such as an industrial hygienist and an occupational health physician. One study revealed that if the mother is dealing with limited oxygen intake, there can be prenatal hypoxia, which impacts brain development and cognitive function with neurodegeneration.[121] With children at the age of two, constant oxygen restriction can impact frontal lobe development. This became apparent when the CDC lowered developmental milestones in children in March of 2022.[122]

When these mask mandates were deployed, I was giving interviews and telling people we were going to see cognitive delay, social delay, increased rashes, bronchitis, pneumonia, hypoxia, hypercapnia, and fungal issues because I already witnessed this in occupational settings from the unsuitable mask and respirator use. Again, respirators are not made for children, and it's written on the box and insert warnings. A talented high school basketball player suffered repetitive hypoxia from overexertion while masking up during basketball practice and gameplay. This high school student has daily pain, sees an array of specialists, and lost his normal quality of life.

In Michigan, parents and teachers have reported children have collapsed from wearing masks in the heat and during prolonged periods of use. That's how dangerous this can be. Any enforcement of masks on children, after known adverse events are reported, is child abuse. I can conceptualize the ignorance of falling for "do what we say" and the fear of retribution, but when you witness children needing medical attention, how do you continue to perpetuate the harm? Before 2020, if a parent forced their child to don a mask or respirator for a flulike virus, in all conditions, every day, all day long, and reusing the dirty breathing barrier, they would expect a visit from child protective services for Munchhausen's syndrome and Munchhausen's syndrome by proxy.

Why would we place masks on millions of children and put them through this form of assault? It's not just the physical harm. We have groomed our children to comply with things they know deep down are unnatural and do not feel right. This can be viewed as a form of grooming the young into a dark place of complying with uncomfortable requests to appease authority. We don't need our children to just shut up and color. My heart breaks as a mother of two to think about what we are doing to our youth. We allowed them to be brainwashed and programmed, and it is completely unacceptable.

QUESTION: Not only are you an expert witness to this atrocity committed en masse, but you are also a victim of it yourself given you have issues from a disability. Because of your expertise, you have testified at legislatures and state court cases throughout the mandates and the pandemic. You have a broad picture of the ferocity with which this has been imposed on people. Can you go through some of the stories and harms you've heard from people where there was no sympathy and they were denied care or service?

KELLY: I had predominantly women come to me who were denied service because they just couldn't cover their faces. It was a highly triggering event to an attack or sexual assault that brought back traumatic memories. That is something I can speak to myself. I was sexually assaulted and sodomized when I was on active duty. The inhumane service members who attacked me placed a bar towel over my face. Since then, I have been unable to forcibly cover my face. If I go to the dentist,

I am under oral and IV sedation because I cannot be placed in a situation where I am forced to cover my face and mouth. It brings me back to that trauma, causing cardiac arrhythmia, altered blood pressure, and vertigo flare-ups. I also have a secondary issue dealing with oxygen deprivation.

One of the most heinous situations I was contacted about was a custody issue involving a child who was in the process of getting a kidney transplant. One parent wanted this child to wear an N95 respirator and the other parent said no. Somehow the nephrologist wanted the child to wear an N95. I thought that was insane. Oxygen deprivation can impact renal function, and the child's kidneys were already in distress.

There are numerous medical issues that preclude you from wearing a mask or respirator. Couple that with people who are already in treatment programs that are regularly scheduled but are denied that treatment because they can't wear a breathing barrier due to the very issue they seek treatment for.

This is a level of discrimination I have a hard time wrapping my head around. The stories come in at all hours of the day. I was contacted by a woman who, while waiting for an x-ray, was placed in a dirty linen closet due to her inability to medically tolerate donning a mask. She was denied utilizing the patient waiting room due to her facial nudity. A Vietnam veteran, who survived lung cancer from Agent Orange exposure, was denied entry into a hardware store because of his reduced lung capacity. Why would anyone place a mask over the face of an individual receiving supplemental oxygen through a nasal cannula? An elderly woman was made to wait outside of a medical facility, wheeled out into below-freezing temperatures while waiting for her appointment.

QUESTION: In the past, they might take your children away from you if you were forcibly covering their nose and mouth with a cloth. But now if you had one parent who didn't want their kids to wear a mask, that would be noted in a custody battle; would the judge side against those parents?

KELLY: It was being classified in the courts as neglect by the parent because we had all these government agencies and people on social media telling you how safe it is to wear a mask all day, in any and all environments, with no regard for anyone's health history. When those in my field attempted to correct the record as expert witnesses, we were told we were not doctors. While we are not dismissed as subject matter experts on exposure control, we were sometimes overshadowed by doctors practicing in a field they are not credentialed in. What the media and government have done is so detrimental to human health, trust in public health, and the field of safety and health. Two decades in this profession should have weight against the unsubstantiated arguments of community masking.

A majority of the litigation sides with us, but the custody issues are the hardest. I've seen parents lose primary custody over these arguments; those who identified harm in masking their children were viewed as conspiracy theorists. If we had been allowed to educate communities about proper control measures, we would have healthier people, have boosted compliance with recommended controls, and you wouldn't see lowered expectations for child development.

QUESTION: What is the feedback you got when it involved an employer or a store or a doctor's office and the person said, "I have a disability and I can't wear a mask"?

KELLY: Just speaking for myself, I haven't worn a mask or respirator at all throughout the pandemic. I explain that I have an Americans with Disabilities Act–protected medical exemption, and sometimes that keyed them into leaving me alone. I don't have special rights over anyone else. I do however have a disability that affects my daily life and I have those protections. Sometimes employees understood ADA Title III protections. My local VA clinic, which actually houses my proof of inability to wear a mask or respirator, has not been respectful of those issues. I have PTSD and battle severe iron deficiency; I was accosted at the door for my inability to wear a mask.

I explained why I cannot comply with their mandate and the VA police observed the conversation; when they saw I was having trouble breathing they allowed me to proceed to my appointment. VA providers and industrial hygienists have admitted they knew that masks do not aid in reducing the spread of SARS-CoV-2. Why aren't they standing up? It is the declining faith in health care systems that is causing an epidemic of patients not reporting medical issues, becoming behind on recurring appointments, and delaying seeking dental care.

QUESTION: You used the term "grooming" earlier. To what end? Was the grooming purposeful or was the policy just bad and did it create the grooming effect?

KELLY: I thought long and hard about this using my experience working for the government for twelve years. I know they knew how dangerous and useless using these control methods was. The fact we substituted a useless control method, which increases cross- and self-contamination and increases the viral load versus recommending engineering controls was self-revealing. We should have incorporated engineering controls in homes and businesses that could have reduced the hazard by 90 percent, I have no other answer than to say that none of this was about health and safety. This level of purposeful negligence cannot be shielded.

If employee and community safeguards were the objective, we would have consulted with the proper experts. I believe this was done to test the compliance of the American people. What will they put up with? Just like public schools are designed to teach children to follow and not have autonomous thought, this cemented why we shouldn't be coparenting with the government. I believe there are nefarious reasons behind this, and I will never understand it, but it was truly grooming children to accept harm to their bodies—whether it be sexual, social, psychological, or physical. It was purposeful. Too many people and agencies in the government knew how dangerous this was, especially to children, and they still brought about this abuse.

CHAPTER 18

J. R. Hoell: How Dare You Heal Your Children Rather than Let Us Experiment on Them?

If a government can control your body, you know what else it can control?

Your children.

Under this new Fourth Reich regime, if you don't agree with the biomedical state—or with their political beliefs in general—then you are a threat to yourself and those around you. Persisting in those views is, therefore, tantamount to child abuse if you are living in accordance with those beliefs around your children.

We have already established that there has been a religious holy war declared on safe, effective FDA-approved drugs like ivermectin. The same doctors who would jab a baby with the mRNA biological products or forcibly mask a child for eight hours in the heat without batting an eyelash also believe that treating a teenager with ivermectin is child neglect. That leads us to our next witness, J. R. Hoell.

Hoell is a principal systems engineer from Dunbarton, New Hampshire. He has also formerly served as a conservative state representative in the New Hampshire House of Representatives, and has been very involved in political causes that threaten the regime, most recently in the medical freedom movement. As a cofounder of ReBuildNH, Hoell was one of the most vocal opponents of the lockdown regime in his state. How coincidental, then, that he suddenly got a knock on the door one day from police at the behest of the state's child protective service—the Division for Children, Youth, and Families (DCYF).

His alleged "crime"? Successfully treating his teenage son with ivermectin.

See, Hoell had committed a "political crime." The attempted punishment that the medical establishment and the state agency tried to mete out was one that was both nefarious and is growing around the country. They wanted to take away all his minor-age children. They wanted to make an example out of him to future regime dissenters.

Medical kidnapping is a growing trend in all fifty states. We have heard numerous stories of hospitals and doctors calling child protective services if they believe the parents are not following their medical edicts, or using the protocols of their political opponents.

In one case in Idaho in 2022, a family temporarily lost custody of their baby simply because they failed to show up for a doctor's appointment (they were all under the weather).[123] It's the worst form of collusion between the medical tyrants and the biomedical state that can result in something worse than jail time—loss of parental rights over one's children.

Although everyone wants to protect those children who legitimately are being abused by parents, we cannot continue a system of guilty until proven innocent whereby one can lose his children for weeks or months based on a political witch hunt. According to the Administration on Children, Youth and Families (ACYF), during FY 2019, child protective services agencies around the country received 4.4 million referrals involving alleged child maltreatment of 7.9 million children.[124] Approximately 3.5 million of these referrals were deemed credible enough to investigate, but just 16.7 percent of the children investigated were found ultimately found to be victims of abuse or neglect. In other words, *just 7 percent* of the original pool of children for whom referrals were lodged were actually found to be in danger.

Those 7 percent badly need intervention, but what about the families of the other children? Now consider that this was before the politics of COVID and political witch hunts introduced an entirely new dynamic to frivolous child neglect claims.

Think about it, if masks and vaccines could be elevated to such lofty omnipotence that they can predominate all laws, human rights, social norms, antidiscrimination policies, Nuremberg principles for human experimentation, and civil rights, they most certainly can be used to abrogate parental rights. What is to stop the government from taking away your children if you don't vaccinate them, mask them, or if you use vitamins and supplements they don't like, or violate any future sacred-cow political obsession we can only begin to imagine?

What if you don't want your children on a ventilator? What if you feel the child is being mistreated in the hospital and desire to discharge him? Indeed, without reforms of the process for child protective service agencies claiming custody of your kid, there is nothing stopping them.

For that reason, we call former state representative J. R. Hoell of New Hampshire to the stand to inform the world about how easy it is for the medical profession to take away your child.

. . . . . .

QUESTION: Let's start out with the timeline of when your son got COVID. You treated yourself and your family very easily and got over the virus. In light of that, what did you do with your son, and what was the reaction of the medical and public officials in your home state of New Hampshire?

HOELL: We saw what was going on in March 2020 and were looking for alternative treatments at that time because I wasn't convinced the medical community had our best interests at heart. It became clear that ivermectin was effective for treating respiratory illnesses and people were using it very successfully early on. Even though the FDA wasn't studying it, I thought it was worth investigating. I started reviewing various medical journals, technical articles, and looking at SARS-CoV-2 virus infection rates and recovery trends in other countries. I realized that certain third-world countries were doing far better at managing the virus than the U.S. and Europe. Fast-forward to August 2021, and one of my employees whom I was working with side-by-side gets COVID. I then treated myself with ivermectin as a prophylactic and didn't become infected with COVID.

Then, right before Thanksgiving, my family came down with COVID. It started with my youngest son, and then it worked its way through the family. I went out and got a test to confirm the diagnosis, and at that point we started using what is now known as the Front Line COVID-19 Critical Care protocol, a protocol designed to prevent and treat COVID in outpatient settings. We recovered swiftly from COVID with no issues. The following week we weren't sure why my thirteen-year-old son wasn't sleeping well after he had recovered. He told us he ingested several Tylenol tablets because he had a headache, and we thought it might be connected so I called poison control.

We went to the emergency room, where they ran a full panel of blood work and the doctors found no evidence of anything that was outside of normal limits. There was no Tylenol in his system, and there was no evidence of any drug toxicity of any sort. After the doctors saw the lab work, they sent us home because there was nothing wrong. The doctor did ask us to do a follow-up visit with our primary care physician to make sure that they were aware of the ER visit. Our son's primary care physician, who is a licensed nurse practitioner, saw him a few days later. After our appointment, she also sent us home.

Several hours later, our nurse practitioner called me and said the disorientation issue with our son was due to ivermectin and that we gave our son "too much." In her opinion, his disorientation was not related to sleeplessness. I discussed with the nurse that the ivermectin was out of his system even before the ER visit, and that it couldn't be detected in his bloodstream. Moreover, sleeping trouble is *not* documented as a side effect in any of the medical literature published regarding this medication. She didn't like my response, and she failed to understand that there is no way to overdose on ivermectin at the levels we were using. We had administered the medicine within the administration limits that Merck had published in the *Physicians' Desk Reference*.

Several minutes later, I received a call from DCYF, New Hampshire's child protective service agency, and that began what was effectively a four-month ordeal that was an attempt to take away my minor-age children (a son and a daughter).

A child having trouble sleeping should not be the reason nurses are calling child protective services!

QUESTION: How did the practitioner even find out your son had taken ivermectin two weeks prior to the Tylenol issue?

HOELL: We were going over the patient history with the nurse and we told her we came down with COVID. We told her our son was still having issues with taste and smell and experiencing other COVID side effects. She immediately concluded it must be the ivermectin, even though these are known post-COVID symptoms, and no side effect data profile on ivermectin supports that hypothesis.

Because I wasn't willing to do exactly as she demanded, the nurse turned us in to child protective services.

Since then, I have been contacted by several other families who were turned in to DCYF for things as simple as failing to show up for a scheduled appointment with a doctor.

QUESTION: In any of your research throughout this ordeal, did you find any indication in published literature that sleeplessness could be a side effect of ivermectin?

HOELL: No. Like most antiparasitic medicines, gastrointestinal issues are the primary side effect of ivermectin. If you take too much, which we did not, the first thing you potentially get is cramps, nausea, and tender/swollen lymph nodes that are sensitive to the touch. In our case, the nurse never physically touched our son, so she had no idea if our son's lymph nodes were swollen.

She never did anything one would expect in an ordinary follow-up visit to properly diagnose the root cause for a trip to the emergency room. On the phone, she demanded I take him to the emergency room right away because, *in her opinion*, he was at risk of coma or death. She literally imagined out of thin air something that was not supported by any actual medical documentation. Competent medical providers routinely complete what is known as a "differential diagnosis." This is when you compare one possible root cause with other potential root causes, and you rank the probability of those options against one another. You come up with pros and cons for all of them. She didn't do any of that, and even if she did, it was not done properly. Instead, she regurgitated the mainstream media narrative that ivermectin is dangerous and that you cannot use it to treat COVID. I should add, for those not familiar with this medication, it has been used for over thirty years and administered several billion times and is on the World Health Organization's list of essential medications. Statistically speaking, ivermectin is safer than Tylenol.

QUESTION: Did she actually warn you she was going to call protective services?

HOELL: No. I received a phone call from an unrecognized New Hampshire state–issued land line, which I took it because I thought it might be important. It was a DCYF worker who insisted I take my son to the hospital right away. I said I would talk with my wife and get back to her about which hospital we would go to. The DCYF worker then called me back a few minutes later and said it was really urgent and that she needed me to pick a hospital right away and that she would meet me there. I let the employee know that we would go to the Elliot Hospital in Manchester. Then, the DCYF worker called back a third time and said I also needed to bring my minor-age daughter to the emergency room as well, even though my daughter was not experiencing any medical issues. I said that was unnecessary, and I would get back to her after I spoke with my wife.

It was at that point I realized they wanted me to take both my kids to the hospital so they could take possession of them in a medical kidnapping, because once you are in the hospital, you can't leave without being released. Consequently, I didn't take either of my kids to the emergency room. My wife and kids left to go visit friends and family, and within twenty minutes, the police and child protective services were at my door attempting to take my kids.

One social worker and two police officers showed up at my front door demanding to be let into our house. They wanted to know where my kids were. I said I didn't know where they were as they were in transit, and I couldn't contact any of them. DCYF said if I didn't turn over my kids quickly, they were going to get a court order to have the kids forcibly removed. A few hours later, they in fact returned with a court order to take possession of my children. There was no chance to argue our case in front of a judge as this order was issued as an ex parte order behind closed doors. They came back and said a judge had ordered for my children to be taken and that I needed to let them into my home to collect our children.

I again stated that my wife and children were not present, and I let one of the officers inside to verify that my children were not present in my home. The police then put the children's names into a National Crime Information Center as missing juveniles, which is normally done for children that have been kidnapped. So, in their attempt to take my children, they accused me of kidnapping my own children, making it near impossible to be present in the state with our children with us.

We remained at that standstill for a full eight days until we could get a court order to allow us to be "temporary custodians" of our own children. Meanwhile, the state remained the legal guardians and this was true for the next four months. After that court hearing, we were able to request that the names of our kids be removed from NCIC so my wife and children could return home. Imagine being forced out of your own home and state because some overzealous state employee thinks that you have given the wrong medication to your children.

What is simply terrifying is that although DCYF knew the very next day that a New Hampshire licensed medical doctor had examined our son and said he was "picture perfect" and in great health, they still continued the witch hunt. Although DCYF had a recorded video call with my son where they were able to ask the questions that they needed to ask to determine that he was fine, they still pursued this case for the next four months.

While they never tried to arrest me for not turning over our children, they did threaten both my wife and I with criminal contempt of court for not turning over the children to the state. I told the judge that the order was not an order to turn in my children; it was a specific court order for the state to come pick our children up. Legally, I wasn't obligated to actively do anything. I also told the judge that the track record of this rogue state agency is such that no loving parent would knowingly render to the state control of children that are being well taken care of.

QUESTION: How were you able to get out of this nightmare without having your kids taken?

HOELL: The state had ordered protective custody of our minor-age children. There were court hearings about this case in December 2021, January, February, and March 2022. In December, we argued that we were a homeschooling family, and the children were fine, so there was no reason to do anything. The judge said he would hold on taking the kids until the final outcome of the case, and that we would have a chance to have our medical witnesses testify at the next hearing. But in both January and February, the judge didn't let our side present any witnesses or evidence at all. He simply ruled against us at the first, second, and third hearings. It was only at the final hearing where we could present our side of the story that the judge ruled in our favor.

In New Hampshire family courts, there are no rules of evidence. The judge has complete discretion about what is shared and not shared in the courtroom. The judge has complete control of what information the case will be decided on. Hearsay is admissible, which is effectively what happened in our case. The nurse made a claim. DCYF took the claim as fact and proceeded to ask for the removal of our children.

The medical system works hand-in-hand with the court system, and it hurts families.

During this series of events, we had four different attorneys working on this for us, but it didn't matter. The judge issued a preliminary finding of child neglect based on our side not being allowed to share the facts of the story. Then at the adjudicatory hearing, the judge ruled:

> *FINDINGS OF FACT: The evidence DOES NOT substantiate the petition: CASE DISMISSED. The petition is dismissed for the following reasons(s): The credible evidence presented by the DCYF did not support the allegations contained in the December 14, 2021 Petition. The father, JR Hoell took his son [redacted] to the Catholic Medical Center Emergency Department (CMCED) at the recommendation of the poison control center after [redacted] disclosed to him he had taken excessive quantities of Tylenol. After being seen at CMCED he was discharged with the recommendation to follow up with his Primary Care Provider (PCP) and to schedule an appointment with a mental health professional. Mr. Hoell scheduled both of these appointments within 24 hours. The PCP, APRN Lauren Goodwin, subsequently conducted a brief appointment with [redacted]. At that time, she made a report to DCYF based on her understanding of what transpired in the Emergency Department on December 4, 2022 and her limited knowledge of [redacted] use of the drug Ivermectin. APRN*

Goodwin opined that [redacted] was in a toxic state as a result of injecting[sic] Ivermectin. During the hearing the overwhelming credible evidence demonstrated that this statement had no medical foundation. The credible evidence also reflected that the parents had not neglected [redacted] in any way, and certainly not in the manner alleged by DCYF....

QUESTION: If you had not had the foresight to send your family away, are you saying you could have been on the hook for losing custody of your children in the preliminary hearing instead of it ultimately being adjudicated to be frivolous?

HOELL: I don't even know if we would have ever been able to successfully argue our case. The state would have held all the cards. The only reason we were able to win this case was we had possession of our children and we were able to fully document that there was never any risk of harm. We were able to document that there was no harm by visiting independent medical professionals (medical doctors, naturopaths, and pharmacists) that were willing to do the right thing and stand up to medical establishment.

Because we were able to push back against the state, DCYF was unable to make their argument. If DCYF had possession of our children, we would never have been able to see other medical doctors to document that our children were in great health other than this sleeplessness issue we were trying to resolve. We would have been in a hostage situation and the state would have been able to dictate what we did and didn't do.

QUESTION: Were the state's actions justified, in your view?

HOELL: No, the state's actions were not justified in our case. I would argue that taking someone's kids away from them is on par with the severity of a felony conviction punishment, but unlike with a criminal case, there is no due process in family court. The judge has complete control of the rules of evidence.

In our case, it was the same judge at all four hearings. We had an emergency room doctor that we hired for the second, third, and fourth hearings sitting in the hallway for three hours waiting to testify and the judge did not afford him the opportunity to speak. Not only did this nurse misdiagnose my son, but it was a fraudulent misdiagnosis to the point the nurse should lose her license. But in New Hampshire, you may or may not be able to testify at the judge's discretion.

The judge can rule that they have heard enough information—which he did in this case—and our witness were never called. We had a three-hour hearing schedule, but after an hour and forty minutes, the judge ruled against us, and then we spent the next hour discussing what to do to get to the next hearing. This could have ended a lot worse had we not acted to keep them from getting their hands on our kids.

QUESTION: What did it cost to win this case?

HOELL: At the time of this interview, we are still paying off the legal and expert witness costs. We spent almost $60,000 just to respond to the state. The good news is that about 75 percent of that cost was covered by generous friends and family who donated and helped.

In hindsight, one wonders if the entire process itself was intended to be a form of punishment that the state can levy against families that do not conform to their tyrannical objectives.

QUESTION: You are somewhat of a known public figure in New Hampshire. You served in the legislature for eight years, and you were one of the founders of Rebuild New Hampshire, which is not just any activist group. It was the largest organization in the state fighting the lockdowns and medical tyranny and mandates. Do you think you were targeted because of your affiliation and activism?

HOELL: I have hard evidence to believe, based on the case files turned over during discovery, that this was a targeted persecution concerning me because of my activism. There is a police report in the file that makes it clear this was a politically motivated witch hunt. Since the trial concluded, I've also had eleven other families contact me who also have been run through the ringer on similar issues.

There is a direct link between the medical industry and the enforcement of child protective statutes under the claim of "in the best interest of the child." But the reality is that the child's best interest is not often the driving motivation. It is a profit-making center for the state. They are incentivized financially to put children into their care because money from the federal government flows down, and that is true in other states as well. They are looking for customers. Each state has its own mandatory reporting guidelines. There are some severally warped incentives to take children out of healthy families, and it needs to be fixed.

That's why I'm coming out of retirement and running for the statehouse again. What is going on here puts children at risk and is not about their mental, physical or emotional health. It is about making government bigger and some level of profit making. It is disgusting.

QUESTION: Do you think homeschool families are at greater risk?

HOELL: Yes, I do. During our final court hearing, we were asked by the attorney representing DCYF whether my wife has her master's degree in teaching. Well, what does my wife's degree have anything to do with the alleged neglect of our children and why is this relevant in a courtroom? Nothing, simply nothing. The only reason that a question like that would be asked would be another fishing expedition to find another reason to keep our children.

In my opinion, the reason that homeschoolers are targeted is twofold.

1. Homeschool children are taught critical thinking skills and not just how to memorize specific information. This makes those children more capable of discussing, evaluating, and dissecting the claims made by the bureaucrats who are employed by government.
2. Homeschool children are not immediately accessible to the state for taking. If your children are going to show up at the public school the next day, the state will have easy access to take them. In the case of homeschoolers, however, this option is not present and therefore they

STEVE DEACE AND DANIEL HOROWITZ

go to extraordinary lengths to make sure that they can take the children directly from the parents.

In our case, our children were never part of a public school system and they have done extremely well. One would think that this is a credit to us, but in our case, the state used the homeschooling against us.

Even though our oldest two children were able to graduate from college with high honors, debt free, having paid for school themselves with grants, scholarships, or on the money they earned while working and going to college, that was insufficient to prove that we were/are good parents. There was nothing that we could do to prove that we were good parents according to DCYF. The good news was the judge eventually saw through the lies and even noted at the last hearing that it was clear that we were good parents and that the state overreacted.

QUESTION: What policy changes do you feel need to be put in place?

HOELL: The problem is there is a secrecy clause for most of what happens in family courts and child welfare cases, and that extends even to matters concerning your own child. They don't allow discussion about anything. In the case of New Hampshire, there are criminal penalties associated with that. We need to bring more transparency surrounding the state's actions. If the state is acting in the best interests of the child, then they should have nothing to hide. Transparency is the key to public policy, especially when nothing short of custody over your own kids is at stake. Time is really of the essence to protect parental rights.

CHAPTER 19

David Martin Asks, "Was It All Part of the Plan?"

The democide committed by the government and medical profession over the past few years would be appalling enough if it were in response to a natural pandemic. However, there is nothing natural about the origins of this virus. It is incumbent that we get to the bottom of who was behind the creation of the virus, who knew what, and when they knew it.

It was known quite early on that the virus is not found in nature and was the result of gain-of-function research. It was also self-evident that the vaccines were not concocted within a few weeks in the beginning of 2020 and that all of the idiosyncratic responses to it—from lockdowns and masking to dashboard counts and the media messaging—were too uniform and too quick to have been germinated serendipitously. How could they have been ready with such a scheme to block natural effective remedies, promote the most dangerous therapeutics, shut down the world, and establish an infrastructure of censorship, enforcement, policy-making, and fear-mongering so quickly?

Was this, in fact, a "plandemic"? Were the same players behind the inhumane response to the virus actually behind the creation and/or release of the virus itself? It is simply astounding that after everything we've learned from a decade of the same players predicting and being involved in gain-of-function research of furan cleavage sites on spike proteins of coronaviruses that there is no commission created in the United States to hold the people responsible accountable.

That entire timeline of the creation of the coronavirus spike protein and the players behind it, warning about it, and planning for it is thoroughly laid out in Peter and Ginger Breggin's 2021 book, *COVID-19 and the Global Predators: We Are the Prey*. For example, on October 18, 2019, an event that was already planned months in advance, the Bill & Melinda Gates Foundation, the World Economic Forum, and Johns Hopkins University hosted "Event 201," a "desktop" simulation on a pandemic.[125] This event was funded by Open Philanthropy, one of the nonprofits funded by Dustin Moskovitz, cofounder of Facebook and owner of Sherlock Biosciences—one of the first CRISPR (gene editing) companies to receive EUA for CRISPR during the state of emergency. This was before anyone knew about a novel coronavirus. The scenario was described as follows.

"Event 201 simulates an outbreak of a novel zoonotic coronavirus transmitted from bats to pigs to people that eventually becomes efficiently transmissible from person to person, leading to a severe pandemic. The pathogen and the disease it causes are modeled largely on SARS, but it is more transmissible in the community setting by people with mild symptoms."[126]

Before anyone knew about a pandemic, Bill Gates tweeted the following message on December 19, 2019. "What's next for our foundation? I'm particularly excited about what the next year could mean for one of the best buys in global health: vaccines."[127] What did he know, when did he know, it, and who else was involved?

Congress and state legislatures must create a commission to get to the bottom of this matter, and to audit any other gain-of-function research coming down the pipeline. For example, in 2022, the Department of Defense finally conceded that it was operating forty-six "Ukrainian laboratories, health facilities, and disease diagnostic sites over the last two decades."[128] We know that many of the same players behind the gain-of-function coronavirus research and the Wuhan lab were involved in the Ukrainian labs.[129] How can we allow this to continue, given all of the destruction this research has wrought on mankind?

In broad daylight, on October 20, 2021, the NIH conceded to Kentucky Rep. Jim Comer that EcoHealth Alliance indeed engaged in gain-of-function research with the Wuhan lab and it was funded by the NIH in 2018.[130] The NIH described the research as a test to see "if spike proteins from naturally occurring bat coronaviruses circulating in China were capable of binding to the humanACE2 receptor in a mouse model." They note that indeed these mice became "sicker," but bizarrely deflected by asserting it was "an unexpected result of the research" that EcoHealth violated the terms of the grant, and that somehow this virus they created was distinct from

STEVE DEACE AND DANIEL HOROWITZ

what was infecting the world. Humanity is owed an answer about the history of this research and what came out of it.

A good starting point is drawing upon the expertise of people like Dr. David Martin. Dr. Martin was an international bioweapons inspector and intelligence analyst who has studied the patents of the various components of the virus and the vaccine for years. He has a story that needs to be shared with the world if we are ever going to get to the bottom of who caused the greatest calamity and destruction of civilization likely in human history. It is for this reason that we call him to the stand to lay out the facts of where COVID, and all its cascading policies, came from:

· · · · · · ·

QUESTION: You have an extensive background in health care, technology, and more. Can you itemize some of that experience for us?

MARTIN: My undergraduate degrees are in biology, psychology, and sports medicine. I have a master's in physiology. My doctorate is in radiology and orthopedic surgery, engineering, and sports medicine at the University of Virginia, which is a top twenty-five university in the country. I joined the med school faculty there in the early 1990s.

Also during the 1990s, I founded and ran Mosaic Technologies, which was a treaty-restricted technology transfer company. Our business was to go into countries that were mostly precluded from exporting offensive military technologies during the Second World War, and the treaties thereafter, and find military technologies that could be exported as civilian technologies.

I've also been very involved in investigating biological and chemical weapons capabilities and violations around the world for the U.S. government. I published the official document on an annual basis that recorded globally all biological and chemical weapons facilities, who was funding them, what they were doing. That work made me familiar with people like Ralph Baric and Anthony Fauci way back in nineties, when they took the spike protein associated with coronavirus and weaponized it to target human tissue—including lung and heart tissue—under the cover of an effort to create a vaccine vector that could be used for an HIV vaccine.[131]

Thus, as you can see, I've had a hand in things ranging from medical technologies, stealth, antenna, radar, nuclear medicine, and all sorts of other things.

QUESTION: Is it your view COVID-19 did not happen spontaneously? That those behind all of this didn't merely take advantage of an organic crisis to advance an agenda, but *caused* the crisis themselves?

MARTIN: Yes, but it's not just my assertion. I have over 4,000 pieces of documented evidence to show that from 1999 until September 2019, this entire terror campaign was organized and funded through National Institute of Allergy and Infectious Diseases (NIAID). For example, in October of 2014, NIAID told the University of North Carolina to continue their gain-of-function work on the spike protein from the Wuhan coronavirus model, despite the moratorium against it.[132] There's not even a question this was premeditated.

The goal early on was finding a way to weaponize what had been for two decades prior a concern of veterinary medicine. Most coronavirus infections prior to 1999 were contained to dogs and pigs, and it was usually a gastrointestinal target, not a cardiac or respiratory one. It was Baric who turned it into a device that could target the human heart and lungs. There is no accident anywhere in this. It is exceptionally clear from the evidence I've been briefing since the early 2000s—that this is a known and planned weapons program. It had nothing to do with public health or any of the alleged nightmarish scenarios we were told in late 2019 and early 2020.

In early 2015, in a critical admission of racketeering and domestic terrorism, Peter Daszak, the head of EcoHealth Alliance, stated to the National Academy of Sciences "to sustain the funding base beyond the crisis we need to increase the public understanding of the need for medical countermeasures such as a pan-coronavirus vaccine. A key driver is the media and the economics will follow the hype. We need to use that hype to our advantage to get to the real issues. Investors will respond if they see profit at the end of the process."[133]

I'm not making an allegation. It is their own admission. I have the documentation. They stated that this was a domestic terror campaign, and they stated it during the gain-of-function moratorium.

QUESTION: Are you suggesting this just about the creation of the virus, or are you saying it about the creation *and* release of the virus?

MARTIN: We need to be precise in this because we are being misled by the cunning use of language. Coronavirus is a model of what is called a clade, or a subspecies of virus. Coronavirus is a descriptor of one type of virus. But the fact of the matter is that there is not a single coronavirus. In 2003, during the first SARS outbreak, which we were told was also an accident, the CDC's first patent that was filed on the genome of SARS coronavirus was ironically the U.S. government seeking to control the genome of the subclade referred to as SARS.[134] What we have had in the past two and a half years has not been a virus outbreak. It has been the deployment of a spike protein weapon that has been known and improved upon over the last two decades since that first patent.

Baric said in 2016, when he was speaking at the Wuhan Institute, that a SARS coronavirus targeting human tissue was poised for human emergence.[135] How would he know that? Because the proverbial guns were loaded and ready to be deployed.

Once again, this is not an assertion. It is an open and shut case. Go back and look at the 2003 patent.[136], [137] The U.S., led by the likes of Fauci and Baric, allegedly took what was described by the Chinese and turned it into an invention owned by the U.S. through the CDC, which was given complete control of the commercial deployment of a coronavirus weapon—specifically the SARS coronavirus, with its corresponding spike protein.

QUESTION: One of the mysteries of this saga from the beginning was the ignoring of thousands of years of preestablished science on natural herd immunity, as well as ignoring decades of post–Spanish flu studies and research on the ineffectiveness of masks. One of the things many always wondered, even back when you would be censored for not accepting a natural origin of the virus, is whether this complete bypassing of established science was a tacit admission the virus was not of natural origin? Therefore, it may not adhere to preestablished natural laws of virology and immunology, which we have observed and recorded. Do you have any thoughts on that?

MARTIN: The fact of the matter is we knew in 2015 that Baric was modifying the Wuhan Institute's coronavirus model to amplify its pathogenicity.[138] We know they were actively aware and conscious of the fact they were constructing a weapon, by inserting into the RNA amino acid sequences that have never been seen in a natural spike protein model of any pathogen—SARS or otherwise. This was architected to be a synthetic chimeric alternative to coronavirus. There never was any attempt to try to make this a herd immunity situation, and what makes that the most damning is the very first patent the University of North Carolina filed on the weaponized coronavirus refers to an "infectious, replication defective" clone of SARS coronavirus.[139] So, this was meant to be a weapon targeting an individual, not a pandemic or immunity structure.

QUESTION: Why? Is it Big Pharma greed? Is it population control? Is it a pretext for broader social control? Is it all the above? Do we yet know why it appears to have been released sometime in 2019?

MARTIN: It wasn't released in 2019. It was introduced more broadly to the population in 2019, but it would take a basic biochemist five seconds to prove the RT-PCR (reverse transcription-polymerase chain reaction) fragments of spike proteins were evident in populations within tissue data banks that go back over the last two decades. It is an easy thing to do, and the reason why nobody does it is because nobody wants to answer the question of how long this has actually been in the population and who has been exposed to it.

The fact of the matter is we know that back in the early days of what is allegedly the pandemic, there were universities in California that were awkwardly finding evidence of what was being called SARS coronavirus in tissue predating patient one in China.[140] Then those efforts were all shut down.

We know that any frozen tissue at any tissue bank, which means any blood sample, could be easily tested for the existence of what we are calling this particular spike protein fragment—and you'd find a relatively high population that has the circulating fragments of coronavirus in tissue samples going back for years. Remember, this disease called COVID-19 is the first and only disease that has ever been invented that has no differential diagnosis. This is a diagnosis by committee. There is no lab test. There is no standard test.

There is nothing that actually says you have COVID, and the reason why is because an enormous amount of people who test positive for the fragment of spike protein have no symptoms. And then a lot of people who have symptoms don't test positive for the fragment of the spike protein, so this is not a causal situation at all.

COVID-19 is a statistical terror campaign. It has nothing to do with any reality, and the spike protein is a weapon and we need to see it through that lens. When you create a weapon and you unleash it on a population, there is no question that the intended outcome is the death of people. If you go back and look at the WHO's global preparedness board document from its vaccine decade preparedness program—which the Gates Foundation, the China CDC, NIAID, the Welcome Trust, and others published in 2011—their goal was a 15 percent reduction in population by 2020, and they even said that was through vaccination programs.[141]

QUESTION: Are you saying this was about herd thinning, not herd immunity?

MARTIN: No question. It was a requirement to reduce the population, and everybody since roughly the year 2000 has signed on to that. You can't achieve immunity with a patented biological weapon that is infectious but replication defective. You have to go back to their own language. Infectious means you get sick. Replication defective means it doesn't transfer to other people. You can't back this into a community health virology storyline that goes awry. This is actually architected to achieve an outcome.

QUESTION: Does this explain why years later there are still people getting sick with this, or does that have to do with the vaccine?

MARTIN: The people who are getting sick and dying are the people getting either the shots or the swabs. You don't get sick and die from a normal, healthy population wandering around doing normal, healthy things. You get sick and die when you are constantly being exposed to having things shoved up your nose, or being exposed to an enormous number of settings where the distribution of the pathogen is being released, which explains the deaths among the injected. The point is proven by the fact that it wasn't until the alleged vaccine trials began that we started seeing excess deaths. Going into the first two quarters of 2020, no life insurance company on earth actually reported excess claims being made. It wasn't until the injection clinical trials got started that we started seeing excess deaths.

QUESTION: If indeed this was purposefully deployed, then what was the purpose of masks and lockdowns?

MARTIN: That's super easy. In April of 2020, so well into the alleged pandemic, the *Journal of the American Medical Association* on its cover page specifically said that a healthy population should not wear face masks at all.[142] The only double-blind clinical trials done on face mask wearing said that influenza-like illness *increased* with mask wearing. So, the only reason you put masks on is to incentivize a population to take the shot and then take the mask off. That was the whole intent.

The mask was the symbol of the terror campaign. If you go back to the early part of the summer of 2021, that was very much the case in cartoons and advertisements and all kinds of other things. "Get the shot and ditch the mask" was kind of the mantra. This was a behavior modification technique. This had nothing to do with health.

There is no question there has been zero evidence in any study ever that says there has been a respiratory transmission case of SARS coronavirus. Thus, the idea of wearing a face mask for something that has never been established as a respiratory pathogen is a rather critical thing to point out, just like when CDC initially tried telling us to wear face masks for monkeypox in June 2022.[143] Monkeypox in most instances comes from direct sexual contact from homosexual men. I'm not going out on a limb to say a face mask won't protect you from a disease spread through gay sex.

This was the fulfillment of a lot of studies on behavior modification techniques, and how you introduce fear into the population.[144] It's the slow rollout of interventions. First, don't travel. Then, stay at home for a few weeks. Wearing masks was part of an architected plan for cognitive dissonance and behavior modification. It is all psychological warfare. It was about studying how to influence people and then executing a plan for that influence. The more cognitive dissonance you put into a person, the more willing they are to say yes to anything.

QUESTION: Let's go back to the COVID vaccines. When did the research on the shots really begin?

MARTIN: Pfizer's first patent on the spike protein coronavirus vaccine was filed way back on November 14, 1990 (US Patent 6,372,224), which is more than a decade before the first SARS.[145] On this particular pathogen, the first development of the injectable form happened mysteriously two days after the CDC filed its aforementioned patent on April 25, 2003.[146]

So, the CDC allegedly invented the SARS genome on April 25, and then a mere two days later, a patent was filed by Sequoia Pharmaceuticals on the vaccine for SARS.[147] If you believe that, I've got a bridge in a swamp to sell you.

QUESTION: Did Moderna piggyback off that work?

MARTIN: Oh, yes. Moderna is distributed and set up as the outgrowth of a ten-year National Science Foundation (NSF) grant that was called—I kid you not—Darwinian Chemical

Systems.[148] That grant was specific to identifying ways you could get RNA, and specifically mRNA, to transfect a genome so you could actually inject mRNA into a cell and change the genome of that cell. For a decade, from 2000 to 2010, that work was financed by the NSF, and in 2010, a set of alleged venture capitalists—who, by the way, no one had ever heard of before, and no one has been able to establish where their money actually came from—formed Moderna.[149] They filed patents on the mRNA technology actually months before the company itself was even started!

This was a setup from the get-go.

QUESTION: Are you suggesting all the pharma companies marketing vaccines for this pathogen knew about the development of this as a bioweapon for many years?

MARTIN: Welcome Trust knew about it because they were part of the campaign since 2011. Pfizer obviously had the largest patent portfolio. Jansen Pharmaceuticals acquired a lot of the early SARS vaccine patents predating the MERS outbreak in 2012 and consolidated a bunch of the spike protein vaccine patents from 2003 to 2008.

The reason everyone knew about it was because when President Trump went to sign the executive order for the Operation Warp Speed vaccine development program, everybody knew that just a day earlier the global preparedness monitoring board at the WHO had said we were going to have a worldwide exercise in the development of a vaccine for an "accidental or deliberate" release of "high-impact respiratory pathogens."[150]

QUESTION: What's the endgame here?

MARTIN: The endgame is ultimately gene editing. COVID is just to get the camel's nose under the tent. You go back to Dolly the Sheep and all the other gene modification technology that was slow rolled over the last decade and a half, the Catholic Church and most evangelical Christians were opposed to it, and most relatively rational human beings were also opposed to the idea of letting people in lab coats engineer humans. This is about gene-editing humans, not getting people treated for alleged pandemic diseases.

That can be for a lot of things. Moderna has a mRNA vaccine platform for what they call opioid addiction. There's an army clinical trial right now for a vaccine for breast cancer avoidance. Among the crowd that Fauci has assembled, there is very strong interest in a world entirely dependent on a chemically engineered vaccine platform. This is to be injected at birth, and then humans will be dependent upon it for the rest of their lives.

This is about getting you hooked into an edited genome to change human experience. Recently, they've been saying this entire exercise is about getting us ready to be rapidly adapted to meet the challenges of climate change and dietary changes. This is a worldview that says humans need to be mechanically evolved faster to adapt to the changing conditions, and the way you do it is to get them dependent on editing their genes in real time.

QUESTION: You understand that what you are describing is extremely—and existentially—sinister stuff, right?

MARTIN: I don't know how else you can say with a straight face that through vaccines, in a decade, we are going to reduce the population 15 percent. That statement says we are going to kill seven hundred fifty million people. Those are the WHO's published objectives in their vaccines publication. And that's signed off on by everybody who is on the WHO board.

QUESTION: Where does Wuhan fit into this?

MARTIN: In 2013, they uploaded what was reportedly a gene sequence called WIV1, which was allegedly a SARS-like virus.[151] The University of North Carolina made a recombinant expression of that virus in 2014, funded by NIAID and amplified by it for the two years of the gain-of-function moratorium. By 2016, they announced to the world that WIV1 spike protein modified recombinant chimeric alteration of the virus was "poised for human emergence." [152]

Wuhan is allegedly where the sample was uploaded and copied into the bioweapons program. The head of the Wuhan lab was the former head of the Chinese bioweapons program.

QUESTION: How much of a coincidence is it that the only therapeutic that got approved early on to treat the virus in patients, remdesivir, happened to also have been developed by the same lab at the University of North Carolina?[153]

MARTIN: Baric, the patent holder, made the weapon and he made the alleged cure you're referring to. Fifty-three percent of the Ebola patients it was given to wound up dying.[154]

QUESTION: When the media started showing images in Wuhan of people collapsing, and then a couple of weeks later the panic coming to Lombardy and New York, you are saying there is a significant number of high-level individuals in our government who knew exactly what was going on?

MARTIN: They weren't befuddled at all. This thing was organized. When you publish that a weapon is poised for human emergence in 2016, and then are shocked it emerges, you are an idiot.

QUESTION: Lest someone reads this and thinks you are addressing this only speculatively, you have actually directly engaged in this battle, including in the legal arena, have you not?

MARTIN: I was sent by the U.S. government to be a biological weapons inspector in 2003 to Slovenia, and then to Tehran in 2005 for the National Bioengineering Summit for Biological and Chemical Weapons manufacturers. I've been doing this for two decades. The reason I can cite all of this without looking at a single note is because it's not just research, but I've been a physical witness of these weapons programs. When anthrax was allegedly released, I was the one who pointed out the fact the army had purchased three hundred million doses of ciprofloxacin in May before the "attack" in September 2001 (the FBI later named an army microbiologist, Bruce Edwards Ivins, as its prime suspect in those attacks[155]).

Regarding COVID, my company was hired to help with the initiative that ended the face mask ordinance on airplanes. And then we did a case in Utah concerning the legality of using

a deceptive term like "vaccine" to promote a public health outcome, when the injection doesn't actually provide any public
health need response. It only allegedly lessens the likelihood
of severe illness or need for hospitalization if infected. It is not
a public health police powers vaccine. It is an elective medical
procedure, so given the fact there has been a misrepresentation
of the use of the term "vaccination," and given the fact it is a
willful act, that is a Class 3 felony in Utah. The government's
response to defend itself from our case is the admission of that
felony, which is why we did it in Utah. The attorney general
is actually compelled to act against a felony admitted by the
federal government.

Which means I'm not just idly or recklessly speculat-
ing here. I've taken the knowledge and documentation I
have regarding COVID-19 and applied it successfully in a
court of law.

**QUESTION: Who do you believe needs to be held respon-
sible for all of this?**

MARTIN: The direct perpetrators who implemented this
plan were Peter Daszak, Ralph Baric, Anthony Fauci, and
former secretary of Health and Human Services Alex Azar.
Those are the four perpetrators who have blood dripping
off their hands. If you take a step back and say they were
funded by other people, then you have the Welcome Trust,
the Gates Foundation, the Open Philanthropy Foundation,
and EcoHealth Alliance. At the end of the day, the core to the
story is that the WHO has been a captive agency since 1952,
which is when Harry Truman signed the executive order that
actually gave the WHO the directive to control the surgeon

general of the United States. Since then, we have been living in a state controlled by the pharmaceutical industry.[156]

QUESTION: How do we protect against this with so many agencies and organizations involved?

MARTIN: You have to have the people informed. We have had a highly corrupt drug-dealing structure that has been far more dangerous than the military-industrial complex. The pharma-industrial complex is far bloodier and damaging. People must wake up to the fact that health care writ large since the 1930s has been chemical drug dealers. When you have drug dealers running a country, you get what we are currently living with. There are a lot of people who just don't want to look at the fact that in the United States, we have been running an active eugenics program for that long. In the 1930s and 1940s, there were headlines asking why we don't manage human populations with the same level of discipline that farmers use to manage their cattle. There's nothing new under the sun. This sinister movement has been around for a while.

I've been pursuing a racketeering and antitrust angle from the beginning because it blows up the shield of immunity for vaccine manufacturers. I want that ended immediately. There should never be any immunity for making a product that kills people. Ever. Until that crime is busted, we can go after the individual hitmen and probably take down some pretty important people. But again, until the blanket immunity is ended, we haven't really accomplished anything. We need to get the public behind the erasure of the liability protection. That's the only way we come out of this alive for ourselves and our future generations.

CHAPTER 20

Vera Sharav: "Never Again" is Now

A s time goes on, there are fewer and fewer people alive who survived the terror of the Third Reich and the Holocaust. Vera Sharav is one of those few remaining gems and she has an enduring lesson for the world: Nazism is not just a specific group of people at a specific time in history. It is a mindset, and she is warning that its legacy is alive and well among the oligarchy ruling what was once concerned enlightened democracies.

Vera was just a young girl when she and her parents were taken to a Nazi prison camp in Romania. Her father died of an illness he contacted in the camp, and she was separated from her mother for years. Luckily, she was able to escape to what is today modern Israel, and eventually immigrated to the U.S. when she was ten.

Different survivors chose an assortment of postwar paths based on the lessons they learned from the genocide they lived through. For Vera, the lessons were quite clear—Auschwitz didn't begin with Auschwitz and the final solution. It began with the mix of scientism, public health nationalism, lack of informed consent, technocratic government authoritarianism, and the elevation of corporate supremacy over individual rights.

It is for this reason she founded the Alliance for Human Research Protection, which is an organization dedicated to upholding the humanitarian values and ethical standards of medicine enshrined in the Hippocratic Oath and the Nuremberg Code. In order to ensure that "Never Again" is more than a hollow slogan, Sharav set out to educate the public on ethical breaches in the principles of informed consent and medical experiments on human beings long before COVID fascism came to life.

Sharav believes that we must understand the underlying ideology and political and ethical framework within the medical community that allowed the Third Reich to grow and eventually culminate with the Final Solution. In order to understand the relevance of the Third Reich to the current discrimination, public health fascism, and unbridled human experimentations (and why we are facing an even more technologically dangerous "Fourth Reich"), we call Vera Sharav to the stand—one of the few remaining people who can speak to the past, present, and future of public health fascism in so-called enlightened countries.

· · · · · · ·

QUESTION: A lot of people recoil from any analogy drawn from the Third Reich, the 1930s, the Nazi regime, and the scientism that they pursued for, in their view, the benefit of public health. As a survivor of the Holocaust who came to

America to escape such horror, what would you say to those people who think such comparisons aren't justified?

SHARAV: The parallels are all too evident. They have to do with the prelude, or the steps that led up to the Holocaust, because it didn't just begin overnight. What is interesting about the children who are being sacrificed now to the Pfizer/Moderna mass injection regime is that the first murder victims of the Nazi regime were German infants and young children under the age of three. Their crime was that they weren't perfect. They were in some way disabled. And the whole public health system was geared toward rounding them up.

At birth, midwives would report the birth of a child who wasn't perfect to the state and it went up the ladder. Doctors were the ones who selected those children whom they deemed unworthy of life. The children were taken away from their parents and they were told their children would receive special treatment to improve their condition.

The special treatment was medical murder.

Some children, before they died, were actually used in starvation experiments, so the doctors could record how long a baby or child would survive without nutrition. What made it possible was the mindset of eugenics, which aims to clear the genetic pool of those they deem unfit. This program expanded to the disabled of all ages. The mentally ill were cleared out of the asylums and the last group were the residents of nursing homes.

Hospitals became state-sanctioned murder ventures. They tested their methods for killing, including Zyklon B for the gas chambers. At a certain point, it had to go underground because when it reached the nursing home group, there was a fuss from the citizenry, but it continued until 1945. When you listen now to some of the people on the advisory committee to the FDA, it is absolutely chilling how disaffected they are about condemning children to death or irreparable damage via the COVID vaccine for absolutely no potential benefit.

There is absolutely no justification whatsoever to expose children to these experimental injections. Children have been proven to be largely unaffected by COVID. So why are they pushing these injections? One possible reason is that it is becoming clear to people that there is no longer an emergency—if ever there really was one—which means that emergency use authorization is essentially illegal.

But the only way the manufacturers could continue to be indemnified from liability for harm is if the CDC puts these injections on the children's vaccine schedule. It is on the backs of the babies that they are trying to maintain their immunity from liability. This is sadly where our society has come to.

QUESTION: Can you take us back to the beginning of your story and how you escaped the Nazis and survived?

SHARAV: I was three and a half when we were deported. All children in such crises develop and grow far beyond their years. I observed a lot. One of the things that was very common in the concentration camps was that although I wasn't in a death camp, death was always around. The fear of being put on a list to be sent to a death camp was constant. In the camp where I was detained, we were left to starve. Under these circumstances, you are left to exist in a subhuman condition.

I lost my father before I was five and I blamed myself for his death. When we were deported, we had to cross a river on a rickety boat and there was fear it would tip over because there were too many people on it. So, my father took off his coat and dropped it into the river. When he died, I was sure it was because he dropped his coat and subsequently got sick from the cold, but I held on to my little toy. Then my mother got wind of a rescue operation in 1944 when they were getting ready to liquidate all the camps. She lied to save my life and registered me as an orphan.

I then spent about ten months as a child without parents. I had to learn how to assess people and whom I could trust to take care of me. I had to *choose*. One of the horrors I remember from that trip is one time we were allowed to get off the train to relieve ourselves. This one girl who was older than the rest of us found a baby in the ditch and she brought it with her back to the train, but the guards wouldn't let her. They beat her off the train with the baby. I was horrified because I knew they would both die.

A lot of such buried memories have come up during this COVID horror. I befriended a family on the train. The ultimate destination was Israel before it was a state. When we got to a harbor city in Romania, there were three small boats waiting for us. I was assigned to the boat with all the orphaned children, but I absolutely refused. Everybody embarked and I was left alone crying my heart out, but I would not budge.

Miraculously, they gave in to me and let me stay with the family I had befriended. The first night out at sea—and I didn't witness this horror because I was asleep—a submarine torpedoed the boat with all of the children on it. There were no survivors. I was supposed to be on that boat.

I didn't say a word the next morning when I found out, but I thought that I had been right not to listen to *authority*. So now as an adult, I certainly hold on to that determination of mine to trust my own instinct—my own informed consent—and not simply to always comply. This whole COVID nightmare would not be happening if people would not comply. If you are a free human being, you have to exercise your freedom.

None of the restrictions during COVID have had anything to do with protecting people's health. On the contrary, they have done the opposite and the evidence is piling up. The countries that have the highest rates of vaccinated people are having the highest rates of sickness and death. It is hard for them to hide it anymore. There are the children, the young men with myocarditis, and the lost pregnancies. This is essentially the worst crime against humanity ever, because this is targeting the entire global human population, not just one group of people or country.

Hitler was helped by a whole slate of corporate allies. American corporations. German corporations. Swiss corporations. U.K. bankers. He was bankrolled with the means to conduct the war and the genocide. Although something unique happened at the end of the war with the Nuremberg trials, it was only a few of the criminals who were tried. Most of the others continued to expand their plots and perfect their methodology.

We've had plenty of hints about this global objective of control. They want the natural resources, the financial resources, and the human resources. Slavery was a very big business during the Holocaust. The most visible leader of the World Economic Forum, Klaus Schwab, had a father whose business relied on slave labor.[157] It's all just a continuing thread.

Most of the perpetrators during the war moved on and many went to the United States. More than 1,600 Nazi scientists and doctors went to the United States with their families.[158] They spread what they did across hospitals and academic institutions and the military. What I'm suggesting is that Germany lost WWII, but the Nazis did not. They have essentially been thriving.

QUESTION: They say the road to hell is paved with good intentions. When you came to America from the camps after losing your father and being separated from your mother for a long period of time, you knew that Auschwitz didn't start with Auschwitz. It was this medical scientism and public health supremacism that was elevated over individual compassion and care and informed consent. Do you feel we are living through that nightmare again?

SHARAV: Until now, I've talked about the uniqueness of the Holocaust compared with other genocides. We had a lot of other genocides in the twentieth century, but none of the others relied so heavily on the medical establishment. That's what we have now. Just like we had in Germany. Without the medical establishment, those babies would not be subjected to what is coming with endless mass therapeutic experiments. The medical establishment gives the veneer of legitimacy to mass murder.

QUESTION: What are some of the tools you see used the last few years that echo or parallel the tools for propaganda that were used by Germany in the 1930s to convince people that their demonic plans were for the betterment of humanity?

SHARAV: The initial weapon was to instill fear in the public with a constant barrage of propaganda. That's what we are living through now. People have been paralyzed by fear of an invisible virus and those who refuse the experimental injection, just like Jews, were demonized as spreaders of infectious disease. It was a lie then and it is a lie now.

QUESTION: One of the actions taken by many of these international governments is the forced lockdown whether you have the virus or not. We even had the camps in Australia and other countries like Canada had quarantine hotels. Then we had the crescendo with the Shanghai lockdowns. Could you describe your experience in the concentration camps when you were a very young child, and how you feel about drawing that parallel?

SHARAV: The first thing is the segregation and deportation. There were more than 4,000 camps of various kinds all over Europe. The main point was to uproot people. Most were not immediately thrown into the death camps. They were more like weigh stations and slave labor camps. We don't have the same thing right now, but it's just a matter of degree. Who knows what the next thing will be?

It happens with an accelerated elimination of civil and human rights and that is done in stages. What is especially disturbing is that the people who are not isolated or sent away look the other way. They pretend they don't see. And what we've seen during these lockdowns is the same kind of thing. People don't want to get involved. They are silent. They don't want to lose their lucrative jobs or respected positions of power. And it has been said over and over again by some of the most prominent Holocaust survivors that the worst crime was *silence*.

The silence of the onlookers got the Nazis to believe that nobody cared. They could just keep pushing the pace of what they were doing. The other thing that is similar to the Nazis today is the medical complicity with technology. Hitler could not have accomplished what he did without IBM. The IBM punch card system was the precursor to today's digital technology. What IBM provided was a conducted census in Germany and all over Europe that identified the Jews. This enabled the Nazis to uproot them, track them, surveil them, and strip them of their assets. If you've seen some of the people tattooed with brands on their arms, those were IBM identification numbers.[159]

IBM machines were stationed at death camps and IBM ran the trains to the death camps so they would arrive on schedule. This was an industrialized genocidal operation made possible by IBM, and IBM today is one of the major producers of digital ID for COVID.[160]

For these days, the vaccines are sort of phase one. What they are really after is for everyone to have a digital ID because that gives them full control where everyone will be a slave. They may have a chip inside the injections. We don't know what is in them. If they get that into your body, that's it, and they control you 24/7.

They aren't even keeping this a secret. One of their so-called philosophers, Yuval Harari, talks about it all the time, as does Pfizer CEO Albert Bourla.[161], [162] Their whole plan is to create transhumans. It is very diabolical and, in that sense, the culture of those planning and pushing all of this are today's Nazis.

Nazism isn't specifically German, or even a country; it's a mindset. They are monsters in human bodies but aren't anything like normal human beings. They have absolutely no empathy. They want to essentially annihilate all that is human in our civilization. They have the hubris to regard themselves as gods.[163]

QUESTION: People never want to believe that they are living in tragic turning points of history like what you are describing here. Pre–World War I, Germany was the most progressive, enlightened, educated, and wealthiest nation on earth. However, the generation that was born during that period would see Germany be the tip of the spear for not one, but two world wars by the time they were in their forties. A lot of Americans are struggling with the idea that such a thing could happen here, now that we are the most enlightened and prosperous nation on earth. Do you see any similar and ominous cultural indicators here in the U.S. that existed in Germany during that era?

SHARAV: The Germans didn't believe something like that was possible and the Jews didn't believe it, either. Until 1938, Jews could still leave Germany. That was five years into the regime, but most stayed until it was too late. When thirty-two countries met in Avion, France, to discuss the "Jewish question," they all decided they could not take in any more refugees. That's what gave Hitler the green light. There are a lot of complicit actors in this crime. The report of the Holocaust Commission to the president of the United States in 1979 warned that with population growth, the Nazi option to slaughter millions of people is real (or justified to curb the excess population).

What I am particularly upset about today is that there absolutely is this concerted effort to prevent anyone from going near the Holocaust and drawing comparisons, and that includes Jewish institutions. What they are doing by keeping the Holocaust out of conversations is making the Holocaust irrelevant when it is the *most* relevant historical episode. The one thing the victims wanted more than anything is for the world to remember so that it wouldn't happen again. They found diaries buried in the ground at Auschwitz written by those who were charged with getting the bodies to the crematorium. They knew that they had only so long to live and then they would be the ones sent there and others would come after them. They wanted a record of it. So those who are trying to prevent a discussion that raises an alarm so people can understand are doing a disservice.

This time it won't be gas chambers. It will be remote. Click, click. It's biotechnology now. That's the weapon of choice because it gives them total control. You really don't need atom bombs now.

QUESTION: Do you think one of the problems with people who talk about the Holocaust is that they diagnose it as an outcome of fascism, and so we need socialism in response or more centralization of power, when your message is that we actually need decentralization?

SHARAV: They actually toyed around with lockdowns back in 2003,[164] but there was a doctor who helped combat smallpox, D. A. Henderson, who actually had a track record of stopping this stuff, and he and others said absolutely no.[165] The worst thing you could do was stop the economy. You isolate only the sick. You don't disrupt life. But then with COVID, we proceeded to do just that. These public officials knew what they were doing. They are taking orders, too.

This has been a purposeful demolition of the economy, especially of the middle class and closing small businesses. They urged everyone to buy everything digitally because they want a digital currency. The worst thing for humanity to do is to give in to central control because that's what they want. The World Health Organization, the United Nations, the World Economic Forum, and the World Bank are all working together here in unison. This is their game. They are intent on eliminating nations and thus eliminating constitutions and constitutional rights. They really want to reduce us to animals. They are treating us as herds.

The trouble is that the education system from kindergarten on has been about training young people to trust authority and be compliant. That's why you are seeing all this obedience. People are even wearing masks where they are no longer required to by ordinance. They don't want to hear the truth. They *want* the controlled narrative. The Biden administration paid $1 billion for the media to only write positive things about the vaccines and they all marched in lockstep. It's not a conspiracy theory. All the leaders in the West have been training by the same script, and they all followed it during COVID. We don't really have elected leaders anymore.

This has been planned for a long time—ever since 1945. They didn't rest. And unfortunately, most of the people have been asleep. I thought they would be shocked and angry to be commanded to stay locked down when they were perfectly healthy. I would have thought Americans, in particular, would value their freedom much more. Yet the United States owns this particular catastrophe. The virus was produced in a lab that we paid for. We've got to undo that.

We were all prisoners. It is unbelievable when you think about it, especially when you know this was not a lethal disease for most people. It was lethal, though, when they put people on ventilators, and when they forbade doctors from prescribing FDA-approved medicine that had been used for decades with a long record of safety. Instead, people died from essentially medical murder.

In March and April of 2020, orders went out to hospitals in Western Europe, Canada, Australia, and at least five states in the United States not to treat the elderly. They were to be sent to nursing homes, where those who were infected would infect the others. It was a genocidal operation. Before Andrew Cuomo gave the order in New York, he predicted the virus in nursing homes would be like fire through dry grass—in other words, *he knew*. So, what happened to him? He made $5 million off a book and he got an Emmy Award.

QUESTION: What would you urge the people to do about this? What would today's Nuremberg Code need to be to put the *never* back in never again?

SHARAV: First of all, they should follow the Nuremberg Code, which is very unique because it emphasized that the individual human being takes precedence over the state. The ten principles essentially laid down what is permissible research with human beings and what is not. The medical establishment and pharma have not been abiding by it. They don't want to hear it. They have other plans.

They use those whom they regard as dispensable people: the mentally ill, prisoners, immigrants, and so on. It's all very dark. These businesses have only grown and a lot of it is under the radar. They have done experiments on mind control with surgical insertions. They have been tinkering on how to control us. Whenever you think something has been laid bare, it isn't. The plan was always to control a vast number of people without having to shoot them and that sort of thing. How to do it in a way where they have cover, both from the medical establishment and from government.

One of the things that most have a hard time trying to grasp is that there are truly, truly evil people. They can't imagine it. They can't imagine that doctors are laying out a vaccine protocol that is going to harm those babies like they voted on at the FDA committee. They don't imagine that those doctors really don't care about those children. A lot of those doctors will say, at best, that they didn't know. But a lot of the doctors, especially at the top, know all too well what they were doing. I've seen this all before.

People aren't listening, though. They are loath to believe that they have been lied to and completely misled. Just like it happened back then also. Some of the Jewish leadership even said Hitler didn't really mean what he said. But they were wrong.

CLOSING STATEMENT

L adies and gentlemen of the jury, from the very outset of
the trial contained in this book, you have been issued
two challenges.

First, obviously starting with a provocative title, *Rise of
the Fourth Reich*, which provokes a very strong reaction—even
among those of you that may have been the most willing to
hear and affirmatively respond to the testimony laid out in its
pages. Using the worst and most evil display of authoritarian
power this world has ever known as a reference point should
not be done cavalierly, let alone for mere rhetorical flourish.

However, and unfortunately, we strongly (and sadly) believe
the testimony contained within this tome reaches such depths
and is therefore a justifiable comparison. If anything, it could
be argued that what Covidstan, the "new normal" of fascistic
western governance, aims to accomplish here, if left unchecked,
might even be worse and here's why. When such authoritarian
evil is relegated to a singular nation-state, or even an axis or
empire, there will naturally be resistance to it. Even if such
resistance is only driven by rival nationalistic ambitions, and
nothing more altruistic, in some or most instances.

But what happens when the authoritarian evil transcends our natural competitions and nationalistic ambitions that would otherwise organically emerge to confront it? What happens when it exists outside our normal geopolitical ebbs and flows? Furthermore, how much havoc can such a power wreak when you can't declare war on it with your military? Or vote it out of office in the next election?

Even Hitler, in all his megalomania, tacitly acknowledged his own mortal limitations in arrogantly proclaiming his Third Reich would last 1,000 years.[166] On the other hand, what's at stake here is nothing less than a new, but technocratic, Dark Ages. An era where the Western civilization that raised humanity from that awful period is all but erased—as are its influences like the Enlightenment, the Reformation, and the American Revolution—and replaced with a transnational alliance of technological elites in both the public and private sector.

Elites who control your lives literally down to the last molecule—if not turn you into nothing but a molecule.

An era when not just individual liberty, but your individual bodily autonomy, are all but extinct. So, no, we don't think *Rise of the Fourth Reich* goes too far at all—though we wished it did. And ladies and gentlemen of the jury, we suspect you're at least open to agreeing with us, otherwise you wouldn't have made it this far into this book.

Which brings us to the second challenge before you, which you will decide after finishing our work. That challenge can be found in our subtitle: *Confronting Covid Fascism with a New Nuremberg Trial So It Never Happens Again.*

We are not a nation of laws, and never have been, but a nation of political will—and we always will be. Which means whatever you incentivize, or don't punish, you will get more of. Whatever tyranny you are willing to comply with will be imposed upon you. This is the very essence of the concept "government by the consent of the governed" mentioned in our Declaration of Independence. We get the very government we deserve.

We do not face an insurmountable army of millions of soldiers with bombs, bullets, and bayonets. If we are to continue allowing a select few evil billionaires and megalomaniac government officials control our ability to breathe freely and live without a biomedical supremacism and surveillance, then shame on us. As Sam Adams, father of the American Revolution, admonished,

> "The truth is, all might be free, if they valued freedom and defended it as they ought. Is it possible that millions could be enslaved by a few, which is a notorious fact, if all possessed the independent spirit of Brutus, who, to his immortal honor, expelled the proud tyrant of Rome and his royal and rebellious race? If, therefore, a people will not be free, if they have not virtue enough to maintain their liberty against a presumptuous invader, they deserve no pity, and are to be treated with contempt and ignominy."[167]

Therefore, we do not ask you merely for a guilty verdict. We ask you to *be the guilty verdict*. Fulfill the subtitle of this book as free men and women in a constitutional republic. Your elected officials will not act en masse to prevent such a tragedy from reoccurring or even taking permanent root without your, shall we say, "encouragement." In order to achieve the en masse of elected officials holding Covidstan's feet to the fire we need, we must first reach a critical mass among the people demanding justice.

Rest assured, reaching a guilty verdict in this trial is not a passive transaction. You cannot render your verdict, and then call it a day. Your work is just beginning if you do, for this is what self-government is all about, and self-government always begins with "self." Just as the Constitution begins with the words "we the people," so must the fulfillment of "never again."

At this point in our tribunal, if we did our job of telling and exposing the truth adequately, your blood is either boiling or clotting. But what are we prepared to do?

Clearly, what we are doing is not working, as the biomedical fascism continues unabated several years after basic science and learned experience repudiated every governmental action taken under the guise of fighting COVID. In our fight for medical freedom, this is our Haggai 1:5 moment: "You have planted much but harvested little. You eat but never have enough. You drink but never have your fill. You put on clothes but are not warm. You earn wages only to put them in a purse with holes in it."

Liberty will not restore itself. The "new normal" of COVID fascism will not revert to the God-ordained self-evident normal of human beings living free of external control, without taking affirmative action against the foundation that has been laid, burning it to the ground, and salting the earth above it. As Sam Adams warned those who initially wanted to avoid confrontation with the English Crown in the early 1770s, "If we are voluntarily silent as the conspirators would have us to be, it will be considered as an approbation of the change."[168]

In other words, it is time for us to up our game.

How can we emerge from the utter destruction of the past few years of Western governments regressing into pre-Enlightenment thinking without any plan of action to immunize ourselves from this disease of biomedical tyranny ever infecting us again? Just like after the Holocaust, when Western governments promised "never again," and established principles to guard against using human beings as lab rats, so too is it incumbent upon our generation to reaffirm certain ironclad principles and construct a legal firewall around these impregnatable principles. If we don't, we will sentence the next generation to even worse.

Sadly, we thought we already inoculated ourselves against such subhuman experimentation and denial of basic human rights seventy-five years ago. Along with the trials at Nuremberg to bring the perpetrators of the Final Solution to justice was a separate doctors' trial held in 1946–1947 to convict those who engaged in experiments for supposed medical purposes. Out of that trial was born an international standard of medical ethics under the newly-adopted Nuremberg Code, in order to make sure that such tortuous experiments would never be carried out under the guise of medicine and science again. And to guarantee that informed consent would serve as the North Star guiding future medical practice, experimentation, clinical trials, and pharmaceutical interventions.

At first glance, someone with only a cursory understanding of the Nazi regime and the Holocaust might be puzzled that there was such a need to adopt medical ethics after the Holocaust. After all, what do a couple of murderous concentration camp "doctors" who tied down starved and abused prisoners, and purposely murdered them, have to do with run-of-the-mill doctors, scientists, and pharmaceutical companies practicing medicine for the good of the general public? Weren't these "doctors" just as unmistakably murderous as the other twelve Nazis sentenced to death at the main trial for carrying out mass genocide? Why did the organizers of the Nuremberg tribunal need a separate, auxiliary trial a year later, rather than mixing them in with the original perpetrators of the Final Solution and the genocide at the concentration camps?

Indeed, they were part of the genocide of Jews, but the prosecutors behind the doctors' trial wanted to make sure that the world understood their actions and intentions were just as diabolical as those who commanded the concentration camps, because the doctors did have their public excuses and defenses.

The main defense of the twenty-three doctors prosecuted for murder was that they conducted, among other experiments, "high-altitude" and "freezing" experiments on prisoners at the Dachau concentration camp in order to help German pilots survive—and were even pivotal to helping U.S. pilots survive in the postwar era.[169] The defense brazenly articulated a view that the "good of the state" takes precedence over the individual. And they even cited, not without merit, the fact that Americans had conducted malaria experiments on prisoners.[170]

To that end, Nuremberg prosecutors wanted to ensure that for the rest of eternity, nobody in the medical field, even those with a legitimate rationale of ancillary benefits inherent in their experiments, could lay claim on another human being's life in order to supposedly save others for "the greater good." Which is why they didn't just create a Nuremberg Code to stop doctors from forcibly tying down patients and injecting them. They understood that in the future, there might be shades of relative gray, where scientists would be so obsessed to legitimately cure an ailment, they'd be willing to deny a patient's proper informed consent about the safety of the therapeutic they were experimenting with.

It's precisely for this reason they state in precept ten of the code: "During the course of the experiment the scientist in charge must be prepared to terminate the experiment at any stage, if he has probable cause to believe, in the exercise of the good faith, superior skill and careful judgment required of him, that a continuation of the experiment is likely to result in injury, disability, or death to the experimental subject."

Yet, if we fast-forward seventy-five years, our own government and medical establishment continued with the lockdowns, school closures, masking, remdesivir, and COVID shots long after it was apparent they needed to be terminated and that the grand human experiment was all pain and no gain.

Brigadier General Telford Taylor, the chief prosecutor at the doctors' trial, stressed in his opening statement, this was "no mere murder trial," because the defendants were physicians who were "exceptionally qualified to form a moral and professional judgment" and who had sworn to "do no harm" pursuant to the Hippocratic Oath.[171]

"It is our deep obligation to all peoples of the world to show why and how these things happened," observed Taylor in his opening statement on December 9, 1946. "It is incumbent upon us to set forth with conspicuous clarity the ideas and motives which moved these defendants to treat their fellow men as less than beasts. The perverse thoughts and distorted concepts which brought about these savageries are not dead. They cannot be killed by force of arms. They must not become a spreading cancer in the breast of humanity."

Taylor's point was that one can fight a murderous army with an equally dedicated military. But how do you fight scientism and biomedical authoritarianism whereby the medical field, working with the state, convinces people that some people deserve less life and that anything and everything goes when it comes to the achievement of scientific, medical, and public health goals—unless it is rooted out legally and intellectually from society, law, and the body politic? General Patton might have been able to defeat the Panzer tanks in battle, but his military success alone could not eradicate the ideology the Nazis were fighting for.

Taylor's concern was not just punishing the Nazis but also ensuring that our own Western societies wouldn't learn from that behavior—perhaps not in a concentration camp but through more subtle means. Hence, Taylor was not only concerned with what the Nazis did in the 1940s in places like Auschwitz and Dachau, but what he witnessed in the lead-up to the Final Solution during the 1930s. That's when the German medical profession played a prominent role in sanitizing the demonic behavior within an otherwise civilized people.

That we have megalomaniac politicians in Western democracies willing to sacrifice lives for power, control, and greed is unfortunately not unprecedented. What is unprecedented, however, is how through COVID, such evil was able to transcend borders and national politics to encompass nearly the entirety of the West just as it once plunged Germany into the Third Reich. With the majority of doctors and the broader medical profession clapping along like trained seals as they enforced this potent zeal and cruelty.

Our entire set of bioethics in modern America is built off the principles of the Nuremberg Code born out of the horrific discoveries during the 1946–1947 Nuremberg doctors' trial. Except those principles were vitiated—anywhere from ignored during a panic to blatantly abrogated during COVID. This marks an eerie return to the darkest ethos of the Third Reich–era doctors and scientists. If we ever hope to reclaim our humanity, there must be a reckoning for the medical profession that not only partnered with but pioneered the Fourth Reich regime of coerced human experimentation, denial of lifesaving care, discrimination against those with disabilities, and the elevation of a medical/scientific authoritarianism over the most basic human rights.

That one should conclude from the Holocaust a person must not be strapped down and physically injected was obvious to the Greatest Generation. What they wanted to craft was a set of ethics that would create an enlightened consent among the public, so they couldn't be manipulated or brainwashed into an experiment, much less threatened, discriminated against, and coerced—either physically or via loss of livelihood and access to public freedoms—into placing a medical device on or in their person. After all, fascism is not initially advertised as barbarism, but as a beacon of hope for bettering the lives of the public as a whole. With such lofty goals as the guiding light of these policies, the leaders of the Nuremberg trials understood that history could repeat itself, and the people could be blinded into supporting barbarism, in pursuit of "perfecting" humanity.

As of this writing, Canadians who didn't get the unsafe and ineffective shots must still drive thousands of miles across their country to see a loved one because they are barred from airplanes. Americans in many parts of the country are still denied organ transplants for not getting the shots regardless of their personal circumstances, risks, and potential benefits from the shots. It is that sort of coercion they wanted to nip in the bud at Nuremberg, and not just for Germany but for the rest of the world.

In crafting a set of medical ethics, General Taylor wrote a memorandum on April 15, 1947, establishing that not only should medical experiments be voluntary in a legal sense, but in an intellectual and social sense as well. "This requires specifically the absence of duress, sufficient disclosure on the part of the experimenter and sufficient understanding on the part of the experimental subject of the exact nature and consequences of the experiment for which he volunteers, to permit an enlightened consent," he wrote.[172]

Decades later, our government has regressed to pre-Enlightenment thinking by openly opposing such framework for an informed consent. In a March 2022 paper coauthored by Dr. Anthony Fauci's wife, Christine Grady (who heads the Department of Bioethics at the National Institutes of Health Clinical Center), she defended the practice of "pressuring employees to get vaccinated" and "embarrass[ing] vaccine resistors."

"Individuals who choose to make the workplace less safe for others through their vaccine refusal should be able to foresee the possibility of this kind of social consequence," wrote Grady along with three other authors.[173] They mention "stigma and ostracization" as potential social consequences.

Meanwhile, they never explain how one could make the workplace less safe if the people who think the COVID shots work have the shots themselves. After all, how can one blame the unvaccinated for failing to protect the vaccinated by not getting the protection that failed to protect the protected?

That is broadly the punchline of the Nuremberg doctors' trial. There is never such a scientific rationale, or moral justification, to assert that person A must take an affirmative action against his body, lest he somehow harm person B who has the same prerogative to take that prophylactic if he so chooses. And even if that person initially agrees, precept nine of the Nuremberg Code notes that he can always withdraw: "During the course of the experiment the human subject should be at liberty to bring the experiment to an end if he has reached the physical or mental state where continuation of the experiment seems to him to be impossible."

The Nazi-era doctors didn't go from zero to one hundred—or from compassionately caring for patients to torturing them in a concentration camp—overnight. Throughout the 1930s, the government promoted a sort of medical authoritarianism and imbued it into the medical field, using national health goals to desensitize doctors to the humanity of the individual patient and acculturating scientists to a culture of the ends justifying the means. It revolved around sacrificing certain *individuals* for the betterment of the state, science, and *public* health. Public health was not just incidental to the Third Reich, but one of the lead ships in their armada of dehumanization and genocide.

Robert N. Proctor, professor of the history of science at Stanford University, noted in his seminal work, *Racial Hygiene: Medicine under the Nazis*, that physicians were seven times more likely to join the SS than German males from other professions.[174] Between the Nuremberg Laws on racial hygiene, euthanasia, and forced sterilization, doctors were groomed into the belief of settled enlightened science being harnessed for the betterment of society.

Indeed, throughout the early twentieth century, Germany was the center of many legitimate medical and scientific breakthroughs while becoming perhaps the most enlightened, progressive, and prosperous nation on earth. This gave mainstream doctors the false sense of the superiority of science, which led to almost treating it as an article of faith. Even before the onset of the Nazis, benevolent authoritarian notions were popular in a nation with such a proud national heritage. Therefore, it didn't take much longer for the Nazis to get them to serve society at large and not the individual patient.

In his book *The Nazi War on Cancer*, Professor Proctor explains the scientific and medical landscape under the Third Reich as follows:[175]

"We know that physicians joined the Nazi party in very large numbers, that about sixty percent of all biologists joined the party, and that roughly eighty percent of all professors of anthropology—most of whom were physicians—were members. We know that the Nazi regime maintained a large medical surveillance capacity, as part of its program to 'improve the strength of the German nation'; we know that there is a curious blend of the modem and the romantic in Nazi culture—a

RISE OF THE FOURTH REICH

blend Jeffrey Herf has characterized as 'reactionary modernism.'"

Again, in examining the backdrop of the Holocaust, Proctor notes how the most genocidal ideology arose not out of the primitive and gruesome tribal warfare in the undeveloped parts of Africa, but in the most scientifically advanced and enlightened society of western Europe. "Part of our story has to be understood in light of the fact that Nazism took root in the world's most powerful scientific culture, boasting half of the world's Nobel Prizes and a sizable fraction of the world's patents. German science and medicine were the envy of the world, and it was to Germany—the 'land of scholars and poets'—that many academic hopefuls flocked to cut their scientific teeth."

Even those not quite as steeped in the intellectual sciences but more in the care and compassion side of medicines, such as nurses, also played a vital role. As the National Holocaust Memorial Museum relates:

> "Many nurses who did not necessarily support the Nazi regime still implemented its discriminatory and murderous policies through the course of their regular, daily work. Engaging with patients more frequently and directly than doctors, nurses were often the ones who actually applied the regime's medical policies. Nurses played a central role in the regime's so-called 'euthanasia' program. Under the program, roughly 250,000 children and adults with mental and physical disabilities

325

were murdered. They were killed by starvation, lethal injection, or gassing."[176]

We have presented eyewitness testimony in this book demonstrating how our government-medical-industrial complex has imbued this same malevolent mentality into the minds of so many mainstream doctors and nurses. If someone doesn't join the experiment, they are subhuman, don't deserve proper care, and in fact deserve to die.

We need not imagine how we could relapse into a eugenics mindset and follow that slippery slope to the gates of hell even in a supposedly civilized country. If it could happen to the Germany of the early twentieth century, perhaps the greatest nation in the world at that time, it can certainly happen to the America of the early twenty-first century.

It's actually far more likely that tragic relapse has already occurred. Absent a reaffirmation of the Nuremberg Code and numerous new laws, policies, patients' rights proclamations, and bioethics codes, it will only continue to get worse.

Proof of such an assertion can be found by our legal system already unanimously adopting a eugenics-era decision of *Jacobson v. Massachusetts* to justify state power to control your body under the guise of public health.[177] Jacobson gave rise to the infamous *Buck v. Bell* decision in 1927, which greenlit forced sterilization.[178] As Justice Oliver Wendall Holmes infamously wrote for the majority at the time:

> We have seen more than once that the public welfare may call upon the best citizens for their lives. It would be strange if it could not call upon those who already sap the strength

of the State for these lesser sacrifices, often
not felt to be such by those concerned, in
order to prevent our being swamped with
incompetence. It is better for all the world,
if instead of waiting to execute degenerate
offspring for crime, or to let them starve for
their imbecility, society can prevent those who
are manifestly unfit from continuing their
kind. The principle that sustains compulsory
vaccination is broad enough to cover cutting
the Fallopian tubes. *Jacobson v. Massachusetts*,
197 U. S. 11. Three generations of imbeciles
are enough.[179]

Notice how immediately before declaring "three generations of imbeciles are enough," that Holmes cites *Jacobson*.
Just know that this is the decision currently being used to
allow governments to do anything and everything to our bodies, without even having to provide evidence of safety, efficacy, and lack of alternatives. Instead, when we demanded to
know where the data was justifying such action, or demonstrating that it's even accomplishing its professed purpose, we
were slavishly told to "trust the experts." During such coer-
cive times, it's only about a five-minute walk from "trust the
experts" to "just following orders."

People often bristle when you draw upon the Nazi comparison to describe what has transpired with COVID fascism. They believe that genocidal fascism is somehow limited
only to the state targeting a particular race or ethnicity. But
fascism doesn't have to always be rooted in race. *Merriam-
Webster* defines fascism as "a political philosophy, movement,

or regime (such as that of the Fascisti) that exalts nation and often race above the individual, and that stands for a centralized autocratic government headed by a dictatorial leader, severe economic and social regimentation, and forcible suppression of opposition."[180]

This is exactly what we are seeing in Western countries via COVID today. It's not a matter of targeting any one race but creating a standard of national interests and proclaiming that anyone who doesn't subscribe to those interests—even if they affect one's body in the most intimate way—is a threat to the nation and needs to be segregated, discriminated against, persecuted, and suppressed.

It's not about equal-opportunity authoritarianism, because it is directed solely at those who don't fit the national standards. Thus, we are witnessing the worst influx of illegal immigration and domestic crime precisely during the time of the most heavy-handed authoritarianism against "some" citizens. This is anarchy mixed with tyranny.

Furthermore, at the same time we suffered from the most autocratic stay-at-home order of all time—to the point that people couldn't properly bury their grandparents with even a modest funeral—we experienced the greatest ubiquitous mass gatherings in history through BLM protests and riots.[181] At the same time that hospitals can deny kidney transplants to those without the shots, Catholic hospitals are being forced to offer castration operations.[182] At a time when schools can expel a student for not covering his breathing or getting the shots, the school is sanctioned from preventing men from entering female bathrooms.[183]

Hence, you are either with the total state and the spirit of the age or you are against them. Nothing less than total submission and compliance will be tolerated, and anything less is considered opposition. And yes, if you are against them, you as may as well be a Jew in Nazi Germany. Nazism doesn't have to be born out of a subhuman regard for one particular race; it can also target a behavior or those who make certain medical, social, or political choices. The goal here is the isolation of "the other" with the intent of later banishing/extincting them. Such evil is unfortunately not unique in human history, it's just unique in our modern age to see it manifested so clearly through political and public institutions like the Nazis did in Germany.

Or like the COVID fascists did throughout Western democracies such as our own.

Thankfully, we had enough pre-existing freedom to eventually force it to de-escalate to some extent before it fulfilled its intended hegemony. But rest assured, malignant tumors left untreated always become a full-blown metastatic cancer—and full-blown cancers once thought to be in remission can return and even spread.

They did this once under the guise of "science"; if permitted they will do it again.

At the time this book was being written, many of the accoutrements of modernity had returned to Western democracies such as our own. But the underlying cancer had not been irradiated. It lingers beneath the surface, waiting for the right time to return and devastate our bodies once more. It uses even obscure ailments such as monkeypox, which is spread only sexually by a scant percentage of the population, to continue its never-ending stream of fearmongering and panic porn. For if a people are perpetually conditioned to live in fear, they can at any strategic point be driven to completely give themselves over to it provided the right malady comes along.

Indeed, the original foundation for biomedical tyranny and eugenics was partially born out of Hitler's own paranoia for diseases. Michael Kater, professor of history at the Centre for German and European Studies at York University in Toronto, proves persuasively in his book, *Doctors Under Hitler*, that "physicians became Nazified more thoroughly and much sooner than any other profession."[184] Professor Proctor posits with regard to the biocratic authoritarianism permeating German in the 1930s, "One could well argue that the Nazis were not, properly speaking, abusing the results of science, but rather were merely putting into practice what doctors and scientists themselves had initiated."[185]

Perforce, what the bioethicists and prosecutors at Nuremberg were trying to preempt was not just the rare doctor who would physically torture a patient on purpose at Auschwitz or Dachau, but the entire culture of scientific supremacism and medical authoritarianism predominating over individual care and compassion that infested the German medical field for a generation.

It is that same sort of trial—and subsequent inoculation in ethics, policy, and law—that we must reaffirm in our times. There would be an urgent need to reaffirm human and bodily rights following the events of the past few years, even if the American and global leaders issued a full-throated repudiation of their past actions. But the reality is that they think they did nothing wrong and plan to do it again. Aside from the Florida governor, dangerously few politicians in either of America's political parties have issued a categorical opposition to any future mass quarantines, masking, discrimination based on medical choices, and use of experimental therapeutics without liability, oversight, and transparency.

In easing some or most of the restrictions, most political leaders merely stated it was time to move on, that the "restrictions" were no longer needed, or that the fatality rate of this particular virus didn't justify the ongoing damage. But the notion that all these policies are illegal, immoral, illogical, and inhumane? Never addressed, which means "never again" will last until the right circumstance presents itself once more. And we'll again see most American politicians, regardless of political affiliation, fall for the next iteration of the biomedical state long before Pfizer can concoct its next magical potion. And if this can happen in America, where there is still some semblance of belief in liberty, imagine how quickly the rest of the world could fall back into barbarism.

Remember, lockdowns, rationing, discrimination, and deeming people unessential are tools that, once legitimized, will not necessarily be limited to pandemics. In June 2022, Sri Lanka used force to block "nonessential" vehicles from accessing fuel as they experienced an economic and debt crisis.[186] French cities banned outdoor gatherings during a heat wave in that same month.[187] Once governments were told by the scientism false prophets that using these barbaric tools was not just permissible in an enlightened world but even imperative and lifesaving, they will never find bitter the taste of such forbidden fruit.

As founding father George Clinton, the very first governor of New York and fourth vice president of the United States, warned at the New York ratification convention in July 1788, "history does not furnish a single instance of a government once established, voluntarily yielding up its powers to secure the rights and liberties of the people."[188]

When Fauci was asked about the most barbaric lockdowns of anywhere in the world—the literal house arrest and starvation of the citizens of China's most prosperous city, Shanghai, in the spring of 2022—one would have expected him to condemn such literal Nazi-like policies with moral clarity. Instead, two years after we understood all of the failures and destruction from lockdowns, Fauci continued to tacitly bless them.[189] His only criticism of China was that he felt their vaccine wasn't good enough that they could emerge from the concentration camp.

But lockdown has its consequences. "You use lockdowns to get people vaccinated so that when you open up, you won't have a surge of infections," Fauci said back then on national television. "The problem is that the vaccines that they've been using are not nearly as effective as the vaccines that are used in the United States, the UK, [the] EU, and other places. So, they don't have the degree of protection that's optimal."

Additionally, he stated that "their approach, the strictest lockdown," is not a viable path here not because it is barbaric, doesn't work, and kills millions long term, but because politically "you'd never be able to implement in the United States."

In other words, according to Fauci, if in his estimation there would be a better vaccine that he, of course, is involved with, and if it would be politically feasible, he would support even the Shanghai genocide. This is two years into hundreds of studies showing lockdowns don't work and that they induced a physical, mental, behavioral, emotional, and child developmental holocaust on society.[190] Such devotion to a proven failure isn't science but dogma. And it's a cult with a big tent, but if you dare think for yourself you aren't in it.

Even as late as April 2022, after it was so clear the shots failed and thus they needed to push a fourth booster, Dr. Paul Offit of the Food and Drug Administration Vaccines and Related Biological Products Advisory Committee essentially said facts don't matter.[191] They now experiment on you first and do the science later.

"It's just sort of fait accompli," said the famed director of the Vaccine Education Center at Children's Hospital of Philadelphia. "I feel that we're in a time, this sort of COVID exceptionalism, where we don't do things the way we normally do it, which is that the science precedes the recommendation. Here, it's the other way around," he said.

We've gone from American exceptionalism to COVID exceptionalism. One puts the individual before the total state, the other the total state before all.

Offit said this even after he himself conceded there were serious risks. Later that month, he wrote in the *New England Journal of Medicine* that boosters are "not risk free" because of myocarditis for younger males.[192] He also warned that for all age groups, there is the potential of "original antigenic sin"—a decreased ability to respond to a new immunogen because the immune system has locked onto the original immunogen.

Translation: continuing to inject people with the COVID shots for an extinct variant risks weakening their immune systems against future tyrants.

Yet, this same venerated vaccinologist, as a member of the relevant FDA advisory committee, voted just a few months later to approve a *three-dose* Pfizer shot for babies out of the gate and suggested they would need boosters.[193] He said it with a straight face as if his prior admissions never happened. You'll be getting the shots just because we say so.

How can they justify this? What is the driving force of their unchallenged certainty, the contrary data be damned?

What we are confronted with today in Western society is an unimaginable quest for transhumanism, the unprecedented technology to implement those perverted ideals, and the clean conscience of the governing elites to pursue them at all costs—all under the guise of creating a class of super humans to control and subjugate the rest.

And if that sounds suspiciously similar to the Nazis' infamous search for the "Übermensch"—it's because it is. There is nothing new under the sun.

The public health supremacism undergirding COVID exceptionalism was ultimately not just about public health trumping human rights, but a grooming tool to acclimatize people to the loss of their bodily freedoms for any global human engineering project in their plans. And trust us when we tell you they have no regrets whatsoever.

As C. S. Lewis once wrote:

> Of all tyrannies, a tyranny sincerely exercised for the good of its victims may be the most oppressive. It would be better to live under robber barons than under omnipotent moral busybodies. The robber baron's cruelty may sometimes sleep, his cupidity may at some point be satiated; but those who torment us for our own good will torment us without end for they do so with the approval of their own conscience.[194]

Nobody expressed this plan to torment our bodies and souls—in the most literal sense—without end and with a clean conscience better than Yuval Noah Harari, the top advisor to Klaus Schwab and the World Economic Forum. In an interview with Israeli media on "The Era of the Coronavirus: Living in a New Reality," Harari plainly stated his intent to undo democracy with transhumanist technology.[195]

"We need to reinvent democracy for this new era in which humans are now hackable animals," he shockingly told Israeli journalist Romi Noimark in October 2020. "You know, the whole idea that humans have, you know this, they have this soul or spirit, and they have free will, and nobody knows what's happening inside me, so whatever I choose, whether in the election, or whether in the supermarket, this is my free will. That's over."

The professor of history at Hebrew University went on to explain exactly what he means by using technology to upend democracy, and even your own sovereignty over your body, soul, and thoughts (emphasis added):

> You have to realize that practically today, we have the technology to hack human beings on a massive scale, and this means you need, we need, to reinvent democracy. We need to reinvent the market. Again, the whole idea of the customer is always right, we just do whatever the customers want, yes, but you can now hack the customers. You can manipulate the customers to want what you tell them to want. So, this whole idea that corporations just serve

the needs of the customers, this is over. You can't hide behind this explanation anymore.

Some governments and corporations, for the first time in history, have the power to basically *hack human beings*. There is a lot of talk about hacking computers, hacking smartphones, hacking bank accounts, but the big story of our era is the ability to hack human beings, and by this I mean that if you have enough data, and you have enough computing power, you can understand people better than they understand themselves, and then you can *manipulate them in ways which were previously impossible*, and in such a situation the *old democratic system stop[s] functioning*.

These chilling comments bring us full circle, and back to the beginning of this closing statement. If you are still naively holding onto the fantasy that our provocative comparison of COVID fascism to the Nazis goes too far, consider these chilling comments were not from *Mein Kampf*—though if such technology existed when Hitler wrote his dark manifesto, they certainly could've been. But these words were said with gusto from a respected academic at a university located in—ironically enough—Jerusalem, Israel!

Which means the cancer has become so widespread that even the people within the nation that should be the most sensitive to mere hints of such precedents have been fully anesthetized into biofascist compliance. Their immunity to authoritarianism has been diminished just as the COVID shots diminish your natural immune system.

That means the time for "never again, again" is upon us. There are not as many of us awake to what is happening as we hoped, but there is far more than they anticipated. Recent elections within several Western democracies, including our own, have shown the masses are growing increasingly disenchanted with the elites driving us towards a new Dark Ages.

Therefore, the time to demand those who have acquired their newfound political power riding the wave of that discontent act accordingly is now. The window for substantive pushback—a mass vaccination drive of human liberty against the pathogen of biomedical tyranny—is open now, but it won't be open forever. The Fourth Reich is upon us, and it will require more from our public officials than a Weimaresque bumbling or buck-passing.

That is where you come in, ladies and gentlemen of the jury.

COVID fascism, and its desire to use anything and everything available through technology to steal our sovereignty as human beings, is not going away. It needs to be ripped up from the ground, root and branch, and tossed onto the ash heap of history. It must be aggressively confronted regardless of where it comes from—government, law, politics, culture, medicine, and science—and using the same force through which it was born.

There must be severe penalties—whether civil, criminal, or political—for those responsible to provide us a legal and political inoculation (one that works much better than the COVID shots) to prevent this from ever happening again. Those responsible are without remorse, so there must be a reckoning. Barring that reckoning, we promise you they will make us remorseful later for not holding them accountable now. They will make our children and grandchildren even more so.

Therefore, ladies and gentlemen of the jury, we urge you to rise to the occasion history has presented us and *be that reckoning*.

APPENDIX

Making the Nuremberg Code Great Again

"**N**ever again" is an empty slogan if we emerge from the past few years—with their violent breach of the Nuremberg Code—and not move to protect human rights, medical freedom, bodily autonomy, and informed consent at all stages of law, politics, and government. What follows is a blueprint, rallying cry, and an emergency agenda that must be championed *immediately* if we are to remain free as human beings.

The first step in repentance is acknowledging the sin, asking forgiveness for it, and resolving to place barriers against a relapse into its commission. To that end, every legislative body—from county council and state legislature up to the U.S. House and Senate—must pass a resolution apologizing for going along with this form of democide we incurred the past few years. They must apologize for the lockdowns, the closure of schools, violation of human rights, denial of early treatment, promotion of dangerous experimental therapeutics, and forcibly masking human beings.

Specifically, the resolution must concede the following points:

- Lockdowns and masks provided only pain and no gain against the virus and must never be used again.
- The COVID injections must immediately be terminated.
- Doctors must never be prevented from prescribing FDA-approved drugs with long-established safety profiles.
- A fund must be created to research the scope of vaccine injury, the best methods for treating it, and monies must be dispensed to compensate those who were injured.
- Nobody should ever be denied a career, education, medical treatment, military service, or any public accommodation on account of not opting to endorse or partake in a particular medical treatment.
- All of the COVID shot manufacturers must be investigated for falsifying clinical trials and withholding information concerning safety and efficacy, and should face indictment for fraud depending on those findings.
- Individuals within government agencies must be held accountable for the gain-of-function research that likely created the virus, for the devastating and failing response measures to the virus, and for working with the pharmaceutical companies on the fraudulent vaccine program.

Next, the resolution of apology must clearly spell out unambiguous rights that are now recognized by government—never to be infringed upon again. They would include:

- The right of every citizen to move freely without being restrained or forcibly vaccinated or masked in violation of his bodily integrity.
- The right of every citizen to responsibly open his or her business without government deciding which ones are essential.
- The right of every citizen to worship freely during a declared emergency.
- The right of every American child to attend school without physical and psychological abuse (or threats thereof).
- The right of every citizen to be shielded from government monitoring of his medical privacy.
- The right of every citizen to move freely and to be free from any quarantine absent evidence of illness or direct exposure to a quarantinable virus (not a respiratory virus).
- The right of every citizen to access basic employment and goods or services without being forced to inject any medical intervention or material into their bodies.
- The right of every citizen to sue for damages resulting from injury from a particular medical device that is either funded by or promoted by government.

Every legislative body, including Congress, must commit in writing to the principle that during a declared emergency—for health or other reasons—individuals absolutely

STEVE DEACE AND DANIEL HOROWITZ

retain the right to be free and independent and maintain their inalienable and fundamental right of self-determination to make their own health and personal safety decisions including, but not limited to, the right to refuse any of the following health-related countermeasures:

- The wearing of masks or other medical devices.
- Vaccination.
- Testing or any physical examination.
- Participation in contact tracing.
- Being indiscriminately monitored and spied upon by governments or corporations using officious technology.
- The involuntary sharing of personal data or medical information.
- Forced quarantine of any individual who has not been infected with an actual disease that has been proven deadly, and has not already proliferated through large portions of the population.

After affirming these rights and recognizing the mistakes of the past in as many legislative bodies across the country as possible, it will then be time for vaccination—to erect legal firewalls to ensure that the sanctuary of the human body can never be attacked by the deadly pathogen of public health authoritarianism.

Constitutional Amendment Banning all Medical Mandates

No government should ever coerce an individual to obtain a medical intervention or utilize a medical product. That is the

safeguard of all human liberty that must never be breached—
ever again.

A constitutional amendment codifying a human right is a
blunt instrument against governmental action with no compromise, exceptions, or discernment. Yet, what we just experienced calls for exactly that sort of strong medicine. What we
have learned clearly from a moral, ethical, legal, and scientific
perspective is that there is never a time when person A's *inactivity* is a threat to another person to the point that said individual must take an *affirmative action* against his or her body
to save person B.

It must be made clear that no government can ever force
an individual to ever wear a mask or get a particular shot or
other medical therapeutic or procedure. No exceptions.

While governments have a right to regulate certain activity and curtail certain actions, they never have the power
to regulate your inactivity and place a positive directive on
your negative state of being. Personal liberty is defined by
Blackstone as "the power of loco-motion, of changing situation, or removing one's person to whatsoever place one's own
inclination may direct; without imprisonment or restraint,
unless by due course of law."[196]

Nobody has the right to mandate a mask or a needle on
or in your body and deny you access to public accommodation
as a result of exercising that right. As Father Ed Meeks of
Towson, Maryland, so eloquently said, "No earthly king or
president or public health official or billionaire technocrat
gets to dictate what we must put into our bodies."[197]

Although the federal Constitution is nearly impossible to
change, state constitutions are pretty easy to change, especially
in a number of red states. In many states, where legislatures

fail to consider the amendment proposal, voters can petition to secure a ballot initiative through voter signatures. The language of the amendment would go something like this: "An individual's right to refuse any medical procedure, treatment, injection, device, or prophylactic may not be questioned or interfered with in any manner. Equality of rights under the law or access to places of public accommodation shall not be denied or abridged to any person in this state because of the exercise of the right under this section."

Pennsylvania State Representative Russ Diamond was the first legislator to introduce a similar amendment, which as of mid-2022, passed the relevant committee in Pennsylvania's House of Representatives.[198]

This entire tragedy came about because the people and their state legislators had no voice in the fundamental transformation of society, when it was impelled upon us in March 2020. Thus, what better way to fix it then by permanently prohibiting any repeat performance—with the state legislatures and the people themselves taking the lead to amend state constitutions at the ballot box?

Reparations and care for the vaccine injured

Our government either mandated or cajoled most people into getting the shots to the point that there was no enlightened consent. Millions have been injured as a result. Congress must establish a fund to compensate those victims. It must also immediately fund research into detecting, diagnosing, and treating those injured. If Pfizer and Moderna were able to get billions of dollars to produce dangerous and counterproductive products, then the people injured by them deserve equal funding.

The right to treat and access treatment

One of the most destructive aspects of the budding Fourth Reich was the ban on accessing lifesaving treatment and the punishing of doctors who, unlike those pushing the experimental shots and dangerous therapeutics like remdesivir, offered patients FDA-approved treatments for COVID with proper informed consent. In order to make sure this can never happen again, we need to pursue a fifty-state strategy to enact the following:

- A ban on any state medical or licensing board taking action against any physician for prescribing clinically indicated, medically necessary, appropriate off-label FDA-approved drugs, for offering their professional opinion on any aspect of the pandemic or its treatment, or for not wearing a mask.
- The process of medical complaints brought before the state boards must be reformed to make them more transparent. These reforms would include making submitted allegations formal affidavits, dismissing anonymous and secondhand complaints, and expedited hearings so that doctors are not suspended for months on end based on a charge they have no ability to combat.
- All medical licensing board officials should be subject to removal by the legislature so that they don't become autonomous tools of tyranny.

- A requirement that all pharmacies fill any prescription of an FDA-approved drug used off-label. Any pharmacist who denies a prescription of a medically necessary drug—unless he has a religious conscientious objection—would face a $500,000 fine or a year in jail.
- Every insurance company must cover COVID-related prescriptions pursuant to the same rules they use for billing of other prescriptions, as well as for coverage of the vaccines and remdesivir. Scope of coverage mandates, whether one agrees with them or not, if they are going to exist, must be applied equally.
- A new patient bill of rights for hospitalized patients, which will allow them to always have one advocate present in the hospital, allow them to access FDA-approved drugs off-label prescribed by a doctor at their own expense if they agree to assume liability, and the right to refuse any hospital-prescribed treatment. There must be a cause of action created to sue any hospital for civil charges and possibly for the district attorney to bring criminal charges against hospitals that deny these rights.

No mandates for school

While access to public school education is not an ironclad fundamental right, the fact public education is the biggest expenditure within each state budget confirms the priority status we have bestowed upon it as a society. Therefore, if the shots are safe and effective, then those with the shots should have no problem with those who opt not to get them for medical or religious reasons. We will not tolerate any longer the fallacy that the success or failure of these products relies upon those who don't use them—beginning with our children. We must ensure in every state, county, and district that children are not discriminated against on account of not receiving any vaccine.

The right to medical privacy

Mix the desire of the medical tyrants to control our bodies with the boundless digital technology, and there is no limit to the pernicious and officious breaches of medical privacy that we will face. In June 2022, when Chinese citizens attempted to withdraw their bank deposits during the barbaric lock-downs, the government had their QR health codes turn red so they were forced back into quarantine and would be arrested for protesting the lock on their bank accounts.[199] We must categorically halt the toxic mix of health tyranny and invasive technology in its tracks. Every state legislature must therefore pass a bill ensuring:

- Nobody's vaccination status should be recorded with-out the explicit affirmative consent of the patient.
- A categorical ban on the authority of any state or county official to issue a stay-at-home order, or to have carte blanche to shut down businesses under the guise of public health.
- A ban on contact tracing or the forced quarantine of any healthy individual who has not been infected with an actual disease that has been proven deadly.
- A prohibition on government tracking, monitoring, or controlling a human being without his consent when there is no probable cause a crime was committed.

- A ban on all health "passports"—digital or otherwise.
- A categorical ban on the funding, creation, and implementation of any "self-spreading" vaccine that could shed the medical intervention from a person who consented to one who has not. Such technology is already being deployed and will be the way of the future if it's not immediately halted.[200]
- A GOP-controlled Congress must also pass federal legislation providing for a cause of action in federal court for any individual or class of citizens to sue the government for breaching such privacy without probable cause of having committed a crime.

Clip the wings of state and county health departments

COVID fascism, like all forms of authoritarianism, flowed from arbitrary, capricious, illegal, illogical, and inhumane executive action—whether at a federal, state, or local level. Not a single one of these detestable policies was instituted by a legislative body in the early days, and even after two years most states and localities never passed a mask or vaccine mandate through a legislative body. To rectify this mistake, and immunize ourselves from arbitrary administrative power in the future, the following objectives must be implemented:

- All state and local health directors must be subject to removal by the respective governing legislative authority.
- Any public health orders issued by the health departments—state or county—are to be regarded as *advisory*

unless they are affirmatively ratified by two-thirds of the governing legislative body.

- No public health emergency declared by the governor may last longer than seven days without the support of two-thirds of the legislature. Any declared emergency would trigger an automatic reconvening of the legislature until the declaration has expired so that we can never repeat the mistake of allowing months to lapse with health directors ruling over our life, liberty, and property without redress through the elected representatives.

- Investigate all actions taken by the federal government under the authoritarian COVID regime. How can we emerge from the Fourth Reich without engaging in retrospection, investigate all the unanswered questions about the origin and response to the pandemic, and shame those responsible for it? Obviously, we need a congressional-level investigation on par with the "9-11 commission," but because so many of the policies were carried out by the state governments, we need state commissions as well. In terms of specific action items:

- Each state should form a temporary COVID committee to hold hearings and audits of all the current actions taken by the federal and respective state governments, predicated on a purported scientific premise about the virus, the vaccines, or treatment. Based on the findings, any policy found to be out of sync with evidence of safety and efficacy must be terminated and permanently banned.

- State legislative health care committees must conduct full investigations of the treatment of patients in hospitals. The scope of each investigation should include an audit and analysis of the therapeutics used, the therapeutics rejected, the deviation from standard and established care for patients in respiratory distress, and any allegations of mistreatment or discriminatory actions taken by hospital staff.
- Every state should pay for a full audit of every individual who died within the thirty-day investigative window of taking the COVID shots, as well as a macroanalysis of excess deaths by category since 2020.
- Every state should establish its own vaccine adverse event database—one that is easier to use than the federal system—and encourage, rather than discourage, doctors to use it.
- Every state must establish a backstop safety net against the FDA for when the FDA approves dangerous products so they will have a process in place to halt the distribution of those products within the state until certain benchmarks of safety and efficacy are established that satisfy state regulators.

Audit all gain-of-function research

It is self-evident that the ban on gain-of-function research wasn't worth the paper it was printed on. Congress must audit every biolab we constructed, fund, or assist throughout the world to root out any efforts to make pathogens stronger or more transmissible or to enable zoonotic viruses to jump to humans. All funding or participation from agencies

RISE OF THE FOURTH REICH

such as BARDA, DARPA, NIAID, and the U.S. Defense Threat Reduction Agency (DTRA) must cease immediately. Congress must stiffen criminal penalties for violations and create a private cause of action for individuals injured by any of these technologies to bring a lawsuit.

Repeal liability for drug companies

If all this new technology they have developed and plan on forcing upon humanity is "safe and effective," then pharma companies should have no problem assuming the baseline degree of liability for defective products that other manufacturers shoulder, right? Imagine if we regulated oil companies or car companies the way we regulate Pfizer? We are so accustomed to endless recalls of car seats and airbags, but never is there a recall of a vaccine.

The original sin to this great human experiment that allowed the vaccine manufacturers to get away with genocide, censorship, and even having their products mandated on human beings without being held liable—and without undergoing the discovery process inherent in lawsuits—is because of the 1986 National Childhood Vaccine Injury Act (NCVIA).

One could defend the idea of absolving vaccines of liability as a well-intended effort to ensure there is a steady flow of cost-effective vaccines in the country. But that was back when we would actually pull a vaccine after the first sign of trouble. The behavior of our government agencies and the manufacturers has voided out the original rationale for that law. The FDA and CDC have proven they cannot be trusted any longer as regulatory bodies.

After all, VAERS was created in the NCVIA as a counter-measure to the liability exemption—in that if people would begin reporting adverse events, it was assumed the government would suspend the vaccine until the reports could be confirmed or denied. It was their job to prove the claims were false before continuing with the mass vaccination. What we witnessed with COVID fascism, however, was that the government continued to fund, market, distribute, mandate, and even expand the scope of availably in age groups of the shots long after over a million adverse events and thousands of deaths were reported to the system.

Furthermore, we now know that the CDC refused to follow through with its promise to publish comprehensive VAERS data that would have compared the rates of adverse events per dose used against other vaccines.[201] The federal government has become a PR department and benefactor of their products, not just the approver or regulator.

Additionally, in 2011, the Supreme Court made it clear that even if there is a design flaw in vaccines, the makers are categorically exempt from all legal action from any such claim. The Supreme Court issued ruled in *Bruesewitz v. Wyeth* that the law preempts all design-defect claims against vaccine manufacturers brought by plaintiffs seeking compensation for injury or death caused by the vaccine's side effects.[202] Any ability to recover damages or even evoke discovery of details in court is extremely limited to the point of irrelevancy.

Finally, as part of the deal to grant manufacturers immunity, the NCVIA required the secretary of HHS to send a report to a House and Senate committee every other year describing the actions of the department "with respect to, the licensing, manufacturing, processing, testing, labeling, warning, use instructions, distribution, storage, administration, field surveillance, adverse reaction reporting, and recall of reactogenic lots or batches, of vaccines, and research on vaccines," in order to reduce the risks of adverse reactions to vaccines.[203] In 2018, HHS acknowledged in a FOIA request that they had never complied with that law in three decades.[204]

Thus, it is quite clear that the 1986 NCVIA is extremely outdated, and must be repealed or seriously reformed and limited.

The NCVIA was aggravated by the Public Readiness and Emergency Preparedness Act (PREP Act), which was invoked on February 4, 2020, by the Trump administration.[205] The PREP Act shields all manufacturers of any diagnostics and treatments (not just vaccines) during a national health emergency from any practical degree of liability.

What this means, according to the Congressional Research Service, is that not only are the manufacturers immune to claims of negligence, but they are immune even to claims of willful misconduct.[206] There are numerous insurmountable hoops one has to jump through in order to sue for willful misconduct, and it can occur only if the DOJ or HHS, which are promoting the vaccine, first commit a legal action against them. As we are all quite painfully aware at this point, asking the government to go after Pfizer is like asking the government to go after itself.

As such, it was known up front that no matter how dangerous or ineffective any COVID product would be, it would never be subject to the same liability process that has perfected the safety of vital products in so many other industries. Thus, all hospital treatments, PCR testing kits, remdesivir, Paxlovid, and molnupiravir were exempt from liability along with the vaccines. Furthermore, the degree of existing immunity conveyed by the 1986 act was expanded by the Prep Act. Both laws must be dramatically reformed.

It's also important to remember that during the 1980s, there were only a few vaccines and very few manufacturers. Now, it is a booming business funded by all the masters of the universe—from governments to Bill Gates. The notion that they need liability protection this broad is insane and downright immoral.

Finally, even if lawmakers cry foul about the potential of multibillion-dollar lawsuits to chill the incentives to develop "cures," a compromise can easily be reached to limit the payouts to those injured just to compensatory damages. However, opening up lawsuits from those injured by vaccines would still have the effect of providing the public with full legal discovery of the science and data behind these products.

Who could oppose sunlight and transparency if they have nothing to hide?

End conflict of interest in drug approval

Generally speaking, a society should desire the least amount of regulation of potentially lifesaving products as necessary to ensure its safety. However, it has become apparent that the FDA is irremediably corrupt and has an incestuous relationship with Big Pharma, as they overregulate some products while greenlighting Big Pharma to unleash dangerous products with the help of government. It is time to sever the impervious bond between Big Government and Big Pharma to ensure the public is never used as lab rats ever again.

To that end, there should be a dual-track regulatory and approval system between those products that enjoy government support and those that don't. Any product that the government plans to endorse, purchase, market, and actively distribute (as opposed to simply approving for use) must be backed by clinical trials conducted by third-party institutions with no conflict of interest or relation to the manufacturer.

Furthermore, the approval must be done by a panel of independent scientists with no ties to either the manufacturer or government. Also, such approval must come with a government slush fund to pay for lawsuits against the product by those claiming injury. Finally, all FDA funding should come from general appropriations, not from user fees, which has created the moral hazard of the pharma companies paying the salaries of the regulators.

In other words, if the government is going to partner with the product, they cannot be the regulator and they must share in the liability.

Transfer public cures research from the medical cartel to study off-label, already-approved drugs

Ever Since President Nixon declared war on cancer in 1971, the National Cancer Institute has spent $90 billion on research of and treatment for the great mankiller. There are several hundred nonprofit organizations they fund with annual budgets topping $2.2 billion.[207] In addition, our convoluted Medicare, Medicaid, and insurance scheme has paid out more money for treatment of the status quo than any other country by a wide margin. Yet, what have we gotten for it?

Recently, Yale researchers analyzed the association between cancer care expenditures and age-standardized population-level cancer mortality rates in twenty-two wealthy Western countries in 2020. Despite the fact that America spent $584 per capita on cancer care—more than any other nation, and double the median spending level of the twenty-one other nations—"cancer care spending was not associated with age-standardized cancer mortality rates."[208]

You can rinse and repeat this dynamic for heart disease, diabetes, Alzheimer's, and autoimmune diseases, and you will find that we get sicker as we spend obscene amounts of money on care and research. Every politician is shamed into funding more "cancer research" without any understanding that they are likely funding the perpetuation of these diseases and the obstruction of a cure.

Big Pharma and Big Government have essentially created a racket in which only therapeutics backed by large randomized controlled trial data (manipulated by the medical cartel) published in high-impact journals (controlled by their allies) get to see the light of day with clinical care protocols. This is how they have, for years, stifled promising results from cheap, safe, off-patent drugs, and milked the taxpayers for endless funds for supposed new wonder drugs that never pan out.

Budding scientists who are truly motivated by the love of science and humanity have no funding to conduct large-scale randomized controlled trials. The only ones who do are the federal government and Big Pharma working together. Thus, while there is so much nascent, promising research on existing cheap drugs possibly working against cancer, they are relegated to in-vitro, animal, and small-scale human observational trials or case studies. These scientists don't have the money to take them to the next level, and Big Pharma would like it to stay that way.

To rectify this circuitous cycle of greed and failure and to take the incentive for control and profit out of the process, Congress (and state legislatures) must allocate a percentage of cancer research *exclusively* to those seeking randomized controlled trials to study off-patent drugs *already* approved by the FDA that have shown mechanistically through preliminary research conceptual efficacy against cancer or other vexing ailments.

In other words, what we all learned from COVID is that Big Government and Big Pharma work together to box out cheap, safe, and effective treatments that are off-label while funding expensive, novel, and often dangerous new drugs. They manipulate the data to suggest whatever they want it to conclude. By allocating some of the funding exclusively for existing off-patent, off-label drugs, it will take the money and politics out of the cures business and attract only those truly seeking the well-being of humanity.

Categorical ban on medical kidnapping

It is an undisputable God-given right for parents to determine the care—medical or otherwise—of their children. In a world where medical "experts" reign supreme and politically motivated accusations run rampant, American parents face a dynamic where they can lose their child without due process based on hearsay and politically-motivated accusations of child neglect.

As such, it's time for every state legislature to affirm the finality of a parent's decision as it relates to medical care for

STEVE DEACE AND DANIEL HOROWITZ

their children. No parent shall be investigated, much less lose parental rights, on account of refusing specific medical treatments, diagnostics, or devices unless there is proof that the parent acted with malicious intent. Refusal to engage in masking or vaccinating a child should never be used as a tool to investigate the parents, nor can it be used as a factor in family court in determining custody arrangements.

Furthermore, it must be clear that a parent, when determining that the child is not getting proper care at a hospital or medical facility, has the right to take the child out and seek care elsewhere without fear of reprisal. There must also be a provision to sue any medical practitioner who calls child protective services, and ultimately, the complaint is found to be frivolous. Not masking or vaccinating a child shall be deemed as a frivolous complaint. Idaho House Bill 821 is a terrific model for affirming parental rights against medical kidnapping sponsored by the state and the medical profession.[209]

Conclusion

There is no greater issue for which there is an urgent need for multipronged policy changes than medical freedom. The survival of humanity quite literally depends upon it. As Bill Gates famously said in 2010 as he lamented about the growing global population, "If we do a really great job on new vaccines, health care, reproductive health services (abortion) we can *lower* that by perhaps 10–15%."[210] At the time, most of us either ignored his comment or didn't take him seriously. Now we know after having lived through his first round of the Fourth Reich. Do we need more to learn our lesson?

During the floor debate over the Fourteenth Amendment, Senator Jacob Howard, one of the primary authors of this civil rights-era constitutional amendment, described a fundamental right affecting an aspect of a citizen "lying at the basis of all society and without which a people cannot exist except as slaves, subject to a despotism."[211]

There is nothing more tyrannical than forcing deadly treatments upon us against our will and denying us the ability to seek proper care for our bodies, especially when the biomedical statists are likely assaulting us with deadly gain-of-function pathogens. We quite literally cannot live free without being subject to despotism until medical tyranny is exterminated from our civilization.

We must vow this: never again will we allow our government to control our bodies under the guise of "science."

To that end, this appendix was specifically constructed so that you, the average American, would have a defined action plan to take to your elected representative and demand they do their job—which is to protect and defend your God-given rights.

Do not let them off the hook. Accept no excuses. We must not just simply move on while the cancer is still there. We must demand nothing less than our elected representatives be the chemotherapy to kill the deadly cells that remain.

We are not a nation of laws, and never have been, but a nation of political will—and we always will be. Our will to demand "never again" must be stronger than their will to do this to us again…and again…and again…

ENDNOTES

1   Payton Iheme, email to Georgeta Dragiou, Becca G. Siegel,
    Tericka Lambert, and Monica Vines, June 15, 2021, https://www.
    icandecide.org/wp-content/uploads/2022/01/Page-35.pdf
2   Department of Homeland Security information leaked to the offices
    of Senator Charles Grassley and Senator John Hawley, June 7, 2022,
    https://www.grassley.senate.gov/imo/media/doc/grassley_hawley_
    to_deptofhomelandsecuritydisinformationgovernanceboard.pdf
3   Spencer Kimball, "Biden Asks Businesses to Proceed with Vaccine
    Mandate after Omicron Variant Arrives in U.S.," CNBC, December
    2, 2021, https://www.cnbc.com/2021/12/02/biden-asks-businesses-to-
    proceed-with-vaccine-mandate after-omicron-variant-arrives-in-us.html
4   Jonas Sandbrink, "As Self-Spreading Vaccine Technology Moves Forward,
    Dialogue on Its Risks Should Follow," *The Bulletin of the Atomic Sciences*,
    June 10, 2022, https://thebulletin.org/2022/06/as-self-spreading-vaccine-
    technology-moves-forward-dialogue-on-its-risks-should-follow/
5   Joseph Cox, "Phones to See If Americans Followed COVID
    Lockdown Orders," *VICE*, March 3, 2022, https://www.vice.com/
    en/article/m7vymn/cdc-tracked-phones-location-data-curfews
6   Antoine Jérusalem, "Mind Control Using Sound Waves? We Ask a
    Scientist How It Works," World Economic Forum, November 7, 2019,
    https://web.archive.org/web/20181107172700/https://www.weforum.
    org/agenda/2018/11/mind-control-ultrasound-neuroscience/
7   Albert Bourla, World Economic Forum 2018, "Albert Bourla
    at World Economic Forum 2018 Is Excited about Electronic
    Compliance Pills, kalibhakta, YouTube video, 1:13, https://www.
    youtube.com/watch?v=1NR1b2NmD4A&feature=emb_title
8   Maajid Nawaz (@MaajidNawaz), "World Economic Forum shill, Yuval
    Noah Harari: 'Covid is critical because this is what convinces people

to accept to legitimize total biometric surveillance. We need to not just monitor people, we need to monitor what's happening under their skin,'" Twitter, May 21, 2022, 6:32 a.m., https://twitter.com/MaajidNawaz/status/1527 975589235376128?s=20&t=NPOvKDeecKEHsZIVTG1thQ

9 Young Americans for Liberty (@YALiberty), "The globalists who want individual rights to be a relic of the past truly believe they are fit to play 'god.' This is a speech given at the World Economic Forum… and it's terrifying. This man's name is Yuval Harari," Twitter, March 18, 2022, 3:30 PM, https://twitter.com/YALiberty/status/150491 8060842450945?s=20&t=TWu8mOGLtFsJqEuoRnL2ew

10 World Economic Forum (@wef), "This is how our lives could soon look. Take a peak [sic]at the future," Twitter, August 17, 2021, 3:00 PM, https://twitter.com/wef/status/1427721919483326470?ref_src=tw src%5Etfw%7Ctwcamp%5Etweetembed%7Ctwterm%5E142772 1919483326470%7Ctwgr%5E%7Ctwcon%5Es1_&ref_url=https %3A%2F%2Fvigilantcitizen.com%2Fvigilantreport%2Ftop-10- insane-wef%2F

11 Andrew Lawton (@AndrewLawton), "Australian eSafety commissioner Julie Inman Grant tells the World Economic Forum we need a 'recalibration' of freedom of speech," Twitter, May 23, 2022, 11:48 a.m., https://twitter.com/AndrewLawton/status/ 1528779966644731906?s=20&t=CcLhCRm_ye4GlVDczHijbg

12 World Economic Forum (@wef), "Welcome to 2030. I own nothing, have no privacy, and life has never been better @IdaAuken," Twitter, April 8, 2017, 6:22 a.m., https://twitter.com/wef/status/85067007 3278812160?s=20&t=NPOvKDeecKEHsZIVTG1thQ

13 Andrew O'Reilly, "Rahm Emanuel on coronavirus response: 'Never allow a crisis to go to waste,'" Fox News, March 23, 2021, https://www.foxnews.com/politics/rahm-emanuel-on- coronavirus-response-never-allow-a-crisis-to-go-to-waste

14 Daniel Horowitz, "Horowitz: 6 times the media credited masks with stopping a pandemic that then spread even more," Blaze Media, July 29, 2021, https://www.theblaze.com/op-ed/horowitz-6-times-the-media- credited-masks-with-stopping-a-pandemic-that-then-spread-even-more

15 Beth Brelje, "Pennsylvania Trauma Survivor, Unable to Wear Mask, Is Denied Medical Treatment," *The Epoch Times*, March 29, 2022, https://www.theepochtimes.com/pennsylvania-trauma-survivor- unable-to-wear-mask-is-denied-medical-treatment_4369511.html

16 Donna Ferguson, "Rape survivors say they are being
    stigmatised for not wearing masks," *The Guardian*, August 10,
    2020, https://www.theguardian.com/society/2020/aug/10/
    survivors-say-they-are-being-stigmatised-for-not-wearing-masks
17 Roger Highfield, "Coronavirus: Hunting Down Covid-
    10," Science Museum Group, April 27, 2020, https://www.
    sciencemuseumgroup.org.uk/blog/hunting-down-covid-19/
18 Hayley Dixon, "No reported case of a child passing coronavirus
    to an adult exists, evidence review shows," *The Telegraph*, April
    29, 2020, https://www.telegraph.co.uk/news/2020/04/29/
    no-case-child-passing-coronavirus-adult-exists-evidence-review/
19 "Australian Health Protection Principal Committee (AHPPC)
    coronavirus (COVID-19) statements on 24 April 2020," Australian
    Government Department of Health and Aged Care, April 25, 2020,
    https://www.health.gov.au/news/australian-health-protection-
    principal-committee-ahppc-coronavirus-covid-19-statements-
    on-24-april-2020#updated-advice-regarding-schools
20 Justin Huggler and Robert Mendick, "Grandparents can safely
    hug under 10s, say Swiss," *Sydney Morning Herald*, April 29,
    2020, https://www.smh.com.au/world/europe/grandparents-can-
    safely-hug-under-10s-say-swiss-20200429-p54o9r.html
21 Sarah Silverberg and Laura Sauvé, "Caring for Children with COVID-
    19," British Columbia Ministry of Health, April 3, 2020, http://www.
    bccdc.ca/Health-Info-Site/Documents/Caring-for-children.pdf
22 "Children, school and COVID-19," National Institute for Public
    Health and the Environment, modified July 16, 2022, https://
    www.rivm.nl/en/coronavirus-covid-19/children-and-covid-19
23 Salomé Vincendon, "'Peu porteurs, peu transmetteurs': une étude
    confirme le rôle minime des enfants dans l'épidémie de Covid-19,"
    BFM TV, May 12, 2020, https://www.bfmtv.com/sante/peu-porteurs-
    peu-transmetteurs-une-etude-confirme-le-role-minime-des-
    enfants-dans-l-epidemie-de-covid-19_AV-202005120233.html
24 Keoni Everington, "Taiwan one of only 6 countries on
    Earth where schools are open," *Taiwan News*, April 1, 2020,
    https://www.taiwannews.com.tw/en/news/3908444
25 "COVIDView Summary ending on May 2, 2020," CDC,
    May 8, 2020, https://www.cdc.gov/coronavirus/2019-ncov/
    covid-data/covidview/past-reports/05082020.html

26 "Nuremberg Code," United States Holocaust Memorial Museum, https://www.ushmm.org/information/exhibitions/online-exhibitions/special-focus/doctors-trial/nuremberg-code

27 Paul Elias Alexander, "More than 150 Comparative Studies and Articles on Mask Ineffectiveness and Harms," Brownstone Institute, December 20, 2021, https://brownstone.org/articles/more-than-150-comparative-studies-and-articles-on-mask-ineffectiveness-and-harms/

28 Philip Ball, "The lightning-fast quest for COVID vaccines — and what it means for other diseases," *Nature*, December 18, 2020, https://www.nature.com/articles/d41586-020-03626-1

29 Harold M. Schmeck Jr., "Swine Flu Program Is Halted in 9 States as 3 Die After Shots," *New York Times*, October 13, 1976, https://www.nytimes.com/1976/10/13/archives/swine-flu-program-is-halted-in-9-states-as-3-die-after-shots.html

30 "Cumulative Analysis of Post-Authorization Adverse Event Reports of PF-07302048 (BNT162B2) Received Through 28-Feb-2021," Pfizer, April 30, 2021, https://phmpt.org/wp-content/uploads/2022/04/reissue_5.3.6-postmarketing-experience.pdf

31 Kenrad E. Nelson, "Invited Commentary: Influenza Vaccine and Guillain-Barre Syndrome—Is There a Risk?" *American Journal of Epidemiology* 175, no. 11 (June 2012): 1129–1132, https://academic.oup.com/aje/article/175/11/1129/140385?login=false

32 "VAERS COVID Vaccine Adverse Event Reports," OpenVAERS, https://openvaers.com/covid-data

33 Ramachandra Naik, "Summary Basis for Regulatory Action," FDA, November 8, 2021, 23 https://www.fda.gov/media/151733/download

34 Joseph Fraiman et al., "Serious Adverse Events of Special Interest Following mRNA Vaccination in Randomized Trials," SSRN, June 23, 2022, https://papers.ssrn.com/sol3/papers.cfm?abstract_id=4125239

35 Venkata R. Emani et al., "Increasing SARS-CoV2 cases, hospitalizations and deaths among the vaccinated elderly populations during the Omicron (B.1.1.529) variant surge in UK," medRxiv, June 28, 2022, https://www.medrxiv.org/content/10.1101/2022.06.28.22276926v1

36 Don Wolt (@tlowdon), "The latest PHE Vaccine Surveillance Report shows UK CoV2 infection rates are as high or higher among the fully vaccinated in all age cohorts ≥40 years old. They're lower in the younger cohorts, but still significant. Vaccine passports are pointless in mitigating spread," Twitter, September 10, 2021, 9:53 a.m., https://twitter.com/tlowdon/status/1436342146538164233?s=20&t=I8A_oywv7psaxm5x3QGtYg

37 Berkeley Lovelace Jr. and Robert Towney, "The leader of CDC just made a rare call to allow Covid booster shots for more people," CNBC, September 23, 2021, https://www.cnbc.com/2021/09/23/covid-booster-shots-cdc-panel-endorses-third-pfizer-doses-for-millions.html

38 Jim Garamone, "Biden to Approve Austin's Request to Make COVID-19 Vaccine Mandatory for Service Members," DOD News, August 9, 2021, https://www.defense.gov/News/News-Stories/Article/Article/2724982/biden-to-approve-austins-request-to-make-covid-19-vaccine-mandatory-for-service/

39 "COMIRNATY," U.S. Food & Drug Administration, https://www.fda.gov/vaccines-blood-biologics/comirnaty

40 Informed Consent Form for "A Study to Evaluate Additional Dose(s) of BNT162b2 in Healthy individuals Previously Vaccinated With BNT162b2," BioNTech/Pfizer, January 4, 2022, 5, https://www.icandecide.org/wp-content/uploads/2022/02/Substudy-C.pdf

41 Matthew E. Oster et al., "Myocarditis Cases Reported After mRNA-Based COVID-19 Vaccination in the US From December 2020 to August 2021," *JAMA* 327, no. 4 (January 2022): 331–340, https://jamanetwork.com/journals/jama/fullarticle/2788346

42 Parent Permission Form for "A Study to Evaluate Additional Dose(s) of BNT162b2 in Healthy individuals Previously Vaccinated With BNT162b2," BioNTech/Pfizer, January 4, 2022, 10, https://www.icandecide.org/wp-content/uploads/2022/02/Substudy-B-Informed-Consent-Form-002.pdf

43 Sonia Ndeupen et al., "The mRNA-LNP platform's lipid nanoparticle component used in preclinical vaccine studies is highly inflammatory," *iScience* 24, no. 12 (December 2021), https://www.cell.com/iscience/fulltext/S2589-0042(21)01450-4?_returnURL=https%3A%2F%2Flinkinghub.elsevier.com%2Fretrieve%2Fpii%2FS2589004221014504%3Fshowall%3Dtrue

44 Ruolan Wang et al., "Potential adverse effects of nanoparticles on the reproductive system," *International Journal of Nanomedicine* 13 (December 2018): 8487–8506, https://www.ncbi.nlm.nih.gov/pmc/articles/PMC6294055/

45 Ramachandra Naik, "Summary Basis for Regulatory Action," FDA, November 8, 2021, 25, https://www.fda.gov/media/151733/download

46 "Package Insert – COMIRNATY (purple cap)," BioNTech/Pfizer, 16, https://www.fda.gov/media/151707/download

47 Lincoln Tan, "Pregnant mum told she can't see her private obstetrician because she is unvaccinated," *NZHerald*, December 4,

2021, https://www.nzherald.co.nz/nz/pregnant-mum-told-she-cant-see-her-private-obstetrician-because-she-is-unvaccinated/XRWK724DZEK4GTLBL42MJR2YEI/

48 "VAERS COVID Vaccine Reproductive Health Related Reports," OpenVAERS, accessed June 8, 2022, https://openvaers.com/covid-data/reproductive-health

49 Geoff Brumfiel, "Why Reports Of Menstrual Changes After COVID Vaccine Are Tough To Study," NPR, August 9, 2021, https://www.npr.org/sections/health-shots/2021/08/09/1024190379/covid-vaccine-period-menstrual-cycle-research

50 Katharine M. N. Lee et al., "Characterizing menstrual bleeding changes occurring after SARS-CoV-2 vaccination," medRxiv, October 12, 2021, https://www.medrxiv.org/content/10.1101/2021.10.11.21264863v1.full.pdf

51 Itai Gat et al., "Covid-19 vaccination BNT162b2 temporarily impairs semen concentration and total motile count among semen donors," *International Journal of Andrology* 10 (June 17, 2022): 1016–1022, https://onlinelibrary.wiley.com/doi/10.1111/andr.13209

52 Principle 18 from "WMA Declaration of Helsinki – Ethical Principles for Medical Research Involving Human Subjects," World Medical Association, July 9, 2018, https://www.wma.net/policies-post/wma-declaration-of-helsinki-ethical-principles-for-medical-research-involving-human-subjects/

53 Daniel Horowitz, "Horowitz: The stifling of COVID treatment: The case study of aspirin," Blaze Media, March 31, 2022, https://www.theblaze.com/op-ed/horowitz-the-stifling-of-covid-treatment-the-case-study-of-aspirin

54 Mostafa Kamal Arefin, "Povidone Iodine (PVP-I) Oro-Nasal Spray: An Effective Shield for COVID-19 Protection for Health Care Worker (HCW), for all," *Indian Journal of Otolaryngology and Head & Neck Surgery* (April 2021): 1–6, https://www.ncbi.nlm.nih.gov/pmc/articles/PMC8026810/.

55 Samantha Berlin, "Some Anti-Vaxxers Are Allegedly Gargling the Antiseptic Betadine as a COVID 'Cure,'" Newsweek, September 14, 2021, https://www.newsweek.com/some-anti-vaxxers-are-allegedly-gargling-antiseptic-betadine-covid-cure-1629091?utm_medium=Social&utm_source=Twitter#Echobox=1631648713

56 Nathan Jeffay, "1 in 4 COVID patients hospitalized while vitamin D deficient die – Israeli study," *The Times of Israel*, June 17, 2021, https://www.timesofisrael.

com/1-in-4-hospitalized-covid-patients-who-lack-vitamin-d-die-israeli-study/

57 Banafsheh Hosseini, Asmae El Abd, and Francine M. Ducharme, "Effects of Vitamin D Supplementation on COVID-19 Related Outcomes: A Systematic Review and Meta-Analysis," *Nutrients* 14, no. 10 (May 20, 2022): 2134, https://www.mdpi.com/2072-6643/14/10/2134

58 Jade Scipioni, "The supplement Dr. Fauci takes to help keep his immune system healthy," CNBC, September 14, 2020, https://www.cnbc.com/2020/09/14/supplements-white-house-advisor-fauci-takes-every-day-to-help-keep-his-immune-system-healthy.html

59 Reviewed by Emily Henderson, B.Sc., "Vitamin D therapy may be a useful addition to the treatment of ovarian cancer, study suggests," News Medical, May 30, 2022, https://www.news-medical.net/news/20220530/Vitamin-D-therapy-may-be-a-useful-addition-to-the-treatment-of-ovarian-cancer-study-suggests.aspx

60 Hassan Yahaya, "Could vitamin D deficiency increase the risk of heart disease?" Medical News Today, January 6, 2022, https://www.medicalnewstoday.com/articles/could-vitamin-d-deficiency-increase-the-risk-of-heart-disease

61 MVP Writing, "COVID-19: Folha de S. Paulo reveals numbers by David Uip. See the comparison with doctors who do early treatment," MédicosPelaVida, May 9, 2022, https://medicospelavidacovid19-com-br.translate.goog/editoriais/folha-de-s-paulo-revela-numeros-de-david-uip-veja-a-comparacao-com-medicos-que-fazem-tratamento-precoce/?_x_tr_sl=pt&_x_tr_tl=en&_x_tr_hl=pt-BR&_x_tr_pto=wapp

62 Estimated based on average CFR from Our World in Data. "Case fatality rate of COVID-19," Our World in Data, January 22, 2020, https://ourworldindata.org/grapher/covid-cfr-exemplars?tab=table&time=earliest&country=~USA

63 Ralph Baric, "Remdesivir, developed through a UNC-Chapel Hill partnership, proves effective against COVID-19 in NIAID human clinical trials," University of North Carolina Gillings School of Global Public Health, April 29, 2020, https://sph.unc.edu/sph-news/remdesivir-developed-at-unc-chapel-hill-proves-effective-against-covid-19-in-niaid-human-clinical-trials/

64 Sharon Lerner and Maia Hibbett, "Leaked Grant Proposal Details High-Risk Coronavirus Research," The Intercept, September 23, 2021, https://theintercept.com/2021/09/23/coronavirus-research-grant-darpa/

65 Jon Cohen and Kai Kupferschmidt, "The 'very, very bad look' of remdesivir, the first FDA-approved COVID-19 drug," *Science*,

October 28, 2020, https://www.science.org/content/article/
very-very-bad-look-remdesivir-first-fda-approved-covid-19-drug

66 Sabue Mulangu et al., "A Randomized, Controlled Trial of
Ebola Virus Disease Therapeutics," *New England Journal
of Medicine* 381 (December 12, 2019): 2293–2303, https://
www.nejm.org/doi/full/10.1056/NEJMoa1910993

67 Jonathan Grein et al., "Compassionate Use of Remdesivir for Patients with
Severe Covid-19," *New England Journal of Medicine* 382 (June 11, 2020):
2327–2336, https://www.nejm.org/doi/full/10.1056/NEJMoa2007016

68 Eamon N. Dreisbach, Gerard Gallagher, and Caitlyn
Stulpin, "Fauci on remdesivir for COVID-19: 'This will
be the standard of care,'" Healio, April 29, 2020, https://
www.healio.com/news/infectious-disease/20200429/
fauci-on-remdesivir-for-covid19-this-will-be-the-standard-of-care

69 Daniel Horowitz, "The $cience of remdesivir vs. ivermectin: A tale of two
drugs," Blaze Media, October 18, 2021, https://www.theblaze.com/op-ed/
horowitz-the-science-of-remdesivir-vs-
ivermectin-a-tale-of-two-drugs

70 "WHO recommends against the use of remdesivir in COVID-19
patients," World Health Organization, November 20, 2020, https://www.
who.int/news-room/feature-stories/detail/who-recommends-
against-the-use-of-remdesivir-in-covid-19-patients

71 Daniel Horowitz, "FDA warns about blood clots from Big Pharma
COVID treatment. Hospitals use it anyway," Blaze Media, September
28, 2021, https://www.theblaze.com/op-ed/horowitz-fda-warns-about-
blood-clots-from-big-pharma-covid-treatment-hospitals-use-it-anyway

72 Pfizer Labs, "Highlights of Prescribing Information," FDA, May 2018,
https://www.accessdata.fda.gov/drugsatfda_docs/label/2018/
203214s018lbl.pdf

73 Max Kozlov, "Merck's COVID pill loses its lustre: what that
means for the pandemic," *Nature*, December 13, 2021, https://
www.nature.com/articles/d41586-021-03667-0

74 Spencer Kimball, "FDA advisory panel narrowly endorses Merck's
oral Covid treatment pill, despite reduced efficacy and safety
questions," CNBC, November 30, 2021, https://www.cnbc.
com/2021/11/30/fda-advisory-panel-narrowly-endorses-mercks-
oral-covid-treatment-pill-despite-reduced-efficacy.html

75 Manas Mishra, "U.S. government to buy $1 billion more worth
of Merck's COVID-19 pill," Reuters, November 9, 2021,

https://www.reuters.com/world/us/us-government-buy-14-mln-more-courses-mercks-covid-19-pill-2021-11-09/

76 Rachel Gutman-Wei, "Paxlovid Mouth Is Real—And Gross," *The Atlantic*, May 5, 2022, https://www.theatlantic.com/health/archive/2022/05/pfizer-paxlovid-covid-pill-side-effects/629772/

77 Igor Chudov, "Did Pfizer Know that Paxlovid will NOT Work in the Vaccinated?" Igor's Newsletter, May 1, 2022, https://igorchudov.substack.com/p/did-pfizer-know-that-paxlovid-will?utm_source=substack&utm_campaign=post_embed&utm_medium=web

78 Paul Farrell, "Anthony Fauci says that he's experienced rebound Covid symptoms after taking a Pfizer's antiviral Paxlovid - which studies now show is NOT effective for people who are vaccinated," Daily Mail, June 28, 2022, https://www.dailymail.co.uk/news/article-10963301/Anthony-Fauci-says-hes-experienced-rebound-Covid-symptoms-Paxlovid-course.html

79 Daniel Horowitz, "The treatment nihilism of our government continues unabated," Blaze Media, January 4, 2022, https://www.theblaze.com/op-ed/horowitz-the-treatment-nihilism-of-our-government-continues unabated

80 "WHO Model Lists of Essential Medicines," World Health Organization, 2022, https://www.who.int/groups/expert-committee-on-selection-and-use-of-essential-medicines/essential-medicines-lists

81 "Press Release," The Nobel Prize, October 5, 2015, https://www.nobelprize.org/prizes/medicine/2015/press-release/

82 Daniel Horowitz, "Horowitz: More VAERS-reported vaccine deaths in our military than COVID deaths," *Blazemedia*, March 21, 2022, https://www.theblaze.com/op-ed/horowitz-more-vaers-reported-vaccine-deaths-in-our-military-than-COVID-deaths

83 "Coronavirus: DOD Response," U.S. Department of Defense, https://www.defense.gov/Spotlights/Coronavirus-DOD-Response/

84 Patricia Kime, "Pentagon Tracking 14 Cases of Heart Inflammation in Troops After COVID-19 Shots," Military.com, April 26, 2021, https://www.military.com/daily-news/2021/04/26/pentagon-tracking-14-cases-of-heart-inflammation-troops-after-COVID-19-shots.html

85 Hannah Kuchler, "The uncertain lessons of Covid: preparing for the next pandemic," *Financial Times*, August 17, 2021, https://www.ft.com/content/84269839-1236-4ef7-ad30-9261f6126553

86 Bloomberg, "Pfizer fights to control secret of $36-billion Covid-19 jab recipe," Business Standard, November 16, 2021, https://www.

business-standard.com/article/international/pfizer-fights-to-control-secret-of-36-billion-COVID-19-jab-recipe-121111600053_1.html

87 Worldwide Safety, "CUMULATIVE ANALYSIS OF POST-AUTHORIZATION ADVERSE EVENT REPORTS OF PF-07302048 (BNT162B2) RECEIVED THROUGH 28-FEB-2021," Pfizer, April 30, 2021, 12, https://phmpt.org/wp-content/uploads/2022/04/reissue_5.3.6-postmarketing-experience.pdf

88 Jonathan Gleason et al., "The Devastating Impact of Covid-19 on Individuals with Intellectual Disabilities in the United States," *NEJM Catalyst*, March 5, 2021, https://catalyst.nejm.org/doi/full/10.1056/CAT.21.0051

89 Louis Lasagna was academic dean of the School of Medicine at Tufts University and coined this version of the Hippocratic oath in 1964. It is used in many medical schools today.

90 "Early Outpatient Treatment: An Essential Part of a COVID-19 Solution, Part II," U.S. Senate Committee on Homeland Security and Governmental Affairs, video, 02:50:26, December 8, 2020, https://www.hsgac.senate.gov/early-outpatient-treatment-an-essential-part-of-a-covid-19-solution-part-ii

91 "YouTube Cancels the U.S. Senate," Newsletter of Ron Johnson, January 29, 2021, https://www.ronjohnson.senate.gov/2021/1/youtube-censored-me

92 Joyce Kamen, "Dr. Pierre Kory: "Barring Dr. Marik from using the medicines he believes will help his patients is unconscionable, contrary to reason and science." (Marik, Part II)," RESCUE with Michael Capuzzo newsletter, November 15, 2021, https://rescue.substack.com/p/dr-pierre-kory-barring-dr-marik-from

93 "Roundtable - COVID-19: How New Information Should Drive Policy," U.S. Senate Committee on Homeland Security and Governmental Affairs, May 6, 2020, video of teleconference, 03:14:35, https://www.hsgac.senate.gov/covid-19-how-new-information-should-drive-policy

94 "Dexamethasone reduces death in hospitalised patients with severe respiratory complications of COVID-19," June 16, 2020, University of Oxford, https://www.ox.ac.uk/news/2020-06-16-dexamethasone-reduces-death-hospitalised-patients-severe-respiratory-complications#:~:text=Dexamethasone%20reduces%20death%20in%20hospitalised,COVID%2D19%20%7C%20University%20of%20Oxford

95 "Press Release," The Nobel Prize, October 5, 2015, https://www.nobelprize.org/prizes/medicine/2015/press-release/

96 Fatemeh Heidary and Reza Gharebaghi, "Ivermectin: a systematic review from antiviral effects to COVID-19 complementary regimen," *Journal of Antibiotics* 73 (2020): 593–602, https://www.nature.com/articles/s41429-020-0336-z

97 Leon Caly et al., "The FDA-approved drug ivermectin inhibits the replication of SARS-CoV-2 in vitro," *Antiviral Research Journal* 178 (June 2020), https://pubmed.ncbi.nlm.nih.gov/32251768/

98 Pierre Kory et al., "Review of the Emerging Evidence Demonstrating the Efficacy of Ivermectin in the Prophylaxis and Treatment of COVID-19," Front Line COVID-19 Critical Care Alliance, updated January 16, 2021, https://covid19criticalcare.com/wp-content/uploads/2020/11/FLCCC-Ivermectin-in-the-prophylaxis-and-treatment-of-COVID-19.pdf

99 Pierre Kory, "Fraudulent Trial On Ivermectin Published By The World's Top Medical Journal. Big Pharma Reigns - Part 2," Pierre Kory's Medical Musings, May 15, 2022, https://pierrekory.substack.com/p/fraudulent-trial-on-ivermectin-published-859?utm_source=%2Fprofile%2F31671068-pierre-kory-md-mpa&utm_medium=reader2

100 Quote by Val Saintsbury in "Nursing: A Nurse Is Not Comfort, Compassion, And Caring Without Even A Prescription?," https://www.bartleby.com/essay/Nursing-A-Nurse-Is-Not-Comfort-Compassion-P3QYP5ECF99X

101 Evan Minton v. Dignitary Health, Appendix, https://www.supremecourt.gov/DocketPDF/19/19-1135/138108/20200313135611202_Dignity%20Health%20Appendix.pdf

102 Victor H. Ferria et al., "Severe Acute Respiratory Syndrome Coronavirus 2 Infection Induces Greater T-Cell Responses Compared to Vaccination in Solid Organ Transplant Recipients," *Journal of Infectious Diseases* 224, no. 11 (December 1, 2021): 1849–1860, https://pubmed.ncbi.nlm.nih.gov/34739078/

103 Hani M. Wadei et al., "COVID-19 infection in solid organ transplant recipients after SARS-CoV-2 vaccination," *American Journal of Transplantation* 21, (April 23, 2021): 3496–3499, https://onlinelibrary.wiley.com/doi/full/10.1111/ajt.16618

104 Brian J. Boyarski et al., "Antibody Response to 2-Dose SARS-CoV-2 mRNA Vaccine Series in Solid Organ Transplant Recipients," *JAMA* 325, no. 21 (May 2021): 2204–2206, https://jamanetwork.com/journals/jama/fullarticle/2779852

105 Dorry Segev, "COVID Vax in the Immunosuppressed: Reason for Concern," Medpage Today, March 15, 2021, https://www.medpagetoday.com/infectiousdisease/vaccines/91631

106 George H. B. Greenhall et al., "Organ transplantation from deceased donors with vaccine-induced thrombosis and thrombocytopenia," *Am J Transplant* 21, no. 12 (December 2021): 4095–4097, https://pubmed.ncbi.nlm.nih.gov/34214257/

107 Dashiell Young-Saver, "What Does 95% Effective Mean? Teaching the Math of Vaccine Efficacy," *New York Times*, December 30, 2020, https://www.nytimes.com/2020/12/13/learning/what-does-95-effective-mean-teaching-the-math-of-vaccine-efficacy.html

108 Paul D. Thacker, "Revelations of poor practices at a contract research company helping to carry out Pfizer's pivotal covid-19 vaccine trial raise questions about data integrity and regulatory oversight," *BJM* 375, no. 2635 (November 2021), https://www.bmj.com/content/375/bmj.n2635

109 Brook Jackson v. Ventavia Research Group, LLC, https://www.documentcloud.org/documents/21206071-brook-jackson-lawsuit

110 "Compilation: Peer Reviewed Medical Papers of COVID Vaccine Injuries," COVID Vaccine Injuries, February 20, 2022, https://community.covidvaccineinjuries.com/compilation-peer-reviewed-medical-papers-of-covid-vaccine-injuries/

111 "Cumulative Analysis of Post-Authorization Adverse Event Reports of PF-07302048 (BNT162B2) Received Through 28-Feb-2021," Pfizer, April 30, 2021, 32, https://phmpt.org/wp-content/uploads/2022/04/reissue_5.3.6-postmarketing-experience.pdf

112 Madison Czopek, "Fact-check: No, using Tylenol isn't killing 'at least 100,000' people per year," *Austin American-Statesman*, May 3, 2022, https://www.statesman.com/story/news/politics/politifact/2022/05/03/fact-check-tylenol-killing-at-least-100-000-people-per-year/9612891002/

113 Jessica Rose, "Let's put the 'it's cuz there are so many COVID shots doled out' argument to bed," Unacceptable Jessica Newsletter, March 25, 2022, https://jessicar.substack.com/p/lets-put-the-its-cuz-there-are-so

114 Fernando P. Polack et al., "Safety and Efficacy of the BNT162b2 mRNA Covid-19 Vaccine List of authors," *New England Journal of Medicine* 383 (December 2020): 2603–2615, https://www.nejm.org/doi/full/10.1056/nejmoa2034577

115 Rose, "When you hear BNT162c(2), run, don't walk, RUN away," Unacceptable Jessica Newsletter, June 19, 2022, https://jessicar.substack.com/p/when-you-hear-bnt162c2-run-dont-walk

116 Megan Ogilvie and May Warren, "'I put my neck on the line': Toronto doctor vaccinated hundreds of kids under 5 'off label,'" *Toronto Star*, May 27, 2022, https://www.thestar.com/news/gta/2022/05/27/how-hundreds-of-kids-under-five-in-toronto-got-covid-vaccines.html

[117] Anthony Fauci, interview by Jon LaPook, *60 Minutes*, CBS, March 8, 2020. Accessed via the *60 Minutes* YouTube channel, https://www.youtube.com/watch?v=PRa6t_e7dgI

[118] Beny Spira, "Correlation Between Mask Compliance and COVID-19 Outcomes in Europe," *Cureus* 14, no. 4 (April 19, 2022), https://www.cureus.com/articles/93826-correlation-between-mask-compliance-and-covid-19-outcomes-in-europe

[119] Jon Williams et al., "The Physiological Burden of Prolonged PPE Use on Healthcare Workers during Long Shifts," Centers for Disease Control, June 10, 2020, https://blogs.cdc.gov/niosh-science-blog/2020/06/10/ppe-burden/

[120] Cecilia Acuti Martellucci et al., "Inhaled CO2 concentration while wearing face masks: a pilot study using capnography," medRXiv, May 11, 2022, https://www.medrxiv.org/content/10.1101/2022.05.10.22274813v1

[121] Natalia N. Nalivaeva, Anthony J. Turner, and Igor A. Zhuravin, "Role of Prenatal Hypoxia in Brain Development, Cognitive Functions, and Neurodegeneration," *Front Neurosci* 12, no. 825 (November 19, 2018, https://www.ncbi.nlm.nih.gov/pmc/articles/PMC6254649/

[122] "CDC's Developmental Milestones," Centers for Disease Control and Prevention, August 17, 2022, https://www.cdc.gov/ncbddd/actearly/milestones/index.html

[123] Ella Kietlinska and Joshua Philipp, "Baby 'Kidnapped' by Authorities Over Missed Medical Appointment, Attorney Says," *The Epoch Times,* accessed May 2, 2022, https://www.theepochtimes.com/baby-kidnapped-by-authorities-over-missed-medical-appointment_4435178.html

[124] Children's Bureau, "Child Maltreatment 2019: Summary of Key Findings," *Numbers and Trends* (April 2021): 2, https://www.childwelfare.gov/pubpdfs/canstats.pdf

[125] "About Event 201," Center for Health Security, accessed August 21, 2022, https://www.centerforhealthsecurity.org/event201/about

[126] "The Event 201 Scenario," Center for Health Security, accessed August 21, 2022, https://www.centerforhealthsecurity.org/event201/scenario.html

[127] Bill Gates (@BillGates), "What's next for our foundation? I'm particularly excited about what the next year could mean for one of the best buys in global health: vaccines," Twitter, December 19, 2019, 9:20 a.m., https://twitter.com/BillGates/status/1207681997612748801?s=20&t=sRbXJs8XkJgESlZcMAnyGA

[128] "Fact Sheet on WMD Threat Reduction Efforts with Ukraine, Russia and Other Former Soviet Union Countries," Department of Defense, June 9, 2022, https://www.defense.gov/News/

Releases/Release/Article/3057517/fact-sheet-on-wmd-threat-reduction-efforts-with-ukraine-russia-and-other-former/

[129] Natalie Winters and Rakeem J. Kassam, "Hunter Biden Bio Firm Partnered With Ukrainian Researchers 'Isolating Deadly Pathogens' Using Funds From Obama's Defense Department," The National Pulse, March 24, 2022, https://thenationalpulse.com/2022/03/24/biden-linked-company-partnered-with-ukraine-biolabs/

[130] Letter from Lawrence A. Tabak to James Comer, October 20, 2021, https://int.nyt.com/data/documenttools/nih-eco-health-alliance-letter/512f5ee70ce9c67c/full.pdf

[131] Ralph S. Baric et al., "Episodic Evolution Mediates Interspecies Transfer of a Murine Coronavirus," Journal of Virology 71, no. 3 (March 1997): 1946–1955, https://journals.asm.org/doi/pdf/10.1128/jvi.71.3.1946-1955.1997

[132] "U.S. Government Gain-of-Function Deliberative Process and Research Funding Pause on Selected Gain-of-Function Research Involving Influenza, MERS, and SARS Viruses," United States Government, October 17, 2014, https://www.phe.gov/s3/dualuse/documents/gain-of-function.pdf

[133] "Rapid Medical Countermeasure Response to Infectious Diseases: Enabling Sustainable Capabilities Through Ongoing Public- and Private-Sector Partnerships: Workshop Summary," National Academies Press, February 12, 2016, https://www.ncbi.nlm.nih.gov/books/NBK349040/

[134] The Associated Press, "Scientists race to patent SARS virus," NBC News, October 15, 2003, https://www.nbcnews.com/id/wbna3076748.

[135] Vineet D. Menachery et al., "SARS-like WIV1-CoV poised for human emergence," PNAS 113, no. 11 (March 14, 2016): 3048–3053, https://www.pnas.org/doi/10.1073/pnas.1517719113

[136] Kristopher M. Curtis, Boyd Yount, and Ralph S. Baric. Methods for producing recombinant coronavirus. U.S. Patent 7,279,327, filed April 19, 2004, and approved October 9, 2007, https://patents.google.com/patent/US7279327B2/en

[137] Paul A. Rota, Larry J. Anderson, William J. Bellini, Cara Carthel Burns, Raymond Campagnoli, Qi Chen, James A. Comer, Shannon L. Emery, Dean D. Erdman, Cynthia S. Goldsmith, Charles D. Humphrey, Joseph P. Icenogle, Thomas G. Ksiazek, Stephan S. Monroe, William Allan Nix, M. Steven Oberste, Teresa C. T. Peret, Pierre E. Rollin, Mark A. Pallansch, Anthony Sanchez, Suxiang Tong, and Sherif R. Zaki. Coronavirus isolated from humans. U.S. Patent 7,220,852, filed April 12, 2004, and approved May 22, 2007, https://patents.google.com/patent/US7220852B1/en

[138] Vineet D. Menachery et al., "A SARS-like cluster of circulating bat coronaviruses shows potential for human emergence," *Nature Medicine* 21 (2015): 1508–1513, https://www.nature.com/articles/nm.3985

[139] Kristopher M. Curtis, Boyd Yount, and Ralph S. Baric. Methods for producing recombinant coronavirus. U.S. Patent 7,279,327, filed April 19, 2004, and approved October 9, 2007, https://patents.google.com/patent/US7279327B2/en

[140] Scott LaFee, "Novel Coronavirus Circulated Undetected Months before First COVID-19 Cases in Wuhan, China," UC San Diego Health, March 18, 2021, https://health.ucsd.edu/news/releases/Pages/2021-03-18-novel-coronavirus-circulated-undetected-months-before-first-covid-19-cases-in-wuhan-china.aspx

[141] Immunization, Vaccines, and Biologicals WHO Team, "Global vaccine action plan 2011-2020," World Health Organization, February 21, 2013, https://www.who.int/publications/i/item/global-vaccine-action-plan-2011-2020

[142] Angel N. Desai and Preeti Mehrotra, "Medical Masks," *JAMA* 323, no. 15 (March 4, 2020): 1517–1518, https://jamanetwork.com/journals/jama/fullarticle/2762694

[143] Lucy Hicks, "Monkeypox: Confusion as CDC Issues Then Rescinds Mask Advice," Medscape, June 9, 2022, https://www.medscape.com/viewarticle/975299

[144] Susan Michie and Robert West, "Sustained behavior change is key to preventing and tackling future pandemics," *Nature Medicine* 27 (2021): 749–752, https://www.nature.com/articles/s41591-021-01345-2

[145] Timothy J. Miller, Sharon Klepfer, Albert Paul Reed, and Elaine V. Jones. Canine coronavirus S gene and uses therefor. U.S. Patent 6,372,224, filed January 28, 2000, and issued April 16, 2002, https://patents.google.com/patent/US6372224B1/en

[146] Paul A. Rota, Larry J. Anderson, William J. Bellini, Cara Carthel Burns, Raymond Campagnoli, Qi Chen, James A. Comer, Shannon L. Emery, Dean D. Erdman, Cynthia S. Goldsmith, Charles D. Humphrey, Joseph P. Icenogle, Thomas G. Ksiazek, Stephan S. Monroe, William Allan Nix, M. Steven Oberste, Teresa C. T. Peret, Pierre E. Rollin, Mark A. Pallansch, Anthony Sanchez, Suxiang Tong, and Sherif R. Zaki. Coronavirus isolated from humans. U.S. Patent 7,220,852, filed April 12, 2004, and approved May 22, 2007, https://patents.google.com/patent/US7220852B1/en

[147] "Sequoia Pharmaceuticals Inc.: Company Information," United States Government, accessed August 21, 222, https://www.sbir.gov/node/305319

148 "Award Abstract # 0434507: Darwinian Chemical Systems," National Science Foundation, accessed August 21, 2022, https://www.nsf.gov/awardsearch/showAward?AWD_ID=0434507

149 Jason P. Schrum et al., "Efficient and Rapid Template-Directed Nucleic Acid Copying Using 2'-Amino-2',3'-dideoxyribonucleoside-5'-Phosphorimidazolide Monomers," *Journal of American Chemical Society* (August 3, 2009), https://molbio.mgh.harvard.edu/szostakweb/publications/Szostak_pdfs/Schrum_et_al_JACS_2009.pdf

150 "A World at Risk: Annual Report on Global Preparedness for Health Emergencies," Global Preparedness Monitoring Board, September 2019, 15, https://www.gpmb.org/docs/librariesprovider17/default-document-library/annual-reports/gpmb-2019-annualreport-en.pdf?sfvrsn=d1c9143c_30

151 Xing-Yi Ge et al., "Isolation and characterization of a bat SARS-like coronavirus that uses the ACE2 receptor," *Nature* 503 (October 2013): 535–538, https://www.nature.com/articles/nature12711

152 Vineet D. Menachery et al., "SARS-like WIV1-CoV poised for human emergence," PNAS 113, no. 11 (March 14, 2016): 3048–3053, https://www.ncbi.nlm.nih.gov/pmc/articles/PMC4801244/

153 Ralph Baric, "Remdesivir, developed through a UNC-Chapel Hill partnership, proves effective against COVID-19 in NIAID human clinical trials," University of North Carolina Gillings School of Global Public Health, April 29, 2020, https://sph.unc.edu/sph-news/remdesivir-developed-at-unc-chapel-hill-proves-effective-against-covid-19-in-niaid-human-clinical-trials/

154 Sabue Mulangu et al., "A Randomized, Controlled Trial of Ebola Virus Disease Therapeutics," *New England Journal of Medicine* 381 (December 12, 2019): 2293–2303, https://www.nejm.org/doi/full/10.1056/nejmoa1910993

155 Scott Shane, "Portrait Emerges of Anthrax Suspect's Troubled Life," *New York Times*, January 3, 2009, https://www.nytimes.com/2009/01/04/us/04anthrax.html

156 Exec. Order No. 10399, presidential papers of Harry S. Truman, September 27, 1952, https://www.trumanlibrary.gov/library/executive-orders/10399/executive-order-10399

157 Johnny Vedmore, "Meet the real Klaus Martin Schwab!," State of the Nation, February 26, 2021, https://stateofthenation.co/?p=54065

158 Jennifer Hunter, "Tracking Nazi scientists who came to America," *Toronto Star*, February 28, 2014, https://www.thestar.com/news/insight/2014/02/28/tracking_nazi_scientists_who_came_to_america.html

159 Jack Smith IV, "This Is the Hidden Nazi History of IBM — And the Man Who Tried to Expose It," Mic, May 9, 2016, https://www.mic.com/articles/142991/edwin-black-ibm-nazi-holocaust-history

160 "Digital Health Pass," IBM, accessed August 21, 2022, https://www.ibm.com/products/digital-health-pass

161 Redpill177617, "Yuval Noah Harari. We have the technology to hack people on a massive scale," Rumble video, March 16, 2022, 4:16, https://rumble.com/vxmdob-wef-yuval-noah-harari.-we-have-the-technology-to-hack-people-on-a-massive-s.html

162 Turning Point USA (@TPUSA), "Pfizer CEO Albert Bourla PRAISED a pill with a chip at Davos…?! Y'ALL WHAT #BigGovSucks," Twitter, May 21, 2022, 12:18 p.m., https://twitter.com/TPUSA/status/1528062810151714816?s=20&t=UQ4pHWq8ks7UHj4ktfhYcQ

163 Thrivetime Show, "YUVAL NOAH HARARI | LEAD ADVISOR FOR KLAUS SCHWAB ARGUES AGAINST THE BIBLE AND GOD'S COMMANDMENTS," BitChute video, March 15, 2022, 1:49, https://www.bitchute.com/video/Qv8hLyXFapOJ/

164 Eric Lipton and Jennifer Steinhauer, "The Untold Story of the Birth of Social Distancing," New York Times, April 22, 2020, https://www.nytimes.com/2020/04/22/us/politics/social-distancing-coronavirus.html

165 Thomas V., Inglesby et al., "Disease Mitigation Measures in the Control of Pandemic Influenza," Biosecurity and Bioterrorism: Biodefense Strategy, Practice, and Science 4, no. 4 (2006): 366–375, http://citeseerx.ist.psu.edu/viewdoc/download?doi=10.1.1.552.1109&rep=rep1&type=pdf

166 "HITLER FORECASTS NO REICH OVERTURN IN NEXT 1,000 YEARS; Proclamation to Nazi Congress Says Movement Won't Yield No Matter What Happens," New York Times, September 6, 1934, https://www.nytimes.com/1934/09/06/archives/hitler-forecasts-no-reich-overturn-in-next-1000-years-proclamation.html

167 Samuel Adams, writing as Candidus, untitled essay in Boston Gazette, October 14, 1771, https://thefederalistpapers.org/founders/samuel-adams/samuel-adams-writing-as-candidus-essay-in-the-boston-gazette-oct-14-1771

168 Samuel Adams, writing as Candidus, untitled essay in Boston Gazette, October 14, 1771, https://thefederalistpapers.org/founders/samuel-adams/samuel-adams-writing-as-candidus-essay-in-the-boston-gazette-oct-14-1771

169 Lucy Soaft, "How Did the Nazi Human Experimentation Project Benefit War Efforts?" The Collector, January 31, 2022, https://www.thecollector.com/nazi-human-experimentation-project-ww2/

170 Esther Inglis-Arkell, "The American medical experiments that the Nazis used as a defense," Gizmodo, December 26, 2013, https://gizmodo.com/the-american-medical-experiments-that-the-nazis-used-as-1488668267

171 "From the Opening Statement by Telford Taylor," United States Holocaust Memorial Museum, https://www.ushmm.org/information/exhibitions/online-exhibitions/special-focus/doctors-trial/opening-statement/charges

172 Evelyne Shuster, "Fifty Years Later: The Significance of the Nuremberg Code," *New England Journal of Medicine* 337 (November 1997): 1436–1440, https://www.nejm.org/doi/full/10.1056/nejm199711133372006

173 Benjamin E. Berkman et al., "The ethics of encouraging employees to get the COVID-19 vaccination," *Journal of Public Health Policy* 43 (March 2022): 311–319, https://link.springer.com/content/pdf/10.1057/s41271-022-00347-9.pdf

174 Robert N. Proctor, *Racial Hygiene: Medicine Under the Nazis* (Cambridge, Massachusetts: Harvard University Press, 1988), 66.

175 Robert N. Proctor, "The Nazi War on Cancer," first chapter in *The Nazi War on Cancer* (Princeton, New Jersey: Princeton University Press, 1999), https://archive.nytimes.com/www.nytimes.com/books/first/p/proctor-cancer.html

176 "The Role of Doctors and Nurses," United States Holocaust Memorial Museum, https://encyclopedia.ushmm.org/content/en/article/the-role-of-doctors-and-nurses

177 Ryan Klaassen et. al. v. Trustees of Indiana University, No. 21-2326 (7th Cir. 2021) at 77.

178 "Buck v. Bell, 274 U.S. 200 (1927)," https://supreme.justia.com/cases/federal/us/274/200/#tab-opinion-1931809

179 "Jacobson v. Massachusetts, 197 U.S. 11 (1905)," https://supreme.justia.com/cases/federal/us/197/11/

180 *Merriam-Webster*, s.v. "fascism (n.)," accessed August 21, 2022, https://www.merriam-webster.com/dictionary/fascism

181 Larry Buchanan, Quoctrung Bui, and Jugal K. Patel, "Black Lives Matter May Be the Largest Movement in U.S. History," *New York Times*, July 3, 2020, https://www.nytimes.com/interactive/2020/07/03/us/george-floyd-protests-crowd-size.html

182 Evan Minton v. Dignity Health, Appendix, https://www.supremecourt.gov/DocketPDF/19/19-1135/138108/20200313135611202_Dignity%20Health%20Appendix.pdf

183 Gloucester County School Board v. Grimm, No. 19-1952 (4th Cir. 2020).

184 Michael Kater, *Doctors Under Hitler* (Chapel Hill, North Carolina: The University of North Carolina Press, 2000), 3–4.

185 Proctor, *Racial Hygiene*, 307.

186 Anusha Ondaatjie and Asantha Sirimanne, "Sri Lanka Under Virtual Lockdown With Fuel Supplies Halted for Private Cars," Bloomberg, June 27, 2022, https://www.bloomberg.com/news/articles/2022-06-27/sri-lanka-is-put-on-virtual-lockdown-as-fuel-supplies-are-halted

187 Tassilo Hummel, "Bordeaux region bans outdoor events as heat wave hits France," Reuters, https://www.reuters.com/world/europe/bordeaux-region-bans-outdoor-events-heat-wave-hits-france-2022-06-17/

188 George Clinton, "New York Ratifying Convention," in Herbert J. Storing, ed., *The Complete Anti-Federalist* (Chicago: University of Chicago Press: 1981), Document 39, https://press-pubs.uchicago.edu/founders/documents/v1ch8s39.html

189 Todd Jaquith, "Fauci touts China's COVID protocol when confronted on Shanghai lockdown: 'Better than almost anybody else,'" BPR Business & Politics, April 15, 2022, https://www.bizpacreview.com/2022/04/15/fauci-touts-chinas-covid-protocol-when-confronted-on-shanghai-lockdown-better-than-almost-anybody-else-1226280/

190 Paul Elias Alexander, "More Than 400 Studies on the Failure of Compulsory Covid Interventions (Lockdowns, Restrictions, Closures)," Brownstone Institute, November 30, 2021, https://brownstone.org/articles/more-than-400-studies-on-the-failure-of-compulsory-covid-interventions/

191 Spencer Kimball, "Scientists divided on need for 4th Covid shot after FDA quietly approved another round of boosters," CNBC, April 6, 2022, https://www.cnbc.com/2022/04/06/scientists-divided-on-need-for-4th-covid-shot-after-fda-quietly-approved-another-round-of-boosters.html

192 Paul A. Offit, "Covid-19 Boosters—Where from Here?" *New England Journal of Medicine* 386 (April 2022): 1661–1662, https://www.nejm.org/doi/full/10.1056/NEJMe2203329

193 Sharon LaFraniere and Noah Weiland, "F.D.A. Panel Recommends Pfizer and Moderna Vaccines for Youngest Children," *New York Times*, June 15, 2022, https://www.nytimes.com/2022/06/16/us/politics/covid-vaccines-fda-children.html

194 C. S. Lewis, *God in the Dock: Essays on Theology and Ethics*, ed. William Hooper (Grand Rapids, Michigan: William B. Eerdmans Publishing Company, 1970).

195 Yuval Noah Harari, interview by Romi Noimark, YouTube video, 35:01, https://www.youtube.com/watch?v=ltJTRnNLYqY

196 "Blackstone's Commentaries on the Laws of England Book the First - Chapter the First : Of the Absolute Rights of Individuals,"

Yale Law School Lillian Goldman Law Library, https://
avalon.law.yale.edu/18th_century/blackstone_bk1ch1.asp

197 Michael W. Chapman, "Catholic Priest: No President or Health Official
'Gets to Dictate What We Put Into Our Bodies,'" CNS News, November
30, 2021, https://www.cnsnews.com/article/national/michael-w-chapman/
catholic-priest-no-president-or-health-official-gets-dictate

198 H.B. 2013, https://legiscan.com/PA/text/HB2013/2021

199 Engen Tham, "China bank protest stopped by health codes
turning red, depositors say," Reuters, June 16, 2022, https://
www.reuters.com/world/china/china-bank-protest-stopped-
by-health-codes-turning-red-depositors-say-2022-06-14/

200 "As Self-Spreading Vaccine Technology Moves Forward, Dialogue
on Its Risks Should Follow," *The Bulletin of the Atomic Sciences*, June
10, 2022, https://thebulletin.org/2022/06/as-self-spreading-vaccine-
technology-moves-forward-dialogue-on-its-risks-should-follow/

201 Josh Guetzkow, "New FOIA Release Shows CDC Lied About Its
VAERS Safety Monitoring Efforts," Jackanapes Junction newsletter,
June 16 2022, https://jackanapes.substack.com/p/new-foia-release-
shows-cdc-lied-about?utm_source=%2Fprofile%2F42568025-
josh-guetzkow&utm_medium=reader2

202 Bruesewitz v. Wyeth, 562 U.S. ___ ; 131 S. Ct. 1068 (2011).

203 Public Health Service Act, Pub. L No. 78–410, § 2127(a)(2)(c), https://
www.hrsa.gov/sites/default/files/hrsa/vicp/title-xxi-phs-vaccines-1517.pdf

204 "ICAN vs. HHS: Key Legal Win Recasts Vaccine Debate,"
Cision PR Newswire, September 14, 2018, https://www.
prnewswire.com/news-releases/ican-vs-hhs-key-legal-
win-recasts-vaccine-debate-300712629.html

205 "Declaration Under the Public Readiness and Emergency Preparedness
Act for Medical Countermeasures Against COVID-19," Health
and Human Services Department, March 17, 2020, https://
www.federalregister.gov/documents/2020/03/17/2020-05484/
declaration-under-the-public-readiness-and-emergency-
preparedness-act-for-medical-countermeasures

206 Kevin J. Hickey, "The PREP Act and COVID-19, Part 1: Statutory
Authority to Limit Liability for Medical Countermeasures,"
Congressional Research Service, April 13, 2022, https://
crsreports.congress.gov/product/pdf/LSB/LSB10443

207 Margaret I. Cuomo, "Are We Wasting Billions Seeking a Cure for
Cancer?" Daily Beast, July 14, 2017, https://www.thedailybeast.
com/are-we-wasting-billions-seeking-a-cure-for-cancer

208 Ryan D. Chow, Elizabeth H. Bradley, and Cary P. Gross, "Comparison of Cancer-Related Spending and Mortality Rates in the US vs 21 High-Income Countries," *JAMA Health Forum* 3, no. 5 (2022), https://jamanetwork.com/journals/jama-health-forum/fullarticle/2792761
209 H.B. 821, 66th Legislature, https://legislature.idaho.gov/wp-content/uploads/sessioninfo/2022/legislation/H0821.pdf
210 stepo, "Bill Gates - Vaccines Health Care System Overpopulation - 2010 Ted Talk," YouTube video, 2:01, https://www.youtube.com/watch?v=fsuxcWt7-vM&ab_channel=stepo, excerpted from Bill Gates, "Innovating to Zero," TED video, 29:32, https://www.youtube.com/watch?v=fsuxcWt7-vM
211 Cong. Globe, 39th Cong., 1st Sess. 2765–2766 (1866).